AF324610

The India Mosaic

The Editors

BIBEK DEBROY is Director, Rajiv Gandhi Institute for Contemporary Studies, New Delhi. He is the author and editor of several books, papers and popular articles. Bibek Debroy's special interests are international trade (in particular the WTO), law reform and the political economy of liberalization in India.

D. SHYAM BABU is a Fellow at the Rajiv Gandhi Institute for Contemporary Studies, New Delhi. His research interests range from national security and arms control to socio-economic problems of Dalits, and Liberalization and Social Justice. A former journalist, Shyam Babu's publications also include a book on Nuclear Non-Proliferation.

About RGICS

The Rajiv Gandhi Institute for Contemporary Studies (RGICS), New Delhi is part of the Rajiv Gandhi Foundation and functions as a think tank. The target audience of the RGICS includes parliamentarians, legislators and representatives of political parties, public policy makers and their advisers, the intelligentsia, the media and various interest groups. To interface with these groups, RGICS uses different modes of communication like books, monographs, working papers, symposia, discussions, talks and lectures. The RGICS research work is focused on international economic relations, law reforms, IT and economic reforms in India.

The India Mosaic

Searching for an Identity...

EDITORS

Bibek Debroy

D. Shyam Babu

PUBLISHED BY ACADEMIC FOUNDATION IN ASSOCIATION WITH
RAJIV GANDHI INSTITUTE FOR CONTEMPORARY STUDIES, NEW DELHI

Academic Foundation

NEW DELHI

Reprint : 2005

First Published in 2004 by

A C A D E M I C   F O U N D A T I O N

4772-73 / 23 Bharat Ram Road, (23 Ansari Road),
Darya Ganj, New Delhi - 110 002.
INDIA.

Phones : 23245001, 02, 03, 04.
Fax : +91-11-23245005.
e-mail : academic@vsnl.com
www : academicfoundation.com

Published in association with
Rajiv Gandhi Institute for Contemporary Studies, New Delhi.

The India Mosaic: Searching for an Identity...
edited by Bibek Debroy and D. Shyam Babu
ISBN 81-7188-355-9

Designed and typeset by Italics India, New Delhi
and printed at Rashtriya Printers, Delhi.

Contents

...Contd....

Authors/Contributors

M. N. Venkatachaliah . . . . Former Chief Justice of India and former Chairman of the National Human Rights Commission of India; recipient of *Padma Vibhushan* (2004).

Sunil Khilnani . . . . Director, South Asia Studies at the School of Advanced International Studies, Johns Hopkins University, Washington DC.

Rudrangshu Mukherjee . . . . . Deputy Editor, *The Telegraph* (Kolkata) and a historian.

B.G. Verghese . . . . A well-known media personality and a Professor at Centre for Policy Research, New Delhi.

Amir Ullah Khan . . . . Fellow at the India Development Foundation, Gurgaon.

Mohammad Saqib . . . . Fellow at the Rajiv Gandhi Institute for Contemporary Studies, New Delhi

Salman Khurshid . . . . Former Minister of State for External Affairs (GoI) and President of the Delhi Public School Society.

Bikramjit De . . . . Teaches at the National University
of Juridical Sciences, Kolkata.

Sagarika Ghose . . . . A well-known novelist and a
journalist with *Indian Express*.

Vinod Saighal . . . . A retired Major General and author
of several books.

Gurcharan Das . . . . An author and columnist with
Times of India and a former CEO
of Procter & Gamble (India).

P. N. Vijay . . . . Heads the Delhi-based P. N. Vijay
Associates, and is a columnist with
Financial Express.

Bibek Debroy . . . . Director, Rajiv Gandhi Institute for
Contemporary Studies, New Delhi
and is a columnist with *Financial
Express* and *Indian Express*.

Arnab Kumar Hazra . . . . Formerly Research Associate with
Rajiv Gandhi Institute for
Contemporary Studies, New Delhi,
is presently Economic Advisor,
Embassy of South Korea.

Bhalchandra Mungekar . . . . . Vice-Chancellor, University of
Mumbai.

D. Shyam Babu . . . . Fellow, Rajiv Gandhi Institute for
Contemporary Studies, New Delhi

Madhu Kishwar . . . . Senior Fellow, Centre for the Study
of Developing Societies (Delhi) and
Founder Editor, *Manushi*

Editors' Introduction

It is customary for an edited volume to have an introduction by the editors. Typically, introductions by editors summarize contents of the papers and weave them together on a continuous canvas. Introductions are thus like appetizers before the main course. However, in this case, the main course is such that an appetizer was impossible and, if attempted, would have spoiled the main course.

This is an edited collection of seminar papers. The idea of India has been interpreted by different people in different ways and perhaps there is no single idea of India at all. Whatever be the interpretation (or interpretations) of the idea of India, there is an unambiguous sense that there is now an attempt to change the idea of India. The resultant discomfort is understandable. The idea that the Rajiv Gandhi Institute for Contemporary Studies (RGICS) should organize a seminar to re-examine the idea of India originated with Dr. Manmohan Singh. Dr. Manmohan Singh planted the seed, B.G. Verghese facilitated the germination and the seminar was eventually held on 10th and 11th May 2003. The seminar was on "The Idea of India" and we left the paper-writers to interpret what they meant by that expression.

Justice Venkatachaliah's keynote address is included in this volume, as are all presented papers but three. Given their other commitments, Mukul Kesavan, Pratap Bhanu Mehta and Sanjaya Baru couldn't submit their papers for inclusion in this volume. RGICS is indebted to all the paper-writers and the participants for having made the seminar and the subsequent output a success. RGICS is also indebted to the Chairpersons of the individual sessions — Dr. Manmohan Singh, Arnab Goswami, Chandan Mitra, Salman Khurshid, Justice Sujata Vasant Manohar, M.K. Rasgotra, Dr. S.P. Gupta and Dr. V.K. Krishnamurthy.

The seminar didn't necessarily intend to find answers. Perhaps there aren't any easy answers. Perhaps there are only questions. There is plenty of food for thought in these papers about what India stands for and about what it should stand for. The world and India are bullish about the Indian economic performance in the next 20 or even 50 years. A recent Goldman Sachs report *(Dreaming with BRICs: The Path to 2050)* is but one instance. The economy is the easy part. But India stands for much more than the overall economic performance alone. And on the overall economic performance, there is the issue of benefits from growth trickling down to disadvantaged sections. And beyond economic performance, there is the question of what India means. There is much in this volume for India's citizens to think about. Over to the main course.

1

Idea of India

M.N. VENKATACHALIAH

As India enters the 21st century, does it do so with a broad revision of a sense of itself? Is there dissolution of the conception of India built over the decades in the past?

These and other questions are raised in Sunil Khilnani's eminently readable *Idea of India*. His answers are dis-comforting. He says that it may seem obtuse and even hubristic to speak of the idea of India in the singular as India "shambles into the new century with so many disparate views of itself and that the idea of India as democratic, tolerant and open minded is in danger of being submerged by more restricted conceptions". Khilnani states the two different perceptions of Indian history:

> ".....one sees India as victim of recurring invasion – whether led by Muslim horsemen or European adventurers or Aryan Tribes or satellite T.V. Muguls. The other views India as an arena of cultural encounters, often uncomfortable, between unequal protagonists, which have produced unique and splendid cultural forms."

But I think the theme is too vast and complex, far more intangible both in depth and range, to admit of facile and neat classifications of the perception of India's past. The metaphor – the Idea of India seems to engage something infinite and baffling and indefinable. The Idea of India is not limited to its massive history, its civilizations, its enduring ways and values of life, its age old sense of community and family as sources of social security, and above all its profound contributions to the irresolvable issues of man's eternal spiritual quest. In short, the "Idea of India" embodies the rare energy for unfailing ultimate solutions, to all the problems that militate against that idea. It is both the problem and the solution.

Indian civilization is underpinned by certain eternal and enduring verities. India and Indians cannot give up those values even if they want to. The roots are deep and they define and condition what it means to be an Indian.

Will Hutton in his work *The World We're In* devoted a chapter to the "Idea of Europe". He spoke of the struggle of Europe against capitalism and free markets of the American brand as distinguished from Europe's own comparatively more humane version. Hutton's definition of the 'Idea of Europe' is consequentialist – He said[1]:

"An effective Europe, delivering at European level what nation-states cannot perform at national level, through political processes that were accountable and transparent, would help to re-legitimize politics and democracy alike. It would do two things. The act of delivering something that could not be delivered at national level would be proof positive that Europe has a raison d'etre that warrants the support of its citizens. It would be government for the people. Second it would, as Jurgen Habermas argues persuasively, begin to identify Europe not as a nation-state in the sense of having a common descent, language and history, but as a civic community that volunteers to have a collective expression in Europe-wide actions. It would be the first step in creating a European civic society which might ultimately be the foundation for a functioning European democracy."

Speaking of what the Idea of Europe should incorporate he said:

"What it must do instead is find ways of returning to Jacques Delors' agenda of positive integration around a social Europe and of organizing a European economic and social space. In short, it has to find ways of defending European values and the best of the European economic and social model – and to be proud and self conscious in what it is doing. In an age of globalization, the priority is no longer negative integration to establish a single market; that job is largely done and has its own powerful momentum. The new injunction is to protect and further the interests of Europe's citizens in an age where the market is king, creating a vibrant and distinct European capitalism that incorporates its history and the views of its peoples.[2]"

In a very poignant further statement on the idea of Europe that could stand for the Idea of India as well — Hutton said, "Above all, it must believe in Europe. It must do so urgently, not only for itself, but for all those who believe in multilateral action to create international public goods – a process which Europe is trail-blazing for the globe." Today's India too must believe in the 'Idea of India' and set a trail-blazing humanism in international relations, development ethos, that will be trail-blazing for the globe. Pluralism, democracy, justice, equality, peace and development are indivisible and inter-dependent.

"Idea of India" also accommodates certain contradictions. It accepts that India lives concurrently in several centuries – both past and future. Therefore the "Idea of India" is incomplete without its historical strengths, its obscurantisms and its own historical and historic weaknesses. In this ancient land many streams in religion saw their unification and confluence. Christianity and Islam interacted - with and occasionally confronted — Hinduism and the result was the realization of the universality of mystic experience. As a scholar observed, "It is well known that in pluralistic societies the common people being exposed to the experience of each other's belief systems and practices, often manage to merge them. People begin by sharing experiences and practices out of neighbourly courtesy. This they manage to do without infringing their own basic belief systems. They accommodate the divergent only to the extent that no major infringement of their own faith might occur. They do often compromise with minor infringements. Quite often, too, fresh myths appear to justify such mutual accommodation at the level of "little traditions".[3]

Ancient India's contribution to Art, Architecture, Aesthetics, Music, Drama, Dance, Sculpture and other brilliant and soul touching manifestations of the finer graces of human imagination and creativity and of the dimensions of curiosity are breath-taking. The whole world looked at the stupendous achievement with wide-eyed wonder and asked itself what kind of a inner civilisational strength, peace and tranquility could have achieved such grandeurs of expression.

In the long harmonious tradition of Hindu-Muslim relations, it is not unusual for Muslim singers to sing in praise of Durga, Rama and Krishna. Accommodation is focused to absorb traditions and forms of older religions into newer religions. Christianity came into India well over a century before it went to Rome. The first Church in India was built within half a century of the Christian Era. "Common humanity asserts itself not only in unifications which occur through a natural process not yet understood."

There were, and still are, it is true, great rigidities of religious practices. Paul Kennedy in his *Rise and Fall of the Great Powers* says:

> "The sheer rigidity of Hindu religious taboos militated against modernisation: rodents and insects could not be killed, so vast amounts of food stuffs were lost; social mores about handling refuse and excreta led to permanently insanitary conditions, a breeding ground for bubonic plagues .....Here were social checks of the deepest sort to any attempts at radical change. Small wonder that many Britons, having first plundered and then tried to govern India in accordance with Utilitarian principles, finally left with the feeling that the country was still a mystery to them."

But then the 'Idea of India' also includes how hope can raise above such self-destructive national impulses. Indian history is replete with manifestations of such power of self-correction and redemption.

The saga of India's Independence was a dramatic event that not only profoundly influenced India but, in a non-trivial sense, transformed the world itself. That was the culmination of the Gandhian spirit. Gandhi's technique of non-violent confrontation became his hallmark. Gandhi's Satyagraha entered into the world – lexicon. Webster's *Third International Dictionary* aptly sums up this technique as "one of the means of achieving social and political reform by means of tolerance and active goodwill coupled with firmness in one's cause expressed through non-violence, passive resistance and non-cooperation".

Gandhiana is itself an inseparable and integral component of the Idea of India. There is woeful lack of understanding in the world of this. In a report on *"Preventing Deadly Conflict"* (Dec., 1997) the Carnegie Commission observed:

> "The world of next century will be markedly more crowded, interdependent economically, closely linked technologically, increasingly vulnerable ecologically and progressively more interconnected culturally. Trends in this direction have long been apparent, but what has only recently come into sharper focus is the importance of managing the pace of change and its widespread repercussions. Contributing to this focus is the highly destructive power and universal availability of modern weaponry."

"Chemical and biological weapons pose new dangers to poor and rich countries alike. Disaffected groups may seek inexpensive weapons of mass destruction, some of which can be produced from ingredients normally sold for commercial purposes."

"An ounce of type A- botulinal toxin, properly dispersed, could kill every man, woman and child in North America.... Just eight ounces of the substance could kill every creature on the planet. Many lethal gases are colourless and odourless and can lead to immediate or slow agonizing death for thousands. These weapons can be delivered in missiles or dropped from planes, exploded in ground ordnance, set in time-delay devices, released via remote control, or put in water supplies. Large concentrations of unsuspecting civilians, especially in urban settings, are vulnerable."

That is the reason for Martin Luther King Junior saying, "the choice is no longer between violence and non-violence. It is either non-violence or non-existence".

Did Gandhi really influence the politics of the world? We see it enacted all over the world. The triumph of spirit over physical might – a kind of re enactment of Gandhi's Salt March. Nehru himself was amazed at the astuteness of Gandhi and his sense of history of the "Boston Tea Party", which was somewhat similar to the Salt March. B.R. Nanda in a deeply moving article on *"Gandhi and Non-violence: Doctrines of Ahimsa and Satyagraha"* refers to this proliferation of the Gandhian technique. Far from being a local experiment, he says, this technique of non-violent confrontation has caught the imagination of the oppressed people all over the world. It deeply influenced and changed the course of political development in many parts of the world like South Africa, USA, Czechoslovakia, Philippines and elsewhere. The second half of the last century saw the Spirit of the Salt March enacted elsewhere in different parts of the globe.

Indian Independence

It was not as if republican forms of government were unknown to ancient India. Indeed, ancient India was studded with republics. Political power was not the monopoly of any caste or group. "It was open throughout Indian history". Monarchy, wherever it existed, was not absolute. Even the Kings were limited in their power against their own subjects. They respected cultural pluralism. There were great harmonizing internal strengths which influenced the inter-relationship between religion, society and politics. A near century of Mauryan rule, crowned by the reign of Ashoka in the pre-Christian era, was a shining example of the great values of ancient Indian polity. The great king spiritualised political power. He did not seek to extend his reign and territories towards 'natural frontiers', but spread the message of his creed of love and humanity beyond his own political boundaries. Indeed, if one were asked as to what is the single most important legacy of ancient India, the undoubted answer is the tradition of tolerance, respect for diversities and reverence for life. It is also the tradition that celebrates peace as a technique for advancement of political, social and even commercial goods.

For the first time in two thousand years, a country grimly struggling to be re-born into a life of dignity after a long spell of foreign domination began to shape its own destiny and work out its constitutional salvation. One remarkable feature was the quality of debates in the Constituent Assembly. The grim aftermath of the partition and the senseless violence it unleashed did not make the debates bitter or acrimonious. On the contrary, the Constitution makers re-affirmed their abiding faith in the 'Idea of India' — the pluralist tradition of the country and passed on to posterity a noble sentiment. The Republican spirit of the Constitution and the assurances to the minorities were affirmations of a great inheritance. The Constitution established a federal, democratic, secular polity and contains guarantees against arbitrary government. It also took note that in a feudal society, only collective action can promise wider benefits. But at the same time, it is to be realized that special interests that hold strategic controls can retard progress. Adult franchise, protective discrimination, aided by cultural and intellectual movements within society helped to impart a 'social depth' to constitutional experiments and concerns. Fifty years of governance in post-Independent India have shown a remarkable constructive capacity, but they have also thrown up great weaknesses.

Amongst the achievements, the most notable is the trend towards a progressive transformation of Indian society. The composition of Parliament itself has undergone a great change. More people from the lower social strata have achieved progressively higher representations. The small man began to assert his place in the sun. Social changes, which were impossible to conceive a century ago, are today's realities in terms of human development.

The 73rd and 74th Constitutional Amendments, when implemented full-steam, will transform rural India and local self-governments. The most notable amongst the achievements is in the area of agricultural production. Between 1950 and 2000, the index of agricultural production increased more than four fold. English wheat took 1000 years to quadruple per hectare. In 1947 India produced six million tonnes of wheat. In 2000 the production was 75.6 million tonnes. The remarkable breakthroughs in wheat and rice production made Dr. William Gadd call the great experiment in India the "Green Revolution". In 1968 a special stamp was released celebrating the "Wheat Revolution". The Index of Industrial production went up from 7.9 in 1950-51 to 154.7 in 1999-2000. This is no mean achievement for a country that relied on food aid until the early 1960s. Prudent fiscal and economic management enabled India to avert the fiscal crisis that many East Asian countries experienced. On the contrary, India's GDP grew annually by 6-8 per cent per annum between 1994-2000, except in the year 1997-98, when it grew by 4 per cent.

The State of Kerala has shown what a society empowered by education, particularly women, and by access to information, can really achieve. About the turn of the century, the life expectancy at birth of an Indian was just 20.9 years. It is now 80 years for the urban female in Kerala. Infant mortality in the beginning of the last century was around 200. It is just 16 in urban Kerala today. Indeed it is said that a child born in Kerala today can expect to live longer than a child born in Washington.

On the positive side, the experience of 50 years has shown that great social and economic changes can be negotiated through institutions of liberal democracy. This is a clear rebuttal of the thesis of Lee Kuan Yew of Singapore that Democracy and Development do not go together.

But then it must be said that while the philosophy of Liberal Democracy has an assured foundation, the techniques of its practice have however thrown up quite a few increasingly disturbing puzzles. There are many forces that we find at work that tend to obliterate all the gains. These are the pervasive criminalisation of politics, politicization of criminals, the deep distortion of the electoral process and pervasive bureaucratic corruption and inefficiency beyond all acceptable limits. Equally disturbing is the slower pace of socio-economic change. India ranks 123rd on the Human Development Index. Only 50 countries in the world have a lower development index. Over a hundred years ago, Vivekananda and Aurobindo cautioned against the neglect of the masses. Equality of opportunity, which is the soul of social equality, is yet an unrealized goal.

As a reaction to the grim events associated with the vivisection of the country, the Constitution makers envisaged a strong centre. This commenced the process of over centralization, with the concentration of power at the higher echelons of political executive and permanent civil services. At the core lies the problem of pervasive political and electoral corruption, which is corroding the values of liberal democracy. Unfortunately, initiative for reform rests in the hands of just those who are the best beneficiaries of the conditions that badly need reform. The deep divisions in the social structure help the clever politician to set up one group against another and confound the real issue. If electoral processes are not reformed, the future of the country is surely doomed.

Chakravarthi Rajagopalachari uttered a prophetic caution eighty-two years ago. Writing in his *"Jail Diary"* while at the Vellore jail, he said that Swaraj either immediately after it is achieved, or even long thereafter, would mean greater happiness for people or better government. He said elections and their corruptions, bureaucratic inefficiency and corruption, tyranny of wealth, will make life hell for the people and that hope could only come from educating people from their childhood in the joy of loving others. At the end however, he uttered some comforting words. He said that he saw greater chances for the culmination of this ideal in India than anywhere else in the world.

Global changes that science and technology usher in are great. An American scholar observed that, "Today the world is divided not by ideology, but by technology. A small part of the globe, accounting for some 15 per cent of the earth's population, provides nearly all of the world's technology innovations. A second part, involving perhaps over half of the world's population, is able to adopt these technologies in production and consumption. The remaining part, covering around a third of the world's population, is technically disconnected......"

The world witnesses oppressive economic inequalities of the international economic order. The key issues however, are the correlation between economic development and social opportunity, particularly in the context of the grim realities of the international economic order and the great transformation that science and technology are ushering in. Inequality and income gap between the top fifth of people in the rich part of the world and the bottom fifth in the poorest was 30:1 in 1960. In 1997 it became 74:1.

There is increasing apprehension about the effect of globalization. In an illuminating analysis, Prof. Amartya Sen made these poignant observations:

"Globalisation has been gathering momentum rapidly across the world. The globe is getting smaller remarkably fast, bringing with it new opportunities as well as fresh problems. Can we make good use of world trade, reap serious benefits from it, without being battered or marginalized? Would economic integration help us in general, or should we do our best to resist it? Will there be losers as well as gainers, and who will they be? How can the threat to the potential losers be reduced or eliminated? Economics is not, of course, the only subject affected by globalisation, and there are in particular, cultural matters."

"It would be a great mistake to see globalisation as being an inescapable harbinger of downfall and misery. Global participation is basically an enhancement of economic opportunity, and its benefits can be plentifully reaped and its costs minimized through appropriate domestic policies, paying particular attention to the availability and distributional equity of economic and social opportunities. If a generalized fear of globalisation is a false alarm, an unreasoned conviction in favour of less governance is a source of real danger. The simple diagnostic slogan that India's problems stem from over-governance is a dangerous half-truth that can wound, on the one hand, while it tries to salvage, on the other."[4]

Science and technology will transform the face of the world. New kinds of property and privileges will emerge. Correspondingly, newer kinds of deprivation and poverty will also emerge. They all require excellent managerial and administrative skills to regulate and handle their social outcomes.

There are in India 400 million children below the age of 14 whose physical and moral upbringing is an enormous responsibility. Over 100 million of them are from the Dalit sections. Nearly 40 per cent of the world's tuberculars are in India; 30 per cent of the world's blind are in India. HIV is a distinct and stable threat.

These problems can be surmounted by a wise deployment of technology. Technology can revolutionize management of Education, Health-Care, Communication and Governance. The key factor is the political will and the realization that corruption and inefficiency in public life are the biggest enemies of development.

Enormous disparities of global wealth between the North and South, the West and the rest, is a reality. There are however, many myths about poverty in the developing world. The problem of the poor in the developing world is not that of lack of wealth, but lack of legal and administrative systems to convert their savings and assets into live capital. In a recent work, Hernando de Soto wrote:

"Even in the poorest countries the poor save. The value of the savings among the poor, in fact is, immense: forty times all the foreign aid received throughout the world since 1945."

"If USA raises its budget for foreign aid to 0.7 per cent of national income, as recommended by UN, it would take that richest country 150 years to transfer to the world's poor the wealth they already possess."

"By our calculations, the total value of the real estate held, but not legally owned, by the poor of the Third World and former communist nations is at least $ 9.3 trillion. This number is worth pondering. $ 9.3 trillion is about as much as the total circulating US money supply. It is very nearly as much as the total value of all the companies listed on the main stock exchanges of the world's twenty most developed countries, forty six times as much as all the World Bank loans of the past three decades, and ninety three times as much as all development assistance from all advanced countries to the Third World in the same period."

Speaking of the poor, he writes:

"The words 'international poverty' too easily bring to mind images of destitute beggars sleeping on the kerb-sides in Calcutta and hungry African children starving on the sand. These scenes are, of course, real, and millions of our fellow human beings demand and deserve our help. Nevertheless, the grimmest picture of the Third World is not the most accurate. Worse, it draws attention away from the arduous achievements of those who triumphed over every imaginable obstacle to create the greater part of the wealth of the society. A truer image would depict a man and a woman who have painstakingly saved to construct a house for themselves and their children, who are creating enterprises where nobody imagined they could be built. I resent the characterisation of such heroic entrepreneurs as contributors to the problem of global poverty. They are not the problem. They are the solution."[5]

Every civilization must absorb some degree of self-criticism and disillusionment; but there are special periods in the nation's history when self-criticism ceases to be an instrument for self-correction; but for self-destruction. Everyone suddenly seems to become too sharp for loyalty. Disenchantment with institutions of governance produces cynicism. Cynicism kills values and shakes the bond that unites people. Eruption of violence is the result if remedial steps are denied for long.

The crisis is crisis of leadership in all fields, particularly religious leadership of all groups. It is a crisis of credibility. It is given to this present day politician, the rare and great opportunity of re-establishing the 'Idea of India' and to earn the eternal gratitude of a grateful nation and of the future generation of Indians. For this, electoral reforms, reform of political parties and legal systems to keep surveillance against unlawful political activity, are fundamental. If the politicians exchange this great opportunity for a mere mess of pottage, he will be, in the words of Shakespeare:

"A poor player that struts and frets his hour upon the stage, then is heard no more."

With him, the grand 'Idea of India' will also be no more.

Two and half thousand years ago Mencius said, "...extend the principle of tender care of the tender ones in your family to the tender ones in others' families; extend the principle of respect to the elders in your family to those in others' families and you will roll a great society in your hands. By the existence of your compassion you can protect all within the four seas. But without it, you will not protect your own wife and children."

This, hopefully, shall remain the enduring Idea of India.

Notes

1. *The World We're In*, Will Hutton.
2. *The World We're In*, Will Hutton.
3. Swami Ved Bharathi, *Unifying Streams in Religion*.
4. *Development as Freedom*, Amartya Sen.
5. *The Mystery of Capital*, Hernando de Soto.

2

Ideas of India in Conflict

SUNIL KHILNANI

I

Conflict is in many ways written into the Idea of India. If the struggle for freedom was characterized by a remarkable non-violence, the actual moment of Independence was after all marked by terrible conflict, of the starkest kind. Conflict is also written into the Idea of India not least because of the decision made by the men and women who worked to make India free, the decision to value choice. Their commitment was to create an India in which Indians, as individuals and as a nation, would have freedom: the freedom to make choices about their economic livelihood, choices about their personal relations and moralities, their values, and choices about who would rule them and in what manner. While there can and must be substantial disagreement about the extent to which this has been at all realized, there can be no disputing that this was the initial commitment. And in the years after Independence, India's leaders very self-consciously and explicitly showed themselves to be choosing: witness the careful deliberations of the Constituent Assembly, as much as anything a theatrical enactment of the act of political choice, in the face of various possibilities.

Now, choices, the making of choices, require alternatives, and must allow for competition between alternatives. Such alternatives frequently will come into conflict, and often these conflicts are between values and practices that are equally worthwhile — that is, they are tragic conflicts, since in choosing, something of value must be sacrificed: think for example of the decision, the choice to relegate Gandhian principles in the Constitution.

Authoritarian political ideologies and orders do not allow for recognition of conflicts in their society, or more precisely, they wish to suppress conflict, through intimidation and terror. Democratic orders acknowledge that ultimately, all there is in politics are conflicts — conflicts about values, about how to achieve those values, as well as conflicts over interests and how to secure these. That just is what politics is, in very large part.

So, in committing India to a democratic order, the founders committed us to learning to live with conflict. But they also tried to show — in the constitutional order they established — that a primary art of politics is the ability to moderate and contain conflicts: to transform them from something base to something richer. That is the alchemical promise of democratic politics. The founders saw that by recognizing the presence of differences, often deep-set ones, one might be able to find ways to contain them, in ways that actually enhance the overall, long-term stability and viability of the Indian project. What their practice also showed was the continual necessity of reflecting on how well we are doing in this respect, and the need also to be inventive, to respond to new conflicts, real and potential, in imaginative ways.

We may feel, as we survey the dissension and bloody struggles that fill the India political landscape today, above all conflicts over our identities as citizens, as members of religious communities, and of caste groups, that that is now a lost art. But I want to suggest that we shall now and in coming years, need more than ever to recover this art — to find ways to recognize and moderate conflicts, and find ways to redirect their energies in creative ways, without imagining that we can abolish conflicts or make them disappear. My remarks will be general in nature — and I will try to move between 3 levels or arenas of conflict: the global, the national, and the individual — levels that are all of course interconnected. My remarks are designed to be suggestive rather than stipulative.

II

I start with conflicts in the global arena, and will be very schematic. There are two quite contrasting views about the nature of global conflict.

Only yesterday it seems, the academic pundits were arguing that globalization was producing a beneficial convergence across the world, draining out ideology from national politics, and leaving governments merely with questions of managing the economy etc. Electronic communications, technology, would connect people into new communities of interest, helping to generate a global civil society. To great fanfare, it was announced that all the major conflicts over ideology and values were now at an end. In the now-notorious phrase of my colleague, Frank Fukuyama, we were at the end of history: liberal democracy, the ideas of peace, democracy and markets now dominated. While there might continue to be skirmishes and resentful reactions against these global processes, the trend was irreversible, the major conflicts about values, and the means to realize these values were declared over and resolved.

There was, all along, plenty of evidence against this over-simple view; but it took the events of September 11 to pull them into focus. Since that day, there has been a swell of opinion going the other way. So we hear claims that we are poised on the edge of — or already in the throes of — major civilizational clashes: a battle between the West and the Rest, the moderns and the anti-modernists, democracy and terrorism, the coalition versus the axis of evil. The conflicts facing the world, it would seem, are ones of basic values. And in these conflicts, technology, the tool that was to bring us all together, suddenly looks threatening: arming these fundamental conflicts with new weapons, instigating new forms of terrorism.

The drift of the first view is to stress integration; the drift of the second view is to stress division. To the first, the World Wide Web is a form of connection; to the second, it can be a kind of trap, a spider's web.

What are these conflicts about, what is their content? Are they conflicts between the modern and the anti-modern? Not really. This is clear if we allow a less simple view of modernization, of the character of the world being created by the processes variously called globalization, modernity etc.

The modernities that are being created across the globe today are multiple, splintered and often self-injuring. Clearly modernity does not come in one form: as for instance the American way of life. The English political philosopher John Gray has put it well (developing a thought set by Berlin): "As societies throughout the world become more modern, they do not thereby become more similar. Often they move further apart. **In these circumstances, we need to think afresh about how regimes and ways of life that will always be different can come to coexist in peace"** (my emphasis).

The belief that the advance of science, of positivist models, will lead to one set of values being accepted everywhere, is proving to be a myth. We are pushed to accept the most important lesson that Isaiah Berlin drove home in his work: that human beings 'have divergent and conflicting values — and we have to learn to live with this fact. Humanity is not destined for a single way of living'.

As well as accepting this general presence of plural and sometimes conflicting ways of living, we need also to see the plural and in many instances self-conflicted nature of the modern world itself. Many of the current sources of conflicts are rooted in the modern world: Al-Qaeda, terrorism, are drawn from Enlightenment sources. As Ian Buruma has recently noted, "the roots of non-Western extremism can often be traced to the West itself", and as he goes on to note that, whether it is "Japanese ultranationalists in the 1930s, Pan-Arabists, Baathists, Islamists, Indian fascists, Russian Slavophiles, and other enemies of liberalism", all have "in common a fatal weakness for illiberal German ideas on race and nation". And one could find many other examples.

From this perspective, fundamental conflicts are deep rooted — they are not remnants or residues of a passing, pre-modern, world: they will remain, intensify, mutate. And all ideologies that promise the passing of conflict, that desire to abolish conflict, should be held in suspicion. How do we find a way for such conflicts to coexist in peace?

For some, like the American analyst Robert Kaplan, faced with international conflicts — over values, resources etc. — the only way to deal with these is by developing a 'warrior politics': a pre-Christian, pagan ethics that is willing to deploy an economy of violence and force (following Machiavelli) to subdue and contain: shock and awe. This is a view which has gained dominance in Washington: the struggles of the modern world as seen as parallel to those in the ancient world (*cf* also historians like Victor David Hanson, popular with Bush). Indeed Kaplan argues that 'there is no 'modern' world', our world is continuous with the ancient world and its conflicts and crises. In a world governed by pagan notions of self-interest and not by virtue, human rights etc, policy must be unsentimental: *e.g.* support democracy where possible, dictatorship wherever necessary. Now there is clearly something to Kaplan's view, especially his deep skepticism of Utopian ideologies — drawing on religion, which promise a moral conquest of the world, rather than acknowledging the clash of irreconcilable elements. And one can see how his pose: go forth, holding a semi-automatic in one hand, and a copy of Thuycidides in the other, is attractive to some.

III

CONFLICTS AND CONTEXTS

Certainly liberalism needs to be hardheaded. But conflicts are never raw, in the imagined pure Hobbesian state, which the Kaplan view suggests. They always take place within contexts that are defined by traditions, institutions, and practices. They exist on a broad spectrum — ranging from verbal disputes to war, civil or between states. And these contexts are mutable, open to human re-shaping, and re-invention.

Changing the context — which is the art of politics — can change the character of conflict. It can turn a potentially or actually violent conflict into a moderated one, which can be negotiated. Think of the example of Europe: long torn by aggressive nationalism, it managed to disarm this over the past 60 years — through creating a new context, the EU and its institutions. The different national identities remain — they are not abolished — but they have been re-framed into a new order. Think also, for example, how one construes secularism, and the arrangements for it that one provides — legal, political, social — that will help to shape the character of religious conflict in the society in question. On this particular point, the critic and writer Leon Wieseltier has wisely written that we need to find ways to transform what are held to be truths (by believers — in religion, ideology etc.) into opinion, *doxa.* We need to change the context to transform truths that are linked to identity, into opinion about one's interests. This is what has always offended critics of democracy: they fear that all is turned to opinion, made relative. But democracy requires opinion, in order to argue and to justify itself. And this is how democracy can learn to live with religious difference — not by seeking to abolish or ignore it, but by re-framing it and putting it a transformative context.

Are there methods for moderating conflicts that are found universally in all societies? This question is asked by the Oxford philosopher Stuart Hampshire in his inquiry into justice. Following Hart, he draws attention to the Latin legal precept: *Audi alterem partem*, 'Hear the other side' — this is the basis of the adversary principle of argument, and the agonistic conception of justice that follows from this. This injunction to hear the other side is both a practical principle of procedure, and a requirement of rationality: how justice is done and seen to be done.

Hampshire's idea of the adversary principle relates to the contrast between antagonistic relations, that is, relations between enemies, and agonistic relations, between adversaries: enemies fight for different ends/values, adversaries contest for similar goals/values. As the pyschoanalyst Adam Phillips has put it, with our enemies we feel superior, but our adversary we must treat as an equal — and accord them that respect. The institutions and contexts of democracy have as part of their purpose the task of converting enemies into adversaries: to change antagonistic conflict into agonistic conflict. Enemies seek absolute victory over each other, full moral and ideological conquest; adversaries seek to persuade each other, to change each other's opinions.

I think it is important to recognize that, contrary to the conventional view that democracy is only about arriving at consensus, on the contrary, part of the purpose of democracy is exactly to value and sustain disagreement: disagreement can itself be a kind of solution. Violence is all too often born from the desire to get rid of disagreement, to purge it, to abolish conflict.

Let me now turn to the frame of the nation, and to saying something about the changing nature of conflicts in India. I'd like to introduce here a distinction between two kinds of conflict: those which are conflicts of interest, where interests can be negotiated, discussed, where people can be persuaded to recognize as interests matter, that they may not have thought of in that way (*e.g.*, the environment). And on the other hand, conflicts of identity: these tend to brook no negotiation, they are all or nothing struggles for indivisible ends. They pursue final victory, not interim compromise.

I fear that what we are seeing in our country today is a shift in the nature of conflict: from conflicts of interest to those concerning matters of identity. And I want here just to try to identify the problem: the tougher question of how we can change the context for these conflicts I leave to others.

The problem becomes apparent if we look at how the meaning of political representation has altered since independence. The spread of democratic politics, in particular through means of regular elections over the past 50 years, has changed the nature of political representation, producing a model of representation that is distinct from the models associated with Gandhi and Nehru (or with Ambedkar and Azad). In the case of these earlier models, we had leaders who acted on behalf of the interests of others: there was a gap between themselves and those for who they acted: leaders and led did not share an identity. In this understanding of representation, the political actor claims to act on behalf of some other group who is disenfranchised (*e.g.*, Gandhi claiming to represent the *Harijans* — argument with Ambedkar over this. But no, even Ambedkar, in three-piece suit, stood at a distance from those he claimed to represent).

What is happening today is sometimes referred to by phrases such as the 'politics of identity', or of 'presence'. Here the leader, the representative, claims to act for, represent his/her own kind — caste, religion, racial or linguistic group — and, at the limit, to act simply on behalf of his or her own self. An identity is postulated between leader and led, which disarms altogether even the possibility of whether leader and led in fact share any interests.

This can generate a politics which, if taken up widely and used persistently, can throw representative government into crisis, and ultimately can force its collapse. For, as those who operate with this understanding of representation see it, their duty as elected politicians is not to act on behalf of anyone else, but themselves and their own supporters — linked by kin, caste or religion.

Previously, a representative (operating with the earlier conception) had to be seen ostentatiously to follow rules and procedures properly on behalf of others — precisely to absolve oneself of the charge of not acting correctly on behalf of others, or of acting in one's own interests. Now, to follow such etiquette under the new conditions of representation is to lay oneself open to the charge of assimilation with an alien elite and of betrayal of one's supporters.

These conditions of representation have yielded up a politics that is hard to contain within the conventional rules of constitutional observance. When the meaning of representation is transformed to signify a politics on behalf of oneself, this is quite unlikely to sustain a larger sense of a political community — of a constitutional social and political order. Such a view proposes no alternative image of the social order, other than that the social order exists simply as a vehicle for serving particular claims, claims made by some groups against other groups within the order.

It yields a politics that seeks to derive power from winning acceptance for a particular claim against others about who one is, and therefore what privileges one might claim, rather than for what one might propose to do with political power. Such a politics of 'identity' or 'presence' is of a radically different kind from the politics that the Constitution envisaged.

Such conflicts of identity, centred around region, caste and religion abound in India. These identity driven conflicts are much harder to manage, and more savage in their form and effects. As Weiseltier has put it, "where faith in God is wanting, there is still religious identity.... The thinner the identity, the louder".

In India as elsewhere, the conflicts and divisions of present politics are shaped by conflicting conceptions of the past. Broadly, there have been two differing descriptions of Indian history. One sees India as a victim of recurring invasions, whether led by Muslim horsemen or European adventurers, Aryan tribes or satellite TV moguls. The other views India as an arena of civilizational encounters, often uncomfortable, between unequal protagonists, which have produced unique and splendid cultural forms. The first sees India's history over the last millennium as a series of rude interruptions: its adherents promise to end all such interruptions, and to return to an original purity. The second celebrates the mongrel character of India's peoples and their histories: instead of hankering for purity, it sees the moments of mixture as the most creative and imaginative ones. It is a view that insists that what was distinctive about India's past was its ability to transform invasion into accommodation, rupture into continuity, division into diversity.

These competing accounts, implicit in the Indian past, of course took vivid — if awkward — territorial shape in the rival nationalisms that, under imperial auspices, helped to partition British India. Since 1947, the Indian subcontinent has contained in uneasy proximity two contrasting pictures of what a modern nation state is. From their inception, Pakistan and India had radically different stories to tell about themselves. Pakistan founded itself on explicitly religious principles, and saw itself as the state of a homogenous people, the first Islamic nation state in the world. Its creation expressed the belief of Muslim religious nationalists that unity must be found in a common culture derived from religion (a belief that many Hindus also shared, but could not at the time act upon). Such views were doubly mistrustful of diversity: they wanted neither to be part of a larger, plural nation, nor to tolerate internal differences, which they saw as an endangering weakness. Pakistan at its foundation was a relatively familiar model of the nation state, in conformity with the classical Western idea; India, though, was much more unusual, and to many external observers looked precarious and unlikely to succeed.

It has, of course, succeeded: but that success is paradoxical. Today, as religious extremists muster their voice, some in India are threatening to make it a Hindu Pakistan. Where once the founding ideas of India and Pakistan constituted a polarity, today they creep toward a parallel symmetry of extremism.

Since September 11, the stakes of extremism in whatever form — whether it be terrorists sponsored by Pakistan and operating in Indian territory, or terror inflicted by the elected government of Gujarat on its Muslim citizens — are higher than ever. The *New York Times* columnist Tom Friedman argues that in the post-September 11 world, the crucial polarity is no longer between East and West, but between what he terms the World of Order and the World of Disorder. The latter — the failed, rogue and messy states — are the breeding grounds for terrorist and criminal networks, while the World of Order, Friedman has suggested, is constructed around four pillars: the U.S., the EU-Russia, China and India. Yet, will India be able to take and sustain a role as a pillar of the World of Order if it adopts a coarse and exclusivist national ideology, one that while promising to abolish domestic differences in the name of mythic unity, would in fact splinter along religious lines India's interconnected diversities and plunge it into internal and international conflict? India remains the one great modernist political success of the non-Western world, and it would be a catastrophic irony — both for its own people and for the international order — if it were now to abandon that hard-won commitment to — and practice of – toleration and moderation.

IV

In fact, the future lines of conflict in India will be many. Just to list some of these, they will encompass: caste injustice; religious differences; economic inequality; environmental degradation and competition for resources; internal migration; political rights and recognition; rural/urban populations; present/future generations; the regions versus the centre; and rival nationalisms and states.

Some of these will be ineradicable. Conflicts around ethnic and religious differences, over the scarcity of natural resources and the collision of rival values, will be persistent causes of division. As John Gray argues, "such conflicts cannot be overcome, only moderated. The checks and balances of traditional sources of government are ways of coping with this fact". It is these checks and balances, the framing devices for which the law is such a rich resource, that we need to focus on, to be inventive about – and to do our best to give strength by observance.

Religion for example will need to be kept in its place. Some in India have argued a case for the putting of secularism in its place. But we need also to put religion in its proper place. We need to do this not merely to protect politics, but equally to protect religion. As Wieseltier, following Benjamin Constant, has pointed out, if we sacralize politics, then the sacred is thereby also politicized; religion is reduced to politics. By keeping religion in its own sphere, we are better able to see that "the most cherished ends of life are not the political ones", and thereby better able to value what religion can truly teach us.

This moves me on to some remarks about the individual as a battleground for conflicts, particularly moral conflicts. We certainly will need institutions and resources to re-frame conflicts, place them in new contexts. But we will also need alternative moralities. These cannot be found readymade — they have themselves to be devised in the midst of struggle and conflict: moralities, if they are to be shared, will emerge by listening to the other side, by argument and justification. There is need to restore the Indian tradition of public reason, developed in the 20th century by Tagore, Gandhi and Nehru. This tradition does demonstrate how moral positions have to be worked out in argument, not merely assumed.

We would certainly need to test moral arguments against, for example, the amoral arguments of a Kaplan — just as, for example, Nehru tested Gandhian ideas about non-violence against the Christian realism of Niebuhr, just as Gandhi and Tagore engaged with interlocutors with whom they shared little in common.

The various protagonists in some of the central conflicts in India today (*e.g.* religious versus secular, upper versus lower caste *etc.*) contain within themselves internal diversities and conflicts — they are themselves internally in conflict. These internal conflicts need to be teased out, because these are often the bridgeheads across the gap between different, opposed positions, and can provide the important first step to hearing the other side. This is so whether one is talking about a political party or movement one opposes, or a rival state.

It helps here to have an ability for self-reflection. Perhaps the most fundamental *ur*-ground of conflict is the individual, each of us: and we are often (always?) internally in conflict. Consider how those of our political and intellectual leaders who have seemed most self-assured and decisive have described their own internal turmoil and moral conflict, e.g. Gandhi, Nehru — in their examples we have a rich resource from which to begin reflection.

V

Let me now move back towards the national horizon. The recognition of conflict, the creation of a context for it that is not destructive, a safe house, is part of the art of crafting a rich and sustainable democracy. Conflict can weaken, but it can also give strength: it can be enhancing. It can help us to understand better what we truly value, and to find better ways of defending what we value. And, by keeping diversity a live and active fact, rather than merely a decorative feature, it can help a nation and state endure.

This is contrary to the view that civilizations/nations based on some single principle are stronger and better adapted for survival. Diversity is a source of strength. We can find this argument of strength in diversity, for instance, in accounts of Europe. The French historian Francois Guizot argued in the early nineteenth century that Europe manifests no single principle: rather, it stood for diversity. This acted as a check against tyranny. Most civilizations have tended to fall under the domination of one value and institution relatively early in their history: but in Europe, one saw a long contest between claims of aristocracy, democracy, monarchy and theocracy. None triumphed completely, resulting in limited government, which did not try to enforce a single set of creeds or practices. Now, it is striking to recognize that we can find a very similar account of the distinctive strengths yielded by India's diversity: in the work of Tagore, and of Nehru.

The founding idea of India sees conflict as fundamental; and saw also the need to provide contexts — institutional, in the form of the legal and political order, as well as moral languages — for these conflicts. It did not dream of an end to conflict, it did not promise to make conflicts disappear. Those visions of India are to be most suspected which promise us a conflict free haven: those which promise a singular selfhood, where deep differences are effaced. A Utopia created through moral conquest, where there is nothing left to enter into conflict with. Such visions of a world without conflict are those which all too often wreak havoc in seeking to realize their vision.

The Indian idea has today its own ground zero, at Ayodhya: the rubble-site of the republic, where professional archaeologists scrape and dig in search of the buried remains of a fabled temple, alleged to have stood beneath the early Mughal mosque. Yet, for those who lull themselves with the hope that such excavation might yield firm ground on which to build a new, grander commemorative temple, the earth beneath their feet is unsteady. Already Jain monks are pressing forward to demand further excavation, in search of the remnants of an ancient Jain temple; and there are potential Buddhist claims too. One might see, in all this earthmoving, an all-too literal, indeed farcical, misinterpretation of Nehru's remarkable image of India as a palimpsest. India, Nehru wrote, "was like some ancient palimpsest on which layer upon layer of thought and reverie had been inscribed, and yet no succeeding layer had completely hidden or erased what had been written previously". That metaphor captures like none other India's past and present reality — yet is itself in danger of being hidden and erased.

3

The Idea of India

Some Doubts and Queries

RUDRANGSHU MUKHERJEE

The doubt about the Idea of India that I want to broach can be simply put. Can one talk about the Idea of India? Is positing one unambiguous and unquestioned Idea of India, suggested by the definite article, the best notion to put forward in the given political context? History and contemporary India throw up many ideas and visions of India and these might be worth thinking about by those of us who value the multicultural and plural character of Indian society and Indian culture.

The Idea of India is linked in history to the idea of empire and at least from the time of the Mughals, is articulated in a Delhi-centric vision of India. This is somewhat inevitable since Clio, as Hegel pointed out, has an overwhelming bias in favour of the State. The importance of Delhi in Indian history is clear from two facts drawn from the 19th century. One is the almost relentless thrust of the British to move towards Delhi from Bengal even though the Mughal capital had ceased to be the real centre of power. Similarly, in the revolt of 1857, Delhi became for a time at least, the principal focus of the uprising and the decrepit Mughal Emperor, Bahadur Shah, the rebellion's titular head. The taking of Delhi by the rebels and its reconquest by the British were interpreted by both participants as turning points of the rebellion. Thus, even when the political importance of Delhi was a thing of the past, its symbolic significance endowed on Delhi an *ersatz* political importance.

Even a movement that was in no way concerned with kings could not quite escape a Delhi-centric view because its aim was to set up a nation state. The Indian national movement was clearly driven by the aim of freeing itself from foreign rule and to establish a modern nation state. The movement for a free India was powered by a well-formulated ideology that argued against the grain of imperialist historiography and propaganda that India was a united country. The vision of a united India was important to the Indian national movement as it allowed the leaders of the movement, under the aegis of the Indian National Congress, to express the position that India, despite its regional and cultural diversity, was a valid political entity which could be ruled by a single political party running a powerful state.

This idea of India, expressed most eloquently for example, in the writings of Jawaharlal Nehru, stressed the cultural continuity of India. From the Indus Valley Civilization there was an unbroken chain which changing political fortunes and conquests had been unable to destroy. In fact, each conqueror and each foreign element had been absorbed to form a new synthesis and unity. This was the soul of India. A similar vision of India's past informed many of the essays and poems of Rabindranath Tagore. But Nehru located a discontinuity with the coming of the British. Colonial rule stifled India's development and impeded the growth of the forces of modernity in India. Consequently, the removal of colonial rule and the setting up of an Independent nation state became the principal task before the nation. The idea of India was thus linked to the idea of Independence and a new nation state and inevitably also to the movement which made the emergence of such a state possible.

It is possible to get a glimpse of a different idea of India and the Indian national movement. Such a possibility is suggested by an almost throwaway comment made by S. Gopal in his preface to the first volume of the *Towards Freedom* project. Professor Gopal, it will be recalled, was the general editor of the series before the present political dispensation removed him from the position. Gopal noted the absence of documents drawn from the regional languages in the *Towards Freedom* volumes and advocated a separate project to make a comprehensive selection of such documents. There is the glint of recognition here that the movements towards freedom in the various regions that make up India could have had different trajectories and rhythms than the ones traced in the *Towards Freedom* volumes. Indeed, a project like the one Gopal mentions could throw up a completely different kind of perspective from the one emanating out of London (as incorporated in the *Transfer of Power* volumes) and New Delhi (the *Towards Freedom* volumes).

An example can perhaps be given here of the way a different perspective can radically alter the understanding of the national movement and the way Independent India was born. Sumit Sarkar has shown in a celebrated essay that in the mid-forties, the Congress leadership was under pressure from a series of mass movements outside its control. Many of the movements were not wedded to non-violence and the mobilization was not along Gandhian lines. The aims and aspirations of these movements were not similar to those of the Congress. Sarkar showed how the decisions taken by the Congress leadership in that period were influenced by these protest movements. Over the negotiations between the Congress and the British fell the shadow of these protest movements. It appeared from this analysis that the Congress, the putative champion of the Indian national movement, had, in its greed for power, been more than enthusiastic about a negotiated and truncated transfer of power. The Independent state of India was thus born after having abandoned a crucial element in the Idea of India — the unity of India.

The possibility that Indian history could move in many different trajectories than the one in which Delhi or *Aryavarta* traveled was present in the nationalist consciousness itself. Bankimchandra argued that Afghan rule in Bengal had brought about a renaissance in Bengal and Mughal rule had been the region's nemesis. He also insisted that the history of Bengal was less influenced by the so-called classical heritage of the Aryans than the rest of north India. There is a suggestion here, as Partha Chatterjee has noted, of an alternative idea of India. An idea different from that of a history dominated by *Arya-Hindu-Bharatvarsha*. This alternative vision does not have Delhi as its centre. Indeed, the idea and the history of India have no centre. This calls into question the entire idea of national history.

Similarly, documents in regional languages might make it necessary to rethink the significance of events and the whole idea of a unified national movement striving towards one unified national goal. The idea of one unbroken national heritage with the same meaning for the entire country might have to be reviewed. The relationship between the national and the regional and the implicit hierarchy between the two may have to be renegotiated. The idea of the national, under one overarching state, might have to yield ground to the confedaral. One unified idea of India — the Idea of India — might itself become a chimera.

Earlier on, I had made a passing reference to Tagore's ideas on India and Indian history and culture. Let me try and elaborate this a little as embedded in Tagore's writings. There is a critique of statist historiography or what I have called a Delhi-centric view of India and Indian history. Ranajit Guha in a recent and remarkable exegesis of Tagore's ideas on history has shown how Tagore privileged the everyday experience of ordinary individuals over political history. The latter repelled the poet. He saw the domain of politics and the state as a scene of intrigues and maneuvers by politicians haggling over sectional and sectarian interests. Away from this and away from the urban centres were the lives of ordinary men and women with its everyday contentment and misery. This was also a shared and therefore a public domain that needed to be captured creatively in the writing of India's history. Tagore appealed for a greater complementarity between literature and historiography.

Tagore's insistence on the importance of the everyday lives of ordinary individuals is echoed, of course, in the views of Gandhi. Gandhi too turned to village India and to ordinary individuals. Men and women, Gandhi believed, had the ability to fearlessly regulate their own lives. In his Idea of India, the state was a redundancy and individuals regulating their lives could live in enlightened anarchy. Gandhi's ideal captured the spirit articulated in one of Tagore's celebrated songs: "we are all kings in the kingdom of our king." This is also what he meant by *swaraj*.

In the ideas of the two foremost minds of modern India, the vision of the country is made independent of that of the state and of those who run it. The privileging of the individual and her experiences made for plurality and deflected Indian culture from a still centre. I am arguing therefore for ideas of India. These ideas have been suppressed in the grand narrative of an emerging nation state and its own will to power. Alternative ways of imagining the nation have been erased or blocked off. Whatever is unconnected with the making of a nation state gets relegated to the margins: they become local, fragmentary, insufficient and inadequate.

The political climate in which we live in India should force us to recognize the dangers of positing a notion like the Idea of India. The most serious threat to the cultural diversity in India comes from today's ruling party. The BJP advocates a monochromatic Indian culture. The colour is saffron. India belongs to Hindus, the majority. The minorities can stay in India, but on terms set by the majority, the Hindus. This has been a running theme in the writings and speeches of V.D. Savarakar and M.S. Golwalkar and their present day *epigoni*. To establish its claims and to establish its own idea of India, the BJP is not unwilling to use violence, even state-sponsored violence as the pogrom in Gujarat revealed. It believes that the Hindu state should be strong and bellicose. The very project of trying to determine the Idea of India is to fight the BJP on its own turf and on its own terms. The positing of a mainstream and the marginal is analogous logically to seeing India in terms of the majority and the minority. This in purely tactical terms may not be the best course to adopt to counter the BJP.

The Idea of India has an official ring to it. India cannot be taken over by one idea of itself or even represented by one idea. The culture and the society are too rich and too plural. Ideas about India will always be in contest with the Idea of India. Imagining India is free and ought to be so.

4

Fraternity and Reconciliation

Next Phase in Nation Building

B.G. VERGHESE

India was an idea long before it became a nation, a celebration of diversity. From ancient times it was an open society, globally connected along the Silk Road and Spice Route. These busy highways of commerce and conquest witnessed a free exchange of culture, faith and invention as caravans, sages and savants traversed mountain and desert and sailed the oceans. Buddhism reached Central Asia and China overland and, together with Hindu influences, was carried by the monsoon winds to Southeast Asia. There was lively intercourse with Persia and the Arab lands, and through them with Rome, Venice and Muscovy, and with the eastern African littoral. This marked one of the great crossroads of the world, enriched by what it received as much by what it gave.

It was an inclusive, accommodative society. Christianity came to the shores of modern Kerala in 52 A.D with St. Thomas, an Apostle of Christ, to found what remains one of the very oldest living churches anywhere in the world. Islam also came early, in the lifetime of the Prophet, along with Arab traders who plied the Malabar coast. Jews and Parsees too found hospitality on these shores centuries ago. Next year, India will celebrate with UNESCO the 3000th birth anniversary of Zoroaster. All these belong and have added to the Idea of India.

Decadence and inwardness led to Western dominance of India and the severance of its age-old ties. These were replaced by bonds separately linking it and other Asian nations to colonial hubs in Europe, only to create a new intra-Asian isolationism. Even up to

1700, India, with China, was amongst the two wealthiest nations in the world. What marked that old society was fraternity, with a sense of togetherness and increasing inter-cultural penetration amid an extraordinary diversity.

Came Partition in 1947 at the end of the colonial interregnum. It was a painful parting, carelessly and callously effected by a hastily departing Imperial power. Yet the hope was that India and Pakistan were separating as sovereign states, but not as people who shared so much and could still work together for the common good. This has sadly not happened - as yet. But that day will come, as it must, sooner rather than later, if India is to rediscover its roots and Pakistan a positive identity. The Kashmir question, that divides them, is not the cause, but the consequence of an emotional disjunction that has long stricken Pakistan, but is now also affecting India even as both sides are striving to sew new nation states from ancient cloth.

There is a defining characteristic of India's plurality that is little understood, though it lies at the very heart of the nation-building project. It is not a melting pot in which different alloys emerge from the cauldron as one metal. Rather, it is a garden in which even the dominant green is of many distinctive shades, interspersed with little tinges and broader splashes of colour, many subtle, others brilliant. The garden once exhibited a more formal design, with everything in its own particular place. No longer. The many hues remain, but the design is undergoing bewildering change.

According to a Japanese saying, "In the garden it is written 'Don't pluck the flowers'. But it is useless against the wind, which cannot read". Strong winds of change are blowing across India and mock social relationships that are frozen in time, cruelly out of place, irrelevant and inimical to the new order into which the country is being reborn. A static social structure based on rigid caste hierarchies is progressively gaining dynamism, with cohorts of a long submerged under-mass or under-class thrusting upwards from Bharat to India to claim their place in the sun. These elements will not be denied. Successive cohorts are asserting a new-found identity and demanding access and participation as equal, sovereign partners in a democratic India. Citizenship and merit must and will triumph over caste, feudal privilege and dead habit.

It is a critical attribute of good governance to usher change. The current upsurge, noisy and untidy as it may seem, represents the making of a new order, not anarchy. It is foolish to treat this churning as a law and order problem. What is loosely called "Naxalism" is no more than a reaction to crass feudal exploitation, with the "law" being used to defend a wholly iniquitous established social order in the name of "stability". The Dalits, tribal India, other backward classes and marginalized groups, sections among the minorities and women are yet to be "liberated".

It is the inability to discern and understand these trends clearly that has long confused the debate on nation building and secularism, the social contract on which the new India must be based. The word "secularism" did not occur in the Constitution until 1976 when the Preamble was amended. However, the idea found explicit mention in the definition of fundamental rights and Directive Principles such as equality before law, prohibition of discrimination on grounds of religion, race, caste, sex or place of birth, equality of opportunity, abolition of untouchability, freedom of religion and conscience, and safeguards for linguistic and cultural minorities.

The secularization of society is a Western concept going back to the renaissance and Age of Reason. It entailed separation of state from Church and Church from school and heralded the process of modernization and scientific inquiry untrammeled by dictates of heresy. The Indian adaptation accepted the first part, but ignored the second. Secularism came to be understood as a policy of state-equidistance from all faiths, but lost the meaning of secularization as a process. Equal respect for all faiths has come to mean pandering to orthodoxy or religious bigotry in the name of keeping faith with "secularism". Thus social and religious reform have, in some ways, become unintended victims of a misplaced Indian secularism, which, like every ism, has acquired a certain rigidity. In practice, equal respect for all faiths has sometimes come to mean equal respect for everybody's communalism. Hence the bizarre spectacle of religious land grab, loudspeakers blaring forth to deaf gods, the invasion of public space, competitive religiosity and, worst, communal vote-banking.

Reservations are a useful and legitimate means of affirmative action. But in the absence of a larger policy frame and bereft of an exit policy, they have created new vested interests and vitiated the attainment of universal primary education, the enforcement of social rights and meaningful social reform. Untouchability persists and the lynching of Dalits in Jhajjar in Haryana in 2002 could still be brazenly passed over with the callous remark that a cow's life is more valuable. The constitutionally-ordained Commission for Scheduled Castes and Scheduled Tribes is a hollow body for which neither Parliament nor successive governments has found much time. Nevertheless, the Dalits and the under-class are on the march. Nothing can halt them, though opposition and obstruction may delay their progress.

The bid to expand the listing of "other backward classes" and empower them through reservations in accordance with the recommendations of the Mandal Commission (1989) was interpreted by the religious right as a sinister bid to fragment and politically weaken Hindu society. This was countered by Hindu mobilization through *rath yatras*, the demolition of the Babri Masjid, the denunciation of "pseudo-secularism" and "minority appeasement". The rise of the Vishwa Hindu Parishad and Bajrang Dal reveals the militant face of the Sangh Parivar. Ayodhya has gained salience but, like Hindutva, seems driven more by politics than faith.

Hindutva has been defined to mean all things to all men. The "cultural nationalism" of Hindu Rashtra is built around the idea of one nation, one flag and one people whose place of origin and holy land is Bharat. This casts Christians, Muslims, Parsees and Jews as "foreigners" or probationary Indians who somehow need to prove themselves. This will be indignantly denied. But one has only to read Savarkar and Golwalkar and the 10th standard Social Studies school textbooks officially brought out and used in Narendra Modi's Gujarat to see that this is so. The appropriation and rewriting of history and the politicized striving to seek present-day revenge for real or assumed historical wrongs have created an "imagined Hindu victimhood" and bred violence and communal discord. This is deeply divisive and has breathed new life into a discredited and discarded two-nation theory.

The genius of India has been accommodation and tolerance despite exceptions. Its plurality and diversity have flourished on the basis of an environment of inclusiveness in which large and little traditions have coexisted and blended to create new harmonies. However,

Hindutva, a narrowly exclusivist, authoritarian doctrine, is a rejection of the Idea of India. The Gujarat holocaust was only possible with the crass complicity of the State. Ideologues have termed it a "successful experiment" in Hindu consolidation that bears repetition.

Recent elections have seen strenuous efforts to stir sectarian passions, whether it be on Ayodhya and other "disputed" temples or on issues relating to cow protection, conversions and the distribution of trishuls through hate speeches, jingoism and inflammatory rhetoric. There have been some gains, but revulsion too. Hindutva is not politically sustainable and India will ultimately triumph. For this to happen, sooner rather than later, there is need to redefine the meaning and practice of secularism and return to that richer, nobler and more meaningful concept of fraternity and togetherness. The language of discourse too must change.

We have to learn to distinguish between religion and culture. The two are by no means synonymous, as mistakenly assumed by some exponents of Indian secularism. Culture is a far wider expression of living experience than faith. Indonesia, the largest Islamic nation in the world, boasts a proud Hindu cultural heritage. Thailand and Cambodia are similarly devoutly Buddhist by faith, but exhibit a strong Hindu cultural underlay in terms of language, art, architecture and so much else.

Likewise, the religious and even linguistic minorities, to whom the Constitution offers special protection, should not be seen exclusively in numerical terms. This immediately translates into political demography, impacting on elections and power equations. That this should be so is understandable in view of the colonial history of separate electorates and representation indexed to numbers that led to Partition. Yet, with the constitutional guarantee of equal citizenship without discrimination on grounds of race, religion, caste, gender or region, this should no longer be a primary consideration. To describe 130 million Indian Muslims — possibly the second largest concentration of followers of Islam anywhere in the world — as a minority, is to strain the meaning of words. Moreover, Muslims, just as much as Hindus or Sikhs or Christians, have multiple identities of which faith may not necessarily be the most important for most and for most of the time. Sikhs, a national minority, constitute a majority in Punjab, but are again a minority in the city of Amritsar.

The politicization of community and caste in relation to numbers has led to vote-bank politics and the competitive exploitation of communal sentiments. This has tended to entrench sectarian tendencies and stoke tensions and negative memories. Being a "minority", more truly represents an attitude towards self and nation. Those who feel weak and inadequate or rejected are liable to feel threatened, irrespective of numbers. Parsees and Sikhs, by and large (1984 notwithstanding), do not behave as "minorities". They are self-assured and competitive. Hindutva spokesmen, however, speak of being oppressed by the minorities, a manifestation of their own minority complex.

Muslim Indians were bewildered and politically orphaned by Partition, which most of them did not seek. Ideology and communal pressures caused some to migrate to what became Pakistan. That flow was stemmed long back. A new generation of more self-assured and increasingly competitive post-Partition Muslim Indians is emerging out of the shell into which the community had retreated. This holds true despite the more recent trauma of periodic riots, lingering discrimination, the demolition of the Babri Masjid and Gujarat-2002. It is noteworthy that no Muslim Indians were found among the Taliban in Afghanistan or have been noticed among the *jehadis* in J&K. Mafia dons there are, but they belong to all communities.

However, the sense of helplessness and despair sweeping the Islamic world over the past few decades, fuelled in part by happenings in Palestine, has fostered what is termed political Islam. This in turn has bred extremist violence and fundamentalism, culminating in 9/11, the so-called War on Terror in Afghanistan, and now Iraq. Pakistan's inability to come to terms with itself has also stoked its proxy war in Jammu & Kashmir. Some of these negative Islamic influences have spread to India, giving a fillip to Hindu fundamentalism and a mythology of hate founded on misconceptions and prejudice against Muslim Indians with little or no validity, thereby setting in motion a vicious cycle detrimental to order and tranquility and the process of social development and modernization in the country.

Secular Muslim leadership in India has to play a more active role in leading the community out of the ghetto and conservatism within which some elements would try and confine it. Education and training in all fields will open up economic opportunities and widen the

Muslim meritocracy at all levels. *Wakfs* should divert funds from ritualistic expenditure and traditional rote learning in *Madarsahs* to more relevant purposes. Children are often enrolled in *Madarsahs* as there is nowhere else for them to go. These institutions are being modernized and upgraded and must be assisted in this process. Muslim reservation, as sought by some, is not to be encouraged. Rather, the State has a duty to assist all deprived communities through targeted education and other opportunities. It is time also for the community to follow the path of *ijtehad* or reinterpretation of the *Sharia* so that Muslim Indians are better able to assume their rightful place in a fast changing world. This is not something others can do for them. Change has to come from within. *Fatwas* will not do.

The nomenclature "Muslim Indian" is more appropriate than the commonly used terminology, "Indian Muslim". The former emphasizes Indianness even while being Muslim, as against an Islamic identity as members of the larger *ummah*.

Hinduism is a richly eclectic way of life made up of multiple strands. It is not a monolithic faith of the Book and cannot be cast in a single mould. It too is in need of reform to end outworn and ritualistic practice and caste oppression. Sanskritisation is a slow process and limited by the caste hierarchy. Hindutva, on the other hand, is power driven and speaks of Hindu consolidation and cultural nationalism in political terms. It is not sufficient for Dalits, tribal peoples and even OBCs to be co-opted into the Hindutva fold. They must be enabled to become full citizens with all the rights and privileges that entails. The answer lies in the social and economic empowerment of the disadvantaged and underprivileged.

Some Dalits have sought a way out of the stranglehold of caste by resort to conversion which, they believe, offers hope of a new beginning within a framework of equality and dignity. Regrettably, the Christian Church has been unable to shake off caste and in a manner of speaking has been instrumental in upholding it by petitioning for continuing reservations for SC Christians, which is a contradiction in terms. Christianity has grown in India since Independence, especially among Dalits and tribals and more particularly in backward and neglected regions. The oppressed and neglected have been attracted by Christian service and caring and, in the case of certain tribal groups have adopted Christianity as a means of differentiation or modernization. Conversion "by force and fraud" is relatively rare. It runs counter to tenets of the faith and is punishable under the law, which should, in such cases, take its course.

One must also deplore the brash conduct of certain so-called revivalist or charismatic churches and missions that exude attitudes of cultural arrogance and fundamentalism that are offensive and unacceptable in a plural society. This is a tendency that the Indian Church must address.

The RSS has in recent years made considerable efforts to work among tribal communities and spread education. This is to be welcomed, but must cause concern if the endeavor is directed towards building political constituencies in a new form of vote-bank politics.

In sum, there has to be social advancement and reform in India across the board. A coalition of enlightened citizens, religious leaders and the State is required to lend momentum to what must become a movement. The Preamble to the Constitution promises Liberty, Equality and Fraternity. Though progress may be halting and disappointing, some efforts have been made to promote political and economic reforms. But the debate on social reform has yet to be fully joined as Indian "secularism" actually discourages forays into what it regards as forbidden ground.

Nothing illustrates this more vividly than the sorry fate of Article 44. This stipulates that the State "shall endeavour to secure for the citizens a uniform civil code throughout the territory of India". This has to be read with Article 25 of the Fundamental Rights chapter, which provides that "subject to public order, morality and health and to the other provisions of this Part, all persons are equally entitled to freedom of conscience and the right freely to profess, practise and propagate religion". Article 26 permits every religious denomination "to manage its own affairs in matters of religion". Again, Article 30 protects the right of any section of citizens "having a distinct culture of its own to conserve the same".

The meaning is clear. Religious codes, customs and cultural practices that are not liable to affect public order, morality and health and do not otherwise offend the Constitution are guaranteed as fundamental rights. The religious and social practices and customary laws of certain other communities such as Nagas and Mizos are also constitutionally protected. Yet, Indian society is rapidly evolving and changing. A variety of traditional communitarian, caste, cultural, regional, ethnic and other barriers and taboos are disappearing as a result of education, social awareness, mobility, technology, inter-marriage and cross-cultural fertilization. In the circumstances, there is not merely room but a real need for an optional uniform civil code that promotes inter-cultural bonding without derogating from multiculturalism.

An optional code will suffice, as Article 44 is hortatory and not mandatory in seeking to foster a uniform civil code, which already exists in Indian criminal jurisprudence. There is in fact a uniform civil code in Goa as a legacy of Portuguese rule. Elements of a uniform code also exist nationally in the form of the *Special Marriage Act*. On the other hand, there is the cruel absurdity of persons other than Hindus (which here includes Buddhists, Jains and Sikhs) being legally unable to adopt children in India in the absence of an adoption law applicable to Muslims and Christians. *The Guardians and Wards Act* is an inadequate substitute.

Tragically, it has not been possible to legislate or even rationally discuss a uniform civil code in India because of bogus "secular" posturising. With the Hindu right arguing the case for "Indianisation" through enactment of a uniform civil code, which in its opinion entails the abrogation of Personal Laws, "secular" lobbies, with the Congress and Marxists in the lead, have been loud in seeking the preservation of Muslim personal law. The fiction that the Hindu right in particular asserts or appears to believe is that the Hindu Code enactments of the 1950s constitute a near approximation to a uniform civil code. This is specious. In fact, during the Emergency, Indira Gandhi retrogressively amended *the Special Marriage Act* to provide that Hindus marrying under it shall be entitled to be governed by *the Hindu Succession Act*.

There are several Hindu codes prevalent in India, and sometimes even within single states. The Hindu undivided family has become a legalized tax haven and Hindu deities are recognized legal persons in whose name property and wealth may be held. Under Article 290A, certain prescribed sums are charged to the Consolidated Fund of Tamil Nadu every year for the maintenance of Hindu temples and shrines transferred to it from Travancore-Cochin under *the States Reorganisation*

Act in 1956. There are legitimate reasons for some of these provisions, but the notion that "Hindu Law" is totally secular or uniform is based on ignorance.

The crucial importance of a uniform civil code also lies in guaranteeing gender justice. All personal laws, almost without exception, discriminate against women in relation to rights and responsibilities, divorce, property and succession. This is equally true of customary law - despite the cover of matriarchy and matrilineality. The women of the Northeast are fighting this battle. One may also therefore suspect a hidden male chauvinist agenda across party lines in diverting attention from the enactment of a uniform civil code that would ensure gender justice. More the pity that the women's movement too has lost its way in the fog.

There is a very strong and urgent case both for the systematic codification of all personal and customary laws, to which little attention has been given, as well as for the enactment of an optional uniform civil code paralleling codified personal codes in a modernizing India. Perhaps the biggest roadblock in the way has been the false conception of Indian "secularism" that has become another doctrinaire "ism" impeding the growth of Fraternity and women's empowerment in India by misguidedly upholding gender discrimination.

In all these cases, the key word is not community, caste, gender or region, but citizenship. "Them" and "us" have to become "we". Reference has earlier been made to mainstreaming. Being on the geographical periphery should not entail being marginalized or considered secondary. There is a certain arrogance in periodically calling upon the Northeast and Jammu & Kashmir to "join the mainstream". These two regions may suffer from the growing pains of nation building; but the "mainstream" is no more than the sum of all the many traditions and cultures of India.

The Northeast is distinctive in-so-far as it is racially neither Aryan nor Dravidian, but of Mongolian stock, with large chunks of territory long constitutionally treated as "excluded areas" under the Raj. Partition relegated them to geo-political isolation. The contending tendencies of national integration and local differentiation on the basis of ethnic identities among peoples still in the earlier stages of becoming Indian posed inherent difficulties and sensitivities. In the years following Indian Independence, many kinds of ethnic assertion and insurgencies have been witnessed. Some, such as a section of Nagas and, for a time, Mizos, have sought sovereignty outside India; others have struggled for separation from Assam and statehood within India; and still others for linguistic and cultural autonomy or economic advancement within Assam or any other of the new states that have come into being in the Northeast. Tactless handling has fanned some separatist movements. Others have burnt out or have been more or less resolved. Some linger, partly as a product of adventurism among alienated and unemployed youth coping with multiple transitions.

The Naga movement is the oldest and strongest of these. Internal factionalism rendered earlier piecemeal settlements infructuous. However, long years of violence, fratricidal killing and suffering have brought about fatigue and a yearning for peace. This triggered intense debate and reflection within Naga civil society as much as among the armed cadres that was mediated by the Naga *hoho* (tribal assemblies), the Church, women's groups and concerned citizens. The result was a Naga Movement for reconciliation and peace, which found space in the ceasefire agreed upon by the two NSCN factions and the Government of India. Though little reported or studied, this has been a remarkable movement to own responsibility, seek mutual forgiveness for injury and error and build trust. The commencement of substantive negotiations between the NSCN (IM) leadership and the Government of India marks a major step forward on what still remains something of a tightrope.

The IM leadership is no longer asking for independence *per se*, but seeks recognition of the Naga peoples' unique history and culture. This demand may be satisfied if the Government were to acknowledge a precedent Naga peoplehood that was possibly involuntarily absorbed into the Indian Union by the tide of history. While this process cannot now be reversed, it has been sublimated by the fact that the Nagas are today co-sovereigns and co-sharers in a democratic republic with no bar on their all-round development and fulfillment in accordance with their own genius. Such a formulation, formally expressed in a solemn concord, could offer a resolution that is just and honorable to both sides.

There is no reason why Nagaland cannot be accorded some further autonomy and certain symbols of identity such as a flag, a Naga embossed Indian passport, special postage stamps and trade and tourist representation abroad. J&K is the only other State that may uniquely qualify for similar consideration. Many Indian Princely States enjoyed such attributes in the past. However, unification of all Naga peopled areas within a single Naga state is not going to be possible. What would be feasible is extension of Naga customary law to Naga-inhabited areas adjacent to Nagaland, without impairing the identity and integrity of these neighboring states. An informal mechanism for social and cultural interaction and consultation among all Naga people could also be institutionalized through a body like the all-Naga *hoho*.

The Naga ceasefire and peace process and subsequent Bodo accord have begun to engender a new mood in the Northeast. Despite continuing violence, insurgency is slowly winding down in the region. The process may take time. While there could be reverses, the changing external environment could exert a positive influence in this regard with the opening up of relationships with Bangladesh, Myanmar and Tibet. These could stimulate the economy, create new employment opportunities and turn their geo-political location to advantage, thereby adding to their sense of self-esteem. The Northeast is hopefully in transition from a neglected periphery to a region of opportunity and a bridge to lands beyond. New policies and a new diplomacy are indicated.

Jammu and Kashmir lies at the other extremity of the country. Here too, there is today a historic opportunity for peace and reconciliation both within and across national boundaries. After months of confrontation and frigidity in mutual relations, a fresh effort is under way to revive an Indo-Pakistan dialogue alongside a new peace process initiated in J&K. Free and fair elections were held to the State Assembly in the autumn of 2002 amid much huffing and puffing by Pakistan and disruptive terrorist strikes. There was a substantial voter turnout despite grave intimidation, and the poll was certified a success by international observers. This has created a new mood which the Chief Minister, Mufti Sayeed has sought to consolidate by imparting a healing touch. The spoilers are feverishly at work, as might be expected, but the people's desire for peace is unmistakable.

A new Prime Ministerial emissary has commenced quiet talks with all sections of the population in order to ascertain views and aspirations across the board. The mandate includes good and humane governance and an economic programme that delivers employment and visibly impacts on the quality of life. But quite obviously, the critical element will be building trust and confidence among alienated communities and reaching an agreement on internal autonomy for the State and regional autonomy within it. This may take time, though it is entirely possible that the process could develop a life and momentum of its own. All the more necessary that the Government and country should not be caught unprepared should events move faster than anticipated.

The peace process is in some ways as important as the agenda. The outcome must be broadly acceptable to the people of J&K and the rest of India, including the Pandits, to Pakistan and to the international community. Quibbles as to whether or not Kashmir is a "dispute" or the discussions are "within the framework of the Constitution" are meaningless. It is not the fact but the nature of the dispute that is essentially in contention. Similarly, both the J&K and Indian Constitutions are amendable and adaptable. The catalyst required is a national consensus.

The nature of the dispute is clear. To restate it is not to indulge in recrimination, but to set the record straight. The plain fact is that Pakistan, though in unlawful occupation of two fifths of J&K by an admitted act of aggression, has for half a century sought to appropriate a further part of the State across the LOC. This pseudo-irredentism is based on the unacceptable and dangerous theory of religious affinity that could equally justify its claiming Afghanistan, Iran or parts of Xinjiang. All else is cant. A plebiscite was offered, but spurned when it was available and practical. That option was extinguished long ago. Overt and covert warfare have failed. There can be no second partition of India.

The people of the unified State of J&K enjoyed *de facto* independence from August 15 to about October 22, 1947 in accordance with *the Indian Independence Act*. This, however, proved unviable in the face of the Pakistan-backed tribal invasion that compelled the Maharaja to turn to India to which he acceded to popular acclaim. India's complaint to the United Nations of aggression in J&K was artfully and willfully dodged by Britain and the US for decades, until Kargil, because by 1949 Pakistan was well on the way to becoming a frontline state, first in the

Cold War, then during the war in Afghanistan and now in waging the so-called War on Terror. Opportunism prevailed over principle and law.[1]

Internal discontents and militancy in J&K are also facts of life. These are being addressed. This is an issue India has to settle with its own people and is one in which Pakistan can have no prescriptive role. The enormity of Pakistan's double-speak so gullibly accepted by assorted apologists, allies and ideologues is evidenced by the fact that there has been little or no self-determination and a wholesale trampling of democratic and human rights in so-called "Azad" Kashmir and the Northern Areas. The latest ploy has been the incessant crying of wolf about an impending nuclear holocaust. This is nothing but nuclear blackmail.

Yet for all that, it must be realistically accepted that Pakistan cannot today simply walk away from J&K. It has to be accommodated in some manner. That too is a ground reality as much as the Line of Control which, incidentally, defines a fairly well-demarcated socio-cultural divide between the two parts of the State and therefore has a certain logic of its own. The LOC can be adjusted within limits to make it a more rational administrative, ecological and defensive boundary, but cannot be wished away. The "gap" in that Line, caused by the so-called Siachen dispute, must also be closed. Otherwise, the entire LOC could unravel as Pakistan thought it well might, with a smash and grab assault on the heights of Kargil in 1998.

It is not well known that the Siachen Glacier is basically on the Indian side of the UN-delineated Cease Fire Line under the Karachi Agreement of July 1949. India acted pre-emptively in 1984 to occupy the Saltoro Ridge, the mountain wall marking the western flank of the Siachen Glacier itself. It did so because Pakistan, gratuitously aided by the US Defence Mapping Agency, had started committing "cartographic aggression" from around 1967 by depicting the CFL as running northeast from NJ 9842, the last grid reference, towards the Karakoram Pass and not "thence north to the glaciers" as the Karachi Agreement unambiguously stipulated. The Cease Fire Line was renamed the Line of Control at Simla in 1972 to give it a political connotation in progression towards gradually becoming an international boundary. The US has only now begun to correct its maps of the region and the attached explanatory legends truthfully to reflect the Actual Ground Position Line as it is called.

Any internal settlement in J&K will stir interest and envy in POK and the Northern Areas and deny Pakistan the leverage it gleefully exploited to meddle in the State. J&K (with Nagaland to some extent) even now enjoys more autonomy than any other Indian State. But a further amendment in Centre-State relations, according it even greater devolution, should be possible. All talk of abrogating Article 370 betrays a lack of constitutional understanding even at high levels. This Article only regulates J&K's relations with the Centre in a federal context. The State stands fully integrated with India as much as any other constituent unit by virtue of Article 1 and Schedule 1, as well as by the corresponding sections of the J&K constitution that happen to be unamendable.

The original heads of accession, namely foreign affairs, defence and communication are themselves widely cast. Many other Entries in the Union List (Schedule 7) confer powers that inhere in any federal government or do not impinge on J&K as such, or are benign by any yardstick. The issues in contention, including the Centre's assumption of concurrent and residuary powers, can be repatriated to the State without impairing national integrity or good governance. Ultimately, the quantum of autonomy will remain a matter of trust - no more, no less.

Regional devolution of power within J&K is also amenable to solution, with an upgraded *panchayati raj* as a basic building block. A look at the process of devolution and according regional autonomy in the Northeast shows how far it has been possible to go in accommodating local cultural identities and safeguarding the economic and political interests of given communities through a process of entrustment. Once the peace process gets under way in J&K, growing confidence and trust will increasingly open new windows.

A marginally adjusted LOC, as may be desirable and feasible, and a lowering of tensions with Pakistan within a wider framework of growing Indo-Pakistan cooperation will not mean a hardening of the J&K divide. What matters is not the fact of an international boundary as much as its nature. The LOC can become a soft international border, admitting of relatively free and easy two-way movement for people to people and cultural exchange, commerce, pilgrimage, tourism and investment and the development of a shared infrastructure across both parts of J&K. It is noteworthy that among the CBMs the Government of India proposed on the eve of the Agra summit was in effect the opening of the Jammu-Sialkot, Uri-Muzaffarbad and Kargil-Skardu routes for cross border traffic.

Common or shared institutions and conventions can be developed to manage an evolving cross-border relationship. Over time, these could be further institutionalized and empowered. Demilitarisation of the LOC could be followed by a thinning down of troops on either side and the creation of zones of peace. An internationally certified Karakoram-Himalaya Glacier Park, stretching from the Karakoram Pass, through Siachen to K2 and Nanga Parbat, would be an early and useful candidate, with Aksaichin and Shaksgam thrown in for good measure should the Chinese agree. An Indus Water-II could be negotiated to supplement the 1960 Treaty in order to optimize the water and energy potential of the Indus basin as a whole. The Jammu-Baramulla railway could in time continue up to Muzaffarbad and along the Neelam valley to link with the Karakoram Highway. International investments could flow to make all of J&K a playground destination with a special personality of its own, as an informal confederation within twin sovereignties.

It is useful to recall that both Jawaharlal Nehru and, more recently, Mr. Advani, have spoken of confederal solutions. All this is as yet no more than a vision. However, the projection opens up exciting vistas down which to travel, overcoming past antagonisms and mistrust.

The question that will be asked is, what is in this for Islamabad? Why should it accept a long-established status quo? The answer is simple. Pakistan would at last be able to redeem its soul and assert a positive identity without need for Kashmir or the Indian "other" for self-definition. It would legitimize its presence in "Azad" Kashmir and the Northern Areas. Further, a honorable settlement in J&K would enable Pakistan to reclaim the role Jinnah wished for it as a modern, liberal, plural democracy and a beacon for the Islamic world. Democratic forces and civil society would thereafter inevitably take control of the levers of state power, gradually returning the Army to the barracks.

Friendship with India and a leading role in a revivified SAARC/ South Asian Community in the making would be another major gain for Pakistan. Abatement of the mutually perceived security threat from the other would facilitate international investment in one or more gas pipelines from Iran and Turkmenistan, through Afghanistan to Pakistan and India. Afghanistan and Iran would be natural members of SAARC in due course, as would Myanmar in the east.

For their part, the people of Jammu and Kashmir on both sides could not expect anything better. They would enjoy the best of both worlds, with a large measure of internal autonomy as well.

Following such a course would lay to rest the ghosts of Partition. Indo-Pakistan reconciliation could give quietus to right wing fundamentalism in both countries. For India the road through Srinagar and Islamabad could also offer a welcome by-pass to Fraternity. A dynamic South Asian Community would allow its constituent units to mitigate or even resolve national problems through optimal regional solutions and enhance regional prosperity and security. South Asia would assume its due place as a global player, representing a sixth of mankind in refashioning a better and more equitable world order.

The Idea of India is written into the truly liberal social charter the Constitution enshrines. The misconceptions, anxieties and animosities of the past need to be quietly but candidly discussed in a newly conceptualized National Integration and Social Development Council. This would provide a suitable forum for an intra-national and inter-faith dialogue to bury the past and point the way to the future. It is in such a setting that Muslim Indians may be emboldened to make a gracious offer to withdraw from the Babri site in order to make way for the construction of a Ramjanambhoomi Mandir, on the explicit understanding that no other "disputed" mosque will be claimed henceforward. The cow slaughter issue stands virtually resolved. But ways must be found to implement the other part of Article 48 calling for modern and scientific animal husbandry. The tens of million stray cattle let loose on the roads and forests of India constitute a health and traffic hazard, a national economic burden and an ecological threat.

Above all, the social charter must and can be implemented within the next 10-15 years. Universal education and poverty alleviation would give powerful impetus to the uplift of marginalized and disadvantaged groups, particularly Dalits and tribals, and gender justice.

We need to move from revenge to reconciliation, from yesterday to tomorrow. We must cultivate Fraternity with Reconciliation. That way lies progress and harmony and fulfilment of the Idea of India.

Note

1. See B.L. Sharma, *The Kashmir Story*, Asia, 1967 and C. Dasgupta, *War and Diplomacy in Kashmir*, Sage, 2002.

5

To Kill the Mockingbird[1] – *Madarsahs* in India: Past, Present and Future

AMIR ULLAH KHAN • MOHAMMAD SAQIB

Introduction

*Madarsah*s (religious schools) and *maktab*s (primary schools) have been providing traditional education in India for over eight centuries now. They have helped in promoting literacy, especially among the Muslims. Over the centuries, they have produced academics and administrators such as Sher Shah Suri, Abul Fazal, Faizi, Todar Mal, and Fatehullah Shirazi, among others. Raja Ram Mohun Roy, the reformer and the founder of the Brahmo Samaj, was educated at a *Madarsah*.

At present, there are several thousand Islamic schools spread all across India[2]. Most mosques have primary religious schools or *maktab*s attached to them, where Muslim children learn the *Quran* and the basics of their faith. For children who desire to specialize in religious studies and train as *imam*s and *maulvi*s, numerous large seminaries or *Madarsah*s exist, with each Muslim sect having its own chain of such institutions. For many poor families, *Madarsah*s are the only source of education for their children, since they charge no fees and provide free boarding and lodging to their students[3]. Given the dismal level of access to education, and the increased mistrust[4] against the curricula of government schools, *Madarsah*s are often the only available educational option for children from poor Muslim families, who have the dubious distinction of being, along with Dalits, the least educated community in India.

The Taliban[5] in Afghanistan and the WTC tragedy[6] in the US have brought *Madarsah*s[7] into the limelight. Labeled as breeding grounds of Islamic terrorism, *Madarsah*s suddenly find themselves under harsh scrutiny. In India, Hindutva groups and sections of the government and the press have started a campaign against the *Madarsahs*, branding them as centers of obscurantism and breeding grounds for 'terrorism.'

Ever since the Bharatiya Janata Party-led coalition assumed power, there has been a spate of attacks on the *Madarsahs* in various parts of the country. Indian intelligence agencies claim that some *Madarsahs* are training grounds for ISI spies and anti-Indian 'terrorists'. The reports suggest that the *muftis*, *maulvis* and *imams* in these religious schools may have been replaced by "highly fanatic agents of ISI", secretly working for the disintegration of India. In May 2001, a ministerial group for the "reform of internal security" headed by Home Minister L.K. Advani, released a 137-page report that recommended a close scrutiny of *Madarsahs*, among other things[8].

According to a report published in the Delhi-based Muslim fortnightly, *Milli Gazette*, the Uttar Pradesh government has issued "a mischievous circular" that suggests that certain vested interests are seriously preparing the ground for a "communal civil war" in the state. The circular, signed by Senior Superintendent of Police, Lucknow, B.B. Bakshi, has been issued to the state police as a guideline on how to keep a vigil on "ISI activities". The circular says that ISI is "leaving no stone unturned" to disrupt life in the state, and is luring Muslim and Sikh youth "to involve them in subversive activities", besides also fanning anti-Hindu sentiments. The circular instructs the Station House Officer of every police station to "prepare a register of Muslim and Sikh families living in his respective area". In particular, the report emphasizes, a list of newly constructed *Madarsahs* and mosques should be kept and these are to be closely monitored.

The *Milli Gazette* sent a team to inspect several of the *Madarsahs* along the Nepal-India border being monitored by the police. It reported that none of the dozen Muslim seminaries that the team visited had any association whatsoever with the ISI. In not one of these *Madarsahs* was any sort of physical training being imparted. The report added that these *Madarsahs* have no history of provoking Hindu-Muslim conflict. In fact, one of them had several Hindu students and teachers on its rolls, while another had several regular Hindu donors. Official sources have so far failed to name the *Madarsahs* involved in ISI activities. The state's Director General of

Police (DGP), Sriram Arun, while asserting that the ISI was active along the Indo-Nepal border, is said to have denied that *Madarsahs* were being used as hideouts. Likewise, the DGP of Rajasthan admitted that *Madarsahs* near the border areas are "neither centers of the ISI nor have they ever participated in any anti-national activities".

According to Asghar Ali Engineer, an expert on Islam, more than 95 per cent of the Indian *Madarsahs* have absolutely nothing to do with the ISI. Most *Madarsahs* only impart basic education of Islam to children. As for the larger *Madarsahs*, these are basically centers of higher Islamic learning. One can differ with them on their syllabus and methods of teaching, but one cannot accuse them of engaging in any sort of political activity.[9]

Some *Madarsahs*[10] may indeed be critical of the policies of the Indian government on issues related to Muslims, such as employment or massacres, but by no stretch of imagination are they pro-Pakistan or anti-India. This is not to suggest that all is well with the *Madarsahs* today[11]. Many *Madarsahs* in Pakistan, for instance, have emerged as breeding grounds for self-styled *jehadists*, including the Taliban in Afghanistan and the Lashkar-i-Tayyeba which wants to emancipate Kashmir. It appears that the experience of *Madarsahs* in Pakistan[12] has fuelled the fear of *Madarsahs* in India, but clearly such a fear is misplaced, as there is no evidence of Indian *Madarsahs* having anything to do with their counterparts across the border, or for that sake, even their counterparts within the country. *Madarsahs* are extremely autonomous institutions and there is no federation or Union that runs or monitors them.

Many teachers as well as students of *Madarsahs* increasingly realize the datedness and irrelevance of their curriculum and methods of teaching. The danger to *Madarsahs* comes not so much from the outside, but from within. This is manifest in the form of animosity and competition among *Madarsahs* of different *maslaks*[13] (schools of thought). Most *Madarsah* graduates are taught to put down the other schools of thought (through an interesting expertise called the *Radd*, which means "to argue against", but in reality translates to "rubbishing"). The *Radd* is not targeted at other religions, but at the various Islamic sects and more specifically at other *Madarsahs* run by rival sects. The other danger is the quality of teaching and instruction in the *Madarsahs* today. Barring the top few, most *Madarsahs* have teachers who have little knowledge of subjects other than that of religious texts.

A Brief History of the Evolution of the *Madarsah* System

Religion is the mainstay of Islamic culture, therefore the importance of religious education. The word *Quran* comes from *Iqra* meaning 'to read'. In numerous verses, the Holy *Quran* has attached great importance to the pursuit of knowledge. In the very first revelation of the book, Prophet Muhammad was given a command to read and write. In a number of sayings, he has emphasized the need to seek knowledge from the cradle to the grave and regard it as a sacred duty. These sayings cover such modern ideas as compulsory education[14] for the sexes, adult and continuing education, and exchanges in the field of education and learning.[15] According to the Prophet, the ink of a scholar is holier than the blood of the martyr. Inspired by these exhortations, early Muslims showed great enthusiasm in the pursuit of knowledge. Important cities of the Islamic world became great centres of learning. The passion for learning was so intense that the Arabs came into contact with the people of distant lands to acquire knowledge about their ways of life, their philosophy, and thoughts.

The major difference between the Islamic system of education and the secular system lies in the attitude towards life itself. While Islam does not regard the worldly life as an end in itself, the latter considers this life and its happiness as the ultimate goal. Also, there is no segregation between the religious and secular education in the Islamic system. Before the invasion and occupation of Muslim lands by the western colonial powers, there was only one type of schooling prevalent through the Muslim world. *Madarsahs* used to impart both religious and temporal education. The system produced young men for the services, trade and industry who were rooted in their religion and culture[16].

In 622 AD, the Prophet Muhammad migrated from Makkah, the city in Saudi Arabia where Islam originated, to Madina, in Saudi Arabia where the Prophet Muhammad is buried, and laid the foundation for the first *Madarsah* of Islam. This *Madarsah* was attached to the first ever mosque constructed in the world; the Masjid-e-Kuba.

The students of this *Madarsah* were called Ashab-e-Sufa. They studied Islam in detail and spread it throughout the world.

The institutions of the *Madarsah* and the *ulema* (class of religious specialists) emerged with the spread of Islam outside the Arabian Peninsula in the years following the death of the Prophet. By the eighth century A.D., large parts of West and Central Asia, in addition to almost the whole of North Africa, had been brought under Muslim rule. A *de facto* division between political and religious power, foreign to pristine Islam, now came into being[17]. Under the Umayyad, and, then later, the Abbasid rulers, while political power rested with the Caliphs, religious authority gradually began being exercised by a special class of men, the *ulema*. The 'ulema set apart from the general body of Muslims, were experts in Islamic theology and law. The two classes worked in tandem with each other[18], the Caliphs providing the *ulema* with protection and official patronage, and the *ulema* seeking to interpret the Islamic tradition in order to legitimize the rule of the Caliphs.

During the Abbasid period, when Islamic civilization and culture was at its zenith, Muslims not only became proficient in the literature and philosophy of the Greek but also became familiar with the Indian sciences and thoughts. It was during this period that institutionalization of learning came about with the establishment of Bait-ul-Hikma (House of Wisdom) set up by Al-Mamun in 830 A.D. However, the first institution which enjoys an enviable reputation throughout the world today was Al Azhar of Cairo, founded by the fourth Caliph of Fatmid dynasty, Al-Muizz (925-975 AD).

It was in this period that *Madarsahs* as specialized institutions for the training of 'ulema emerged, first in West Asia, and then, as Muslim rule spread, in Africa, southern Europe and South Asia. *Madarsahs* were subsidized with permanent sources of income, such as land grants by the state or by endowments (*awqaf*) by rich Muslims. Although *Madarsahs* were known to have existed before the tenth century[19], the first major *Madarsah* after Al Azhar, dates to 1065, when Nizam-ul Mulk, the great *vazir* of the Sajuq Sultans, ordered the construction of the grand Nizamiah *Madarsah* in Baghdad. The Nizamiah school was the forerunner to *Madarsahs* that were set up in other parts of the Muslim world, and were intended to train bureaucrats for the royal courts and the administration, as well as judges (*qazis, muftis*), who were appointed by the state. Typically, teachers as well as students were drawn from the elite, while there seems to have been little provision for the education of children from the poorer classes. Since one of the primary aims of the *Madarsahs* was to produce a class of bureaucrats and, particularly judges, as employees of the state, the teaching of Islamic law (*fiqh*) came to occupy a major position in the *Madarsah* curriculum.

Among the Sunnis, who now account for some ninety per cent of the world's Muslim population, four schools of jurisprudence developed—the *Hanafi, Hanbali, Maliki* and *Shaf'i*. Each of these schools had its own chain of *Madarsahs*. In addition to law, Arabic grammar and prose, the other subjects taught were logic and philosophy. Theology (*deeniyat*) and mysticism (*tasawuf*), subjects that one would have expected religious seminaries to specialize in, received little attention.[20]

In South Asia, Muslim rulers made elaborate arrangements for the setting up of *Madarsahs*[21] to train a class of 'ulema attached to their courts. In addition, most mosques had schools (*maktabs*) attached to them, wherein children were taught to recite and memorize the *Quran*, a pattern that continues till this day. No standardized syllabus was employed in the *Madarsah*s, however, and each school was free to teach its own set of books.

The learning consisted largely of commentaries on classical works on Islamic law. With the general consensus of the 'ulema that the 'gates of *ijtihad*', or creative understanding of the law in the light of changing conditions, had been 'closed' following the collapse of the Abbasid Caliphate in the late thirteenth century, the *Madarsah* curriculum lost its earlier dynamism and vigor. It began degenerating into a seemingly timeless warp. New books, attuned to the very different context in which Muslims found themselves in India, ceased to be written and read, and a blind conformity to the classical works was sought to be rigidly enforced.

Signs of change emerged in the late seventeenth century, when the Mughal Emperor Aurangzeb Alamgir commissioned a team of 'ulema to prepare a compendium of Islamic law, named after him as the Fatwa-i-Alamgiri. Aurangzeb granted one of the 'ulema associated with this project, Mulla Nizamuddin, an old mansion owned by a French trader, the Firangi Mahal[22], in Lucknow, where he set up a

Madarsah, which soon emerged as the leading centre of Islamic studies in north India. Mulla Nizamuddin prepared a fresh curriculum for study here, which came to be known after him as the *Dars-i-Nizami* or the 'Syllabus of Nizami'. The focus of the *Dars* was on what were called the 'rational sciences' (*ma'qulat*), subjects such as law, philosophy and grammar that would benefit prospective bureaucrats. Three centuries later, the *Dars-i-Nizami* continues to be the syllabus of most *Madarsah*s in South Asia today, although an increasing number of books on the 'revealed sciences' (*manqulat*), such as theology and the traditions of the Prophet (*hadith*) have been added.

While in Mughal times the *Madarsah*s served the purpose of training intellectual and bureaucratic elite, leaving the poorer classes largely out of their purview, things began to change with the onset of British rule[23]. By the early nineteenth century, the British had replaced Persian with English as the language of officialdom and Muslim *qazis* and *muftis* with lawyers and judges trained in English law. The eclipse of Muslim political power in the region now meant that the 'ulema and their *Madarsah*s were now bereft of sources of political support and patronage. In many cases, the British revoked the vast grants that Muslim rulers had provided the *Madarsah*s. In this rapidly changing context, the 'ulema now began to turn to Muslim society for support.

With the march of modernity and secularisation, *Madarsah*s were now seen as centres of obscurantism and superstition, and as one of the principal causes of Muslim decline at the hands of the West. In different Muslim countries the attack on the *Madarsah* system took different forms. In Turkey, for instance, a government decree in 1925, soon after the Republicans under the staunchly secular Kemal Attaturk took power deposing the last Muslim Caliph, ordered the closing down of all *Madarsah*s in the country with a single stroke of the pen. This policy was followed in several Muslim countries that had come under communist rule in the aftermath of the Russian revolution in 1917, such as Albania and other countries in the vast Muslim belt in Central Asia. In other countries, such as Morocco and Algeria, while the state continued to base its legitimacy on Islamic appeals, Islamic education was sought to be 'modernized', with departments of Islamic studies in modern universities taking the place of traditional *Madarsah*s. In 1961, the socialist and Arab nationalist Jamal Abdul Nasser, in his impatience with the traditional Muslim 'ulema, whom he saw as a major challenge to his modernization efforts, transformed the world-renowned Al-Azhar in Cairo, the oldest, largest and most respected *Madarsah* in the world, into a modern university. South Asia, where over half of the world's Muslim population lives, followed a slightly different course. While the *Madarsahs* were left largely untouched, the effective delinking of *Madarsah*-education from the job market led to the declining popularity of traditional Islamic schools.

The 1980s witnessed a rapid revival of the *Madarsahs* in much of South Asia[24], in terms of numbers as well as power and influence. In India, the number of *Madarsahs* is now estimated at some thirty to forty thousand, with a similar figure in Pakistan and probably a slightly smaller number in Bangladesh. In Pakistan and Afghanistan, *Madarsahs* today play a crucial role in national politics. Pakistan has several 'ulema-based political parties with millions of supporters. The Taliban regime in neighboring Afghanistan was entirely 'ulema-based, products of Deobandi *Madarsahs* in Pakistan's North-West Frontier Province and Baluchistan[25]. In India, the 'ulema and their *Madarsahs* wield no political influence. However there are a few outside the *Madarsah* system who are active in Indian politics, and they, however, exercise an enormous influence on Muslim public opinion. The massive agitations that India witnessed against what was seen to be an attack on Muslim Personal Law in the 1980s were led principally by the 'ulema[26].

Geographical Spread of *Madarsahs*

India

There are a large number of *Madarsahs* in northern and western parts of the country. There are various estimates about their number. Estimates range from a figure of eight thousand to thirty to forty thousand religious institutions in the country. According to Home Ministry sources, there are 721 *Madarsahs* catering to over 1,20,000 children in Assam, 1,825 *Madarsahs* catering to over 1,20,000 children in Gujarat, 961 *Madarsahs* catering to 84,864 children in Karnataka, 9,975 *Madarsahs* catering to 7,38,000 children in Kerala, 6,000 *Madarsahs* catering to over 4,00,000 children in Madhya Pradesh and some 1,780 *Madarsahs* catering to over 25,000 children in Rajasthan[27]. In Uttar Pradesh, the number of *maktabs* is more than 15,000 and the number of *Madarsah*s is above 10,000. There are over 3,500 *Madarsah*s in Bihar[28], including 1,111 under government control where the Bihar government pays the salary of the teaching and non-teaching staff[29]. There are 507 *Madarsah*s affiliated to the West Bengal *Madarsah* Board in which about 2,00,000 boys and girls study. Besides, there are many unregistered seminaries.

Pakistan

The number of *Madarsah*s in Pakistan is estimated to be in the vicinity of 30 to 40 thousand[30]. According to other estimates, there are more then 15,000 *Madarsah*s in Pakistan and about one million students are studying there. Furthermore, there are about 2,512 *Madarsah*s in Punjab Province alone, which is the most populous province of Pakistan.

Bangladesh

At present, Bangladesh has 10,500 *Madarsah*s, of which 7,500 are funded by the government[31]. Till 1999, there were a total of 7,122 registered *Madarsah*s supported with government grants, including three full-fledged government ones.

*Madarsah*s in India: 1780 onwards

With the collapse of the Mughal Empire, the British gained supremacy. The British rule brought about a new administrative and educational set up which changed various aspects of Indian life. The Muslim nobility lost its political power and started getting squeezed economically and educationally. This gave a serious jolt to the traditional educational set up as it was now deprived of endowments in the form of free land properties and was left to depend on its own resources.

The board of directors of the East India Company in the early days of British domination in India, while sympathetic towards attempts to revive Indian learning, entertained no idea of introducing any system of education in the country. At the same time, the British realized that it was inescapable not to study the existing knowledge systems, especially laws, of the natives before any reforms could be introduced in the new administrative set up.

In 1781, Warren Hastings established the Calcutta *Madarsah* College for Muhammedans for the study of "Muhammedan law and such other sciences as were taught in Muhammedan schools". In 1792 Jonathan Duncan, resident at Benares, obtained permission "to establish a college in the holy city for the preservation and alleviation of laws, literature and religion of Hindus, for recovering and collecting books on the most ancient and valuable general learning and tradition now existing in perhaps any part of the globe"[32].

Interestingly, both the *Madarsah* in Calcutta and the Sanskrit College at Benares had one common objective: to study the local law. Before the introduction of the Anglo-Saxon juridical system in India, the Company's magistrates and judges had to depend on Hindu *pandits* and Muslim *qazis* for the administration of justice. Thus, in spite of the general disinclination of the Company's board of directors to introduce any system of education, the local government had to introduce both Hindu and Mohammedan systems of education to perform the basic duty of administering law and justice.

The British rulers commissioned surveys of the educational institutions in the regions under their control, *viz.*, Bengal, Bombay and Madras Presidencies. William Adam surveyed the native schools in Bengal and Bihar in the years 1938-40. In his reports, Adam reported that there were a good number of native schools in Bengal and Bihar in which both Hindus and Muslims studied together. The British followed the policy of strict neutrality in religious matters. The Education Commission of 1882 reiterated this position. The Indian University Commission of 1902 and the Calcutta University Commission 1917-19 also maintained the same stance of religious neutrality "in view apparently of the difficulties of the problem in a country where religion seemed to be a source of strife and disunion."

The replacement, as mentioned earlier, of Persian by English in 1837 as the language of the courts was another blow to the *Madarsah* system. The Great Indian Mutiny of 1857 and the subsequent transfer of authority of governance of India from the John Company to the British Crown had a very profound impact on Muslim education in India.

Muslims had to face many formidable changes along with the general animosity of the British rulers. They had to counter the proselytizing activities of the Christian missionaries. The 'ulema, with considerable help from their flock, initiated some serious responses. A large number of *Madarsahs* were set up in the latter half of the 19th century. The more important and famous among them were[33]:

(1) Darul Uloom, Deoband, 1866.

(2) Mazaheral Uloom, Shaharanpur, 1866.

(3) Madarsah Baqyatris Salehat, Vellore, Tamil Nadu, 1883.

(4) Jamia Mazharul Uloom, Benares, 1893.

(5) Darul Uloom Nadwatul Ulema, Lucknow, 1894.

(6) Madarsah Ameenia, Delhi, 1897.

(7) Darul Uloom Khalilia Nizamia, Tonk, 1899.

(8) Jamia Arabia Hayatul Uloom, Mubarakpur, 1899.

(9) Madarsah-ul Islah, Sarai Mir, Azamgarh, 1909.

(10) Jamia Darus Salam, Umnabad, 1924.

Darul Uloom, Deoband

The premier religious university in the sub continent, the Darul Uloom, at Deoband, in Saharanpur district of UP in India, is popularly known as the Deoband *Madarsah*. The Deobandis arose in British India, not as a reactionary institution but a forward-looking movement to unite and reform Muslim society in the wake of oppression the community faced after the 1857 revolt. According to the historian Mushirul Hasan, "The Deobandis opposed Partition, rejected the two-nation theory and strongly supported the nationalist movement led by the Congress." Deobandis set up *Madarsahs* all over India. By 1879 there were 12 Deobandi *Madarsahs*. By 1967 when the Deobandis celebrated their centenary, they had 1,000 *Madarsahs* in South Asia (India, Pakistan, Bangladesh).

Nadwatul - Ulema, Lucknow

Nadwatul - Ulema at Lucknow draws a large number of Muslim students from all over the country. Nadwa's avowed objective was to bring a middle path between classical Islam and modernity. In the annual convocation of the Faiz-i-Aam *Madarsah* at Kanpur in 1893, Islamic scholars like Muhammad Ali Mongiri, Ashraf Ali Thanwi and Mahmud-ul-Hasan felt the need of preparing a group of 'ulema conversant with the conditions and events of the contemporary world. With an idea to counter the Aligarh movement as well as Western

(Contd. ...)

(...Contd. ...)

education, this institution was an updated version of Deoband. The choice of the name Nadwa was inspired by a hall in Mecca, where the nobility would assemble and deliberate. Nadwa was eventually shifted from Kanpur to Lucknow in 1898, when it also revised its Islamic curriculum with English, modern sciences and vocational training.

Dar-ul-Ulum Manzar Islam, Bareilly

Dar-ul-Ulum Manzar Islam, which was founded by Ahmed Reza at Bareilly in 1904, is another prominent Islamic institution in India. Its followers, known as Barelwis, are spread all over India and in the Punjab province of Pakistan. Its founder, an Islamic scholar of repute, was strongly opposed to the Deobandi movement for its aversion to saint-worship and the Sufi cult, accepted by most people as Islamic traditions. In 1903, he even issued *fatwas* against the founding members of Deoband for their opposition to celebration of Muslim customs like the birth anniversary of Prophet Mohammad and tomb worships of Sufi saints. Ahmed Reza had also opposed the Khilafat movement and his followers owed allegiance to the Muslim League during the Freedom Movement.

In the last fifty-five years, the abject failure of the education system in particular, and the skewed nature of economic development in general, have left the Indian Muslim disgruntled. Most Muslim scholars allege that after Independence, the secular school curriculum was given a communal texture in the Hindi belt. As a result, Muslim children kept away from government schools. Also, the Urdu language was banished from the government educational set up, which consequently contributed to the growth of religious institutions like the *Madarsahs*[34].

Today, *Madarsahs* across the country provide free education to the poor Muslims. According to a study[35], around 36 per cent of all school age children in the age group of 6-18 years study in *Madarsahs* in India. During initial years of schooling, more than half of the Muslim children are sent to *Madarsahs*. However, of those who seek enrolment in *Madarsahs*, only 22 per cent of boys and 17 per cent of girls and 20 per cent of total students manage to reach up to Class VIII.

Structure of the *Madarsah* System

Institutions known as *Madarsah* may be divided into three categories:

- *Maktab*

- *Madarsah*

- *Jamia*

Maktabs provide instruction in religious as well as secular subjects up to primary stage. They function from a *masjid* or a small modest building. *Madarsahs* are institutions that impart education generally up to the senior secondary level. *Jamias* are institutions of higher learning providing instruction up to post-graduation and specialization level. Every *Madarsah* follows its own pattern in the matter of study structure. There is no uniformity with regard to subjects, books or emphasis. Secondly, there is no uniformity in the number of years for preparing students for various degrees.

Let us take the example of the Bihar Madaris Education Board which is government funded and has a semblance of an organization structure[36]. It entails 17 years of study for graduating as a Fazil, the equivalent of an M.A. The road to Fazilat degree under this system of education follows the following sequence:

Standard	Equivalent to	Period of Study
Tahtania	Primary Education	Four Years
Wastania	Middle Education	Four Years
Foqania	High School	Two Years
Moulvi	Intermediate	Two Years
Aalim	B.A.	Three Years
Fazil	M.A.	Two Years

The pattern is a little different in U.P.:

Standard	Class Level	Equivalent to
Tahtania	Up to Class V	Primary Education
Foqania	VI to VIII	Middle/Upper Primary
Munshi/Moulvi	IX-X	Secondary/High School
Aalim	XI-XII	Intermediate/Sr. Secondary
Kamil	B.A.	Graduate
Fazil	M.A.	Post-Graduate

The *Madarsah* Board Curriculum also provides for transfer of *Madarsah* boys to the general schools at various stages. For example, a student having completed Wastania could join a high school of the general educational system.

Table 1
Different Periods of Schooling for the Same Degrees in the Major Indian Madarsahs

S. No.	Madarsah	Degree	Period of Schooling
1.	Jamia Salafia	Fazil-e-Adab	2 years
		Fazil-e-Shariah	2 years
		Alimiat	3 years
		Fazilat-e-Tibb	2 years
2.	Mazahirul Uloom	Durusul Ausat	3 years
		Darja Alia	4 years
3.	Darul Uloom Ashrafia	Fazilat	7 years
		Ikhtesar fil Uloomil Islamia	2 years
		Ikhtesar fil fiqh al-Hanfi wal-Ifta	2 years
		Ikhtesar fil Adab-al-Arabi	2 years
		Ikhtesas fil Ulomm al-Aqlia	2 years
		Qura'at Saba	2 years
4.	Nadwa	Derasat-Ulya (Shariah)	2 years
		Derasat Ulya (Arabic Lang. & Lit.)	2 years
		Al-Dawah	1 year
		Alimiat	4 years
5.	Darul Uloom Deoband	Fazilat	8 years
		Takmeel	1 year
		Ifta	1 year

(Adapted from Manzoor Ahmed, *Islamic Education*)

What the *Madarsah*s teach - the Curricula[37]

The development of Islamic curricula in India started around the 12th century A.D. During the times of Ghayasuddin Balban and Allauddin Khilji, Delhi became the centre of Muslim education. Historian Ziauddin Burney names 46 scholars in the times of Allauddin Khilji in India who were leaders in their fields in the world. During the reign of Firozshah, two eminent scholars Najmuddin Samarqandi and Jalaluddin Dawwani from Central Asia came to India. Dawwani was appointed the principal of the Royal Madarsah at Delhi.

The development of the *Madarsah* curriculum in India can be divided into four periods:

1. 13th century to 15th century: In this period there was a great emphasis on language and literature, *Fiqh* (law), logic, *tasawwaf* (philosophy) and *tafseer* (understanding the *Quran*). However, remarkably, the study of *Hadith* (the sayings of Prophet Mohammad) was not emphasized.

2. 16th century: In this period, Sheikh Abdul Haq went to Hijaz and came back after studying the tradition of the prophet for three years and tried to renew the emphasis on the study of the *Hadith*.

3. Late 16th to early 17th century: In this period, subjects like physiology, physics, mathematics as well as *Hadith* received greater attention.

4. Late 17th century: This was the most important period for the development of the Islamic curricula in India. It was now Nizami who compiled the Dars-e Nizami or the Nizami system. For its age, it was a revolutionary system. It laid emphasis on mathematics, algebra, astronomy, physics, and physiology. The contemporariness of the Dars-e Nizami can be gauged from the fact that Mullah Nizamuddin included a book by Mullah Zahid, which had been completed and published just as the curriculum was being designed.

Unfortunately, in the last three hundred years, the Dars-e Nizami has remained almost unchanged. It has, therefore, become largely anachronistic. The first person to raise a voice in this regard was Maulana Shibli Naumani. Because of his views on the modernization of the *Madarsah* syllabus, Nadvatul Ulema came into being in Lucknow in 1894. The 'ulema were now convinced that the Islamic curricula need revolutionary change.

Present Scenario

At the moment, it is difficult to make any generalized statement about the *Madarsah* curriculum. Every *Madarsah* follows its own pattern in the matter of curriculum. There is no uniformity with regard to subjects, books or emphasis. Secondly, there is no uniformity in the number of years for preparing students for various degrees.

After examining the curricula of the 14 well-known *Madarsahs*, Manzoor Ahmed[38] observes that the subjects taught in these *Madarsahs* can be divided in four categories:

1. Languages and Literature

2. Contemporary Learning

3. Commentary and Discourse

4. Law and Jurisprudence

In the language section, Urdu, Persian, Arabic language and literature, and at places Hindi and English are taught in various *Madarsahs*[39]. In contemporary learning, Mathematics, General Sciences, Hygiene, Geography, History, Economics, Political Science, and Philosophy are taught. In the third category, Sarf-o-Naho, Mantiq, Falsafa, Balaghat, Hayyat, Tafseer-e Quran, and the art of manazirah are taught. The fourth category consists of Fiqh, Usool-e Fiqh, Hadith, Usool-e Hadith, Aqeeda, etc.

Some of the major problems of curricula in *Madarsahs* are:

1. The curriculum puts undue emphasis on memorization drill and repetition. It fails to create the width of vision, a scholarly objectivity and freedom of thought that are essential for scholarly work.

2. There are wide differences in the emphasis laid on the study of subjects taught in various *Madarsahs*.

3. There is not much emphasis on the study of the Holy *Quran*. The syllabus of Arabic literature is old and archaic, and modern writers hardly find any place in it. *Fiqh* (Jurisprudence) is taught in a partisan manner, creating *Maslaki* differences (among the various Islamic schools of thought).

4. Contemporary subjects are taught in a slip-shod manner.

Reforms

For a long time now, there has been a debate on the need for reforms in *Madarsah* syllabus[40]. At the root of the inertia is the fear of change. However, things are changing now, albeit a little slowly. Some Islamic scholars and educational bodies are trying to update the syllabus. One of the most interesting efforts has come from the U. P. Arabi Farsi Board. Commissioned by this board, Dr. Ghulam Yahya

Anjum of Jamia Hamdard, New Delhi has come up with a revised syllabus[41]. This syllabus has been implemented across all those *Madarsah*s in UP that are supported by the government. Dr. Anjum claims that the revised syllabus can make a student of the *Madarsah* system at par with the student of a modern secular institution.

Profile of Students and Teachers

Most *Madarsah* students come from poor families. For such families, *Madarsah*s are the only sources of education, since they charge no fees and provide free boarding and lodging to their students. Given what is said to be the dismal level of Muslim access to education, *Madarsah*s are often the only available educational option for children from poor Muslim families. *Madarsah*s have thus been playing an important role in promoting literacy among the Muslims, who have the dubious distinction of being, along with Dalits, the least educated community in India.

Today what is imparted in *Madarsah*s is mostly Islamic knowledge. Some institutions have, however, realized the need to introduce modern disciplines like economics, political science, education, etc. Unfortunately this change is too slow to bring about any worthwhile result. Availability of competent teachers to teach these subjects is also a problem. Unfortunately, most of the *Madarsah* teachers are untrained and there is no provision of training, pre-service or in-service. Therefore, *Madarsah* teachers are unaware of the modern techniques of teaching.

Generally, the management adopts an insulting attitude towards teachers[42]. Students study aimlessly and teachers teach arbitrarily, without any enthusiasm. Only a few of the graduates get admission in universities for higher studies. Some of them go in for professional courses such as in Unani Medicine & Surgery, Arabic-Urdu translations, *etc*. Some go into teaching and most of them go back home.

One of the major reasons for this unimpressive performance is the educational infrastructure available. Both teachers and students live in cramped quarters, without proper lighting, fans, beds, desks and chairs, and toilets. Most of them neither have playgrounds nor any library. Salaries are low and stagnant. Most of the teachers are untrained. Capital punishment is the norm. Students of different ages study in the same class. There is hardly any motivation to excel. Learning by rote is the only way known to teachers and students. Very few teachers use blackboards and other teaching aids. All these issues make the learning poor and tardy.

Financials

For the thousands of *Madarsahs* that operate in India, there are three sources of funding available:

1. Charity

2. Government Grants

3. Overseas charity

All *Madarsahs* are charitable institutions[43]. Most *Madarsahs* have their designated *"Safeels"* (charity collectors) who go door to door to collect money. Sometimes, some individual chooses to give a *Madarsah* a big grant. People donate their *zakat* and *fitra* (religiously ordained taxes to be paid by individuals for the poor) to these seminaries. During Id-ul-Azha, Muslims often donate the *charm-e qurbani* (the skin of the slaughtered animal) to the *Madarsahs*. Some *Madarsahs* have permanent sources of income, such as land, buildings and other property that produce regular returns. Almost all *Madarsahs* depend on charity.

In some states, such as Bihar, Bengal, and U.P., there are *Madarsah* boards, just like the school boards. The government in these states allocates some funds to those *Madarsahs* that are registered with the *Madarsah* board[44]. The number of such *Madarsahs*, however, is very low[45]. Most *Madarsahs* choose to survive without government grants because of two basic reasons: one, they feel government funding would lead to governmental intervention in their work, jeopardizing their independence; and two, the teachers of such government supported *Madarsahs* start behaving like government employees (having the assurance that whether they work sincerely or not, they will get their salaries)[46].

There are really a very limited number of *Madarsahs* that fall in the third category.[47] Rich Arabs from the Middle East bankroll most of these *Madarsahs*. These are the ones who are charged, mainly by other *Madarsahs*, for propagating the Wahabi[48] brand of Islam in the country. The annual budgets of *Madarsahs* range from a few lakhs to a few crores of rupees. For example, the Darul Uloom Deoband spends Rs. 3 crore annually, Jamia Salfia. 1.5 crore a year, Jamiatul Falah 10 lakhs a year and so on[49].

The Nadvatul Ulema is an interesting case in point. The school has 4,000 students on its rolls. Admissions are open to children who are at least 10 years old. These students predominantly from Bihar, but also from UP, Kerala and Assam, are short-listed based on their mailed application. These short listed ones then go through an entrance test. Those who qualify are offered admission. The better off pay Rs. 300 a month towards their food expenses, and Rs. 12 a month for electricity. Most students are not charged even this amount. The sixty faculty members are paid between Rs. 3000 and Rs. 6000 a month. The Nadva also maintains a huge library, and a big mosque. This institution has steadfastly been refusing any government aid or control, and generates all its money through its own network of sponsors, and is therefore able to maintain its reputation as an important seat of learning all over the Islamic world.

Issues of Reform

Modernization of Madarsahs in India

The goal of *Madarsahs* traditionally has been not to produce engineers and doctors or technocrats, but to produce scholars who would interpret Islam in relation to the demands of the specific time. For example, what a Muslim scholar needed to know was not quite the same in the early nineteenth century as it is today. In other words, the *Madarsah* equips a scholar not for simple scholastic interpretation of the Holy *Quran* and the traditions of the Prophet of Islam, but to cater to the changing needs of the Muslim society[50]. This brings us to the second issue, which is to see how the *Madarsahs* from the days of early colonial rule have been handling this demand.

Reforms in Curricula

Madarsahs in India have been undergoing slow reform and insufficient in the recent decades and that is why they have been unable to get their graduates keep pace with the fast changing world[51]. The Islamic seminary Darul-uloom at Deoband introduced computer applications in its curriculum in 1994. Apart from computers, a few other technical courses have also been given included in the curriculum of the seminary[52].

The Darul-uloom Deoband syllabus includes Modern Indian History, Islamic History, Civics, Geography, General Sciences, principles for health care, the Indian Constitution, principles of economics, philosophy, life history of modern philosophers and computer applications[53]. At the Dar-uloom Nadwat-ul-ulema at Lucknow, a fair knowledge of the English language has been a special feature. Right from its inception, the seminary has adopted English Language and Literature as one of the elementary subjects. In a total of 16 years of study, it lays emphasis on English Language and Literature at par with other Islamic disciplines. From the primary level, it teaches various modern disciplines, especially English, Hindi, Science, Indian History, and Economics almost up to the graduation level.

Madarsahtul-Ishah, which is the living expression of the dream of Allama Shibli and Allama Hameeduddin Farahi, emphasizes modern disciplines. It includes in its curriculum English Language and Literature, history of classical and modern philosophy almost up to the graduation level. Other *Madarsah*s like Jamiatul-hidaya in Rajasthan teach Business Management, Commerce and Agriculture as well, and the Jamia Mohammadia Mansura at Malegaon produces medical practitioners, as medical science is one of the distinguishing features of this *Madarsah*. Looking at the present curricula of above-mentioned *Madarsah*s, one could argue that *Madarsah*s in India have already been modernizing their syllabi. However, this is a far cry from what the modern technology driven market demands.

Apprehensions

Many Muslim scholars apprehend that in the name of modernization of *Madarsah*s, the government may have been trying to deprive them of their independence and autonomy. The core of the *Madarsah* education must remain religious and, therefore, by definition 'modernization' or 'secularization' has its measurable limits[54]. Only some elementary courses in languages like Hindi, English, (or the regional language), arithmetic, geography, history and social studies need to be added as the major *Madarsah*s have been doing by themselves over the last century. The major *Madarsah*s have also been restructuring their programme of studies in a manner that if a student wishes to leave the *Madarsah* mid-stream and take the middle or high school examination or enter a university for undergraduate or postgraduate education, he may do so. Some *Madarsah*s have introduced vocational courses so that their products do not depend solely on finding employment as teachers or Imams.

The Madarsah Modernization Scheme

The Ministry of Human Resource Development, Government of India, had a series of meetings with representatives of the *Madarsah*s discussing the desirability of their modernization and clarifying that it would not entail either compulsion or interference by government. After being satisfied with the result of these discussions, the Ministry formulated the scheme of modernization of *Madarsah*s[55].

The main features of the scheme, launched in 1993-94, are as follows[56]:

1. The objective of the scheme is to encourage traditional institutions like *maktab*s and *Madarsah*s to introduce teaching of science, maths, social studies, Hindi and English in order to provide opportunities to students to acquire education comparable to the national system of education.

2. The process of modernization is entirely voluntary.

3. In the first phase, primary classes of middle and secondary level *Madarsah*s were to be covered. In the second phase (during the 9th Plan), the coverage was extended to institutions providing education equivalent to secondary stage.

4. The scheme covered the following items in the first phase:

   a. 100 per cent assistance for appointment of qualified teachers,

   b. assistance for book bank and strengthening of libraries,

   c. provision of science, math kits and essential equipment.

5. Only registered voluntary organizations, which have been in existence for three years, were considered for assistance.

6. The performance of the scheme was to be reviewed after three years of its operation.

The scheme has been criticized by many Muslim intellectuals for its hidden agenda. The ostensible purpose of the Scheme administered by the Ministry of Human Resource Development was to persuade the *Madarsah*s to revise their conventional curriculum to add 'modern' subjects – English, Hindi, Science, Mathematics and Social Studies, including History and Geography. Certainly, there can be no objection to the idea of reforming the *Madarsah* curriculum. What has made people wonder is "this sudden interest in up-gradation of *Madarsah*s by the authorities which are reluctant to provide modern educational facilities, even at the primary level, in Muslim-concentration areas and which simply refuse to divulge available data on Muslim educational backwardness and which, by carefully manipulating the levers of power, change curricula, particularly related to language, syllabi, school culture and medium of instruction so as to make Muslim parents more and more reluctant to send their children to government schools."[57]

The scheme failed to interest most *Madarsah*s, as they were ill equipped to deal with the bureaucracy. Thus, the total annual outlay under the scheme has been of the order of a few crores with a few hundred beneficiaries[58]. The National Council of Educational Research and Training undertook a study of existing curriculum in *Madarsah*s and published a report in the year 2000, based on data collected from some *Madarsah*s, most of them government-aided, from 3 states UP, MP and Kerala. The recent Report by the Group of Ministers of Reform of Internal Security has linked *Madarsah* education with national security and this clearly was a cause for concern among people already wary of a State that was seen as being partisan and inimical to minority interests. It didn't help the government's image much, when in addition to scrutinizing *Madarsah*s closely, a large section of the BJP party workers were demanding the closing down or strict regulation of Christian schools too.

The report says: "Funded by Saudi and Gulf sources, many new *Madarsah*s have come up all over the country in recent years, especially in large numbers in the coastal areas of the West and in the border areas of West Bengal and the North east...*Madarsah* education is a part of a Muslim child's religious tradition. Steps should be taken to encourage these institutions to add inputs on modern education also. Efforts should be made for providing increased facilities for modern education, particularly for the border areas where such facilities are lacking... The Central Sector Scheme for giving financial assistance for modernization of *Madarsah* education... should be strengthened... A Central Advisory Board may be set up for *Madarsah* education instead of leaving this critical matter to different State Level Advisory Boards. The Ministry of Human Resource Development (HRD) should take necessary action in this regard."

As Shahabuddin notes, the motive of the government largesse is clearly neither to benefit the *Madarsah* students to become more employable and more useful to society, nor to upgrade the standard of *Madarsah* education. It is to penetrate the *Madarsah* system, to monitor what goes on there, what is taught, whether the students are motivated to become militants and trained in the use of fire arms, whether the *Madarsahs* serve as shelters for the ISI! This explains the persistent and well-orchestrated propaganda against the *Madarsahs* (and the *masjids*) at the official level, with numerous searches and detentions of teachers and students on trumped up charges. None has been convicted so far. The most dangerous proposal that the Group of Ministers has made now is that a Central Advisory Board of *Madarsah* Education may be set up under the Ministry of HRD. Obviously, the advisory role can be transformed gradually into a regulatory and control role, in the name of up-gradation and uniformity of syllabus, standardization of education (*e.g.*, in Bihar). Since the financial bait is there, some *Madarsahs* – at least some management, may fall for and accept official intrusion.

The Way Ahead

According to Syed Shahabuddin, the community should provide basic Islamic instruction to all boys and girls in *maktabs*, as in Kerala, and rationalize the *Madarsah* system for quality education and for producing the Islamic scholars it needs; this it can do on its own.

The government should, on the other hand:

- Establish primary, middle and secondary government schools in villages, Blocks, *mahallas* of Muslim concentration in accordance with national norms.

- Modify its policy on medium of instruction (in Urdu-speaking States) and on languages, the contents of the textbooks and the school culture, so that an orthodox Muslim does not apprehend any distortion of or threat to his ward's religious identity in government schools.

- And allow continued freedom to the community to establish and run its *Madarsahs*.

Dr. Syed Hamid, the former Vice Chancellor of Aligarh Muslim University and a renowned Muslim educationist, has come up with the following suggestions[59]:

- *Madarsahs* need to revise and update their syllabi; they need to integrate contemporary knowledge with religious education.

- The emphasis should be on intellectual learning, not on learning by cramming.

- *Madarsahs* need to streamline and organize their poor funding structures; teachers should not be underpaid.

- *Madarsahs* should be able to attract the best of talents; and not just the residue among the students.

- Well-educated and trained teachers should be employed.

- Industrial, technical, and professional training should also be provided.

- *Madarsahs* should aim to have three streams: stream of pure religious education; stream of religious and contemporary education; and stream of religious education and technical training. Students should be free to choose any one of these streams.

Case Study - We don't Produce Terrorists; We Feed and Educate Poor Children[60]

On a hot sweltering Sunday afternoon, we stand in front of the Jamia Arabia Shamshul Uloom, opposite the Shahdara Railway Station, in east Delhi. Between the *Madarsah* (seminary) and the asphalt road, runs a *nullah*, flanked by a series of low buildings, including two houses, a urinal, and a garbage bin. Qari Zubair Ahmed Jamai (Maulana Zubair), the founder of the *Madarsah*, has confirmed on his cell-phone that we will be escorted inside by one of his colleagues.

Soon the escort spots us. He takes us to the *Madarsah* through an arched gate, made of red bricks. The gate opens into a courtyard, half of which is a cemented platform, forming the verandah of the mosque.

The prayer hall, which also acts as the reading room during non-*namaz* hours, is connected on the three sides to a series of reading rooms. The three hundred students of this *Madarsah* dine, read and sleep in this two-storied structure. The third floor is under construction.

On the right hand, adjacent to the main gate sits *Maulana* Zubair, the director. We leave our shoes at the door, and take our seats on a carpeted floor after shaking hands with him. "Where have you come from and what do you want to know?" asks the *maulana*. We are curious researchers wanting to know more about the *Madarsah* system of education.

The *maulana* listens very carefully. He is reclined on a *gao-takiya*, picking his teeth. When we have finished speaking, he reaches for a spittoon. Two of his assistants sit in a corner, poring over account books.

The *maulana* is satisfied with our intentions. "The misconceptions about *Madarsahs* are a shame. People don't know the reality. If they knew, they'd never treat us with any suspicion," he says. "I am glad that you are here to explore the truth about *Madarsahs*. Our gates are always open to those who want to see how we live and what we do."

He tells us the history of his *Madarsah*, that he established in 1971 with his colleague, *Maulana* Shoaib Anjum. The seminary earlier operated from a mosque in Old Delhi. Soon the number of students swelled and they had to shift the campus to the present location. Back then, the *maulana* tells us, this place was a disused mosque. They took over this place, a property of the Delhi Wakf Board, and nurtured it to its present status.

After this brief history, he gives us the statistics. The structure houses three hundred students, 21 teachers and 5 workers. For us it was difficult to imagine how so many people lived in a 2000 square yard structure, till we were shown their cramped accommodation. The institute runs on charity. It is a sheer miracle that 300 kids are fed and educated here without any regular support.

Zubair tells us about the educational pattern and syllabus of the seminary. A nine or ten year old child enters the seminary after passing a written test. He is admitted to the *Tehtaniya* (primary school). At primary level, the students are taught Arabic, Persian, English, and Hindi. After a study of four years, he is promoted to the

Ustania classes (middle school). If a child pursues further studies, he gets certificates such as *Maulvi/Munshi* (equivalent to Matriculation), *Alim* (B.A.) and *Fazil* (M.A.).

We are then taken around the campus. We come out of the small dingy room. We start from the primary classes, and are led into bigger classes that are faculty rooms. Students, mostly teenagers inching towards manhood, sit cross-legged rocking on their haunches as a teacher takes them through an interpretation of a religious text. All students and teachers sit on straw mats on the floor. Surprisingly, none of them carry any writing material. It is entirely oral education.

The rooms are darkly lit. They are the same rooms where students and faculty sleep. The working hours start from daybreak. Studies begin after the morning prayer, and continue till the night prayers. The only let up is the lunch break and the evening break.

The library is a small room lined with a few books. Most of them are religious texts. There are no reading desks there. We are then taken to the kitchen where two cooks are busy preparing the dinner. We see a heap of kneaded flour on a big tray and a cauldron simmering on a brick-layered stove. There are a couple of LPG cylinders sitting in a corner. What's cooking in there, we ask. *Dal*, we are told. *Dal* and *roti* is the staple diet here. "Seldom have we had a generous donor. Then we have some variety," the *maulana* tells us. "We have the best food during *ramazan*. That is when people send us other delicacies," he says.

Thursdays are half working days. Friday is the only off day of the week. The seminary provides a summer break. But the students are so poor, mostly belonging to Bihar, Bengal, and Assam, that they don't have the money to visit their homes. "The railway ministry has withdrawn concessions to our students," says the *maulana*. Under Jaffer Sharif and Paswan, the railways would not differentiate between students, and *Madarsah* students would get the standard 50 per cent rate cut. But under the new government, *Madarsah* kids are suddenly not eligible. It is indeed a sign of our times that on the one hand a Shahnawaz Husain doles out subsides to the rich adults going for *Haj*, while Nitish Kumar withdraws concessions to the poor child. This is another example of the familiar issue of subsidies reaching the better off, and good intentions resulting in gross misuse.

We reach the rooftop. Some labourers are busy constructing the walls of a new room. We look down. "We are situated in a Hindu *mohalla*, but we never give a reason for complaint," the *maulana* says. He points to the minaret of a mosque at a distance. "There, you have some Muslim families." Now we understand why there are no day scholars in this seminary.

Finally, we come down to the director's room. We are served tea. *Maulana* Zubair sends for one of his erudite scholars to give us the history of *Madarsahs* in India. He soon comes, an old, bearded man, his neck half titled to one side. He briefly tells us the history of *Madarsahs*. "If you are writing a research paper, I can dictate the same along with the relevant sources," he says. The director is visibly proud of the scholarship of his employee.

Soon it is time for the afternoon prayer. After the prayer we take leave. "You must tell others that we do not produce terrorists here. We are trying to produce angels," the *Maulana* beseeches. "And if they have any doubts, ask them to visit us anytime."

We assure *Maulana* Zubair and come out of the seminary. He escorts us till we finally depart from the place. We have the feeling that we have come out of an orphanage. We wonder: If these people had a little more money, they would eat better food and perhaps buy some more books, and surely some notebooks too. If you don't believe this, go see for yourself.[61]

Madarsahs

A Brief Timeline

830	The establishment of Bait-ul-Hikma (House of Wisdom) set up by Al-Mamun
925-975	Reign of the fourth Caliph of Fatmid dynasty, Al-Muizz, the founder of Al Azhar of Cairo, the first Islamic institution which enjoys a wide reputation through out the world even today
1065	The first major *Madarsah* was set up, when Nizam-ul Mulk ordered the construction of the grand Nizamiah *Madarsah* in Baghdad
1748	Death of Mulla Nizamuddin; Mughal Emperor Aurangzeb Alamgir had granted one of the 'ulema, Mulla Nizamuddin,

(Contd. ...)

(...Contd. ...)

	an old mansion owned by a French trader, the Firanghi Mahal, in Lucknow, where he set up a *Madarsah*, which soon emerged as the leading centre of Islamic studies in north India. Mulla Nizamuddin prepared a fresh curriculum for study here, which came to be known after him as the *Dars-i-Nizami* or the 'Syllabus of Nizami'.
1781	Warren Hastings established the Calcutta *Madarsah* College for Muhammedans for the study of "Muhammedan law and such other sciences as were taught in Muhammedan schools".
1866	Darul Uloom, Deoband and Mazaheral Uloom, Shaharanpur were established.
1894	Darul Uloom Nadwatul Ulema, Lucknow, was established.
1925	In Turkey, a government decree, soon after the Republicans under the staunchly secular Kemal Attaturk took power deposing the last Muslim Caliph, ordered the closing down of all *Madarsah*s in the country with a single stroke of the pen.
1961	The socialist and Arab nationalist Jamal Abdul Nasser, in his impatience with the traditional Muslim *'ulema*, transformed Al-Azhar in Cairo, the oldest, largest and most respected *Madarsah* in the world, into a modern university.
1980	The 1980s witnessed a rapid revival of the *Madarsah*s in much of South Asia, in terms of numbers as well as power and influence.

A Note on *Madarsah*s and Women's Education

The gender bias in education has been extremely pronounced in India, and especially among Indian Muslims. In comparison to the male students in *Madarsah*s, the ratio of female students is very low. This trend generally correlates with the female literacy levels in the country. At the national level, male literacy is 64.13 per cent, whereas female literacy is only 39.29 per cent (Census, 1991). According to a sample survey, the percentage of urban muslim female literacy is 40.1 per cent whereas the rural muslim female literacy is 23.9 per cent[62].

For the purpose of illustration, let us take a look at the figures in the UP State. In 78 *Madarsah*s in *Tahtania* classes (primary), there are 12920 boys and 8333 girls (60.70 and 39.21 per cent respectively). Their drop-out rates are 54.41 and 45.59 per cent respectively.

In *Fauqania* classes (VI to VIII), total number of boys is 2360 and girls are 1039 (67.88 and 32.12 per cent respectively). The drop out rate is 950 boys and 578 girls, totaling 1528.

Table 2

Distribution of Madarsahs by 'Boys', 'Girls' and Co-educational Institutions in UP

Type of *Madarsahs*	Number of *Madarsahs*	Percentage
Exclusively for boys	45	57.69
Exclusively for girls	09	11.54
Co-educational		
i. Up to *Fauqania*	*15*	*19.23*
ii. Up to *Munshi/Maulvi*	*09*	*11.54*
Total	78	100.0

Source: *Evaluation Report on Modernization of the Madarsah Education Scheme (UP)*, Hamdard Education Society, New Delhi, 2003.

APPENDIX

Evaluation Report on Modernization of the *Madarsah* Education Scheme (UP), Hamdard Education Society, New Delhi, 2003

Major Findings and Recommendations

The findings and recommendations emerging from the Evaluation have been mentioned in detail in the preceding paragraphs. We would conclude on emphasizing some of the more important points as follows:

1. Although the Modernization Scheme was introduced without proper groundwork and although detailed guidelines seeking to ensure uniformity in standards were not issued, the performance under the scheme has on the whole been fairly satisfactory. Since the take-off stage has been reached, now the provision for the Tenth Five Year Plan should be radically augmented. It is learnt that the relevant Working Group for the Ninth Five Year Plan has recommended a provision of Rs. 91.65 crores for the Modernization Scheme. The amount actually provided was Rs. 48 crores. The total amount released does not exceed Rs. 16 crores. The releases, further, were tardy and intermittent and bristled with difficulties and avoidable expenses for the applicant *Madarsahs*. In most cases it took a

year for the *Madarsahs* to receive assistance whereas they had to make monthly payments to teachers of modern subjects. This causes considerable hardship and dissatisfaction. It is therefore necessary that *Madarsahs* should be paid grant every month and asked to submit the utilization certificates every quarter. This would make both the management and the teachers happy and contented and give a fillip to the Scheme which proceeded haltingly because of glitches and impediments in release of funds. To maintain the momentum and to make the Scheme viable an allocation of at least Rs. 500 crore should be made for the Scheme in the Tenth Five Year Plan.

2. One teacher is much too insufficient for teaching four or five modern subjects to students for whom the subjects and modern method of teaching have virtually been unknown. Two teachers should be sanctioned for each *Madarsahs* under the Scheme. One teacher could take up Science and Mathematics, and the other English, Hindi and Social Studies. Even more important than Mathematics and Science for personality development and modernizing of attitudes will be Social Studies. All the five modern subjects should be made compulsory. Introduction of computer education would require a third teacher. Provision of computers should also be funded.

3. The time–table of *Madarsahs* which choose to include modern subjects has got to be revoked centrally in consultation not only with the representatives of *Madarsahs* but also with the expert of the education methodology. They will of course take into account experience gained so far and evolve a time-table which takes care in a balanced way both of religious and modern subjects.

4. Most of the teachers appointed to teach modern subject in *Madarsahs* are raw and untrained. It seems essential that a training programme, specifically drawn up by NCERT in consultation with SCERTs and representatives of *Madarsahs* should be mounted as early as feasible. The training should be pre-service and in-service, the former covering a period of 3 to 6 months and the latter of 2 to 3 weeks. For facilitating the latter, special assistance may be provided to the *Madarsahs*. Those already serving the *Madarsahs* may be given an opportunity to acquire the qualification.

5. A Central Board of *Madarsah* Education may be established by Ministry of Human Resource Development. The Board should be empowered not only to monitor the implementation of Modernization Scheme but also the functioning of *Madarsahs* that opt for the supervisory role of the Board. Considering that *Madarsahs* and *Maktabs* in large number are spread all over the country, the proposed Board can bring about standardization of

education and elevation of standards. It will also effect integration between traditional knowledge and modern knowledge. The programme is so important and introduction of modern subjects in traditional institutions so complex and their number and the catchment area of the Scheme so large that for a proper implementation of the programme a Central *Madarsah* Board is essential.

6. In affiliated *Madarsahs*, the teacher-pupil ratio for modern subjects, as revealed by the limited sample, was 1:40 whereas the religious subject 1:30. The respective ratios for unaided but affiliated *Madarsahs* were 1:36 and 1:28. This is just the reverse of what it should have been. This would suggest strict implementation of the provisions reported to have been made by Government that the number of modern subject teachers should be linked to the number of students. What the scheme requires is three properly trained and adequately paid teachers.

7. The Study revealed that modern subjects are being taught up to Class VIII only. It is important that the scope is extended to Classes IX, X, X and XII.

8. The evaluation for Class VII should be done centrally by the state authorities as there is no safeguard against over-liberal marking. This is a new scheme and the control of the Head of the *Madarsah* over the modern subject teachers is not likely to be very effective. Apart from evaluation, a tab has to be kept on the quality of teaching as well.

9. The Scheme should provide a liberal book grant. The Study has revealed that out of 690 *Madarsahs* assisted under the Scheme, only 109 were given grant for setting up a book bank. Only 31 *Madarsahs* were given science and mathematics kits. A proper programme for providing kits to all the *Madarsahs* and teaching its use should be formulated.

10. The Study has revealed that as far as subjects taught are concerned, out of the 78 *Madarsahs* surveyed, 22 have taken up Science, Mathematics, English and Hindi. This reinforces our point that all the five subjects including Social Studies may be made compulsory simultaneously ensuring that teachers are trained and necessary equipment is provided.

11. As regards the Academic Session, *Madarsahs* observe it from *Shaaban* to *Shawwal*.

12. Concurrent monitoring of the functioning of the scheme would need to be done. This would require evaluation of the scheme in a few more states in different zones.

13. The Scheme should also aim at strengthening the infrastructure of *Madarsahs*. Libraries should be properly stocked. Facilities to the extent feasible for games and sports have to be provided. The students have generally demanded vocationalisation of their education. This will make them more productive members of the society. An ambitious plan of vocational education should be drawn upon on the pattern of Jamiat-ul-Hidaya which has three academic streams, viz. (a) religious education and modern education; (b) religious education and vocational training in job-oriented courses; (c) religious education alone.

14. Arrangement for computer literacy has got to be made. The present Study reveals that only 6 *Madarsahs* out of 78 have extended this facility to their students.

15. It is not fair to release funds at the end of year on an annual basis. *Madarsahs* find it extremely difficult to pay salaries monthly from their own resources.

16. An anomaly occurred in the implementation of the Scheme when the *Madarsahs* assisted by the Arabic and Persian Board were included in its scope. The teachers in these schools have been getting much higher salaries than the consolidated salary of Rs. 3000/- provided under the Scheme. This is obviously causing heartburn. It seems that this fact has escaped the Government's attention. If the intention was to strengthen the existing modern subject teaching in the Board *Madarsahs* it should be put to an end as early as possible. Another anomaly is that some mainstream schools that had been teaching modern subjects appear to have added religious subjects in order to attract the benefits of the Scheme. This point would have to be reviewed. The consolidated salary sanctioned for modern subject is ridiculously low viz. Rs. 3000/- p.m. It should be raised to Rs. 6000/- and Rs. 5000/- respectively for *Madarsahs* and *maktabs* and should be paid directly to them by cheque. Similarly the amount sanctioned for Science and Maths kit should be raised and a provision made for the *Madarsah* library.

17. Instructions should be issued for facilitating admission of *Madarsah* products into mainstream institutions.

The following *Madarsahs* which were included in the list of *Madarsahs* scheduled to get the benefit of Modernization Scheme do not exist:

(a) Jamia Sawabi Islam, Kachehri Road, Lucknow.

(b) Darul Uloom Maarif, Chowdhry Tola, Aliganj, Lucknow

(c) Madarsah Arabia Ansaria, Mohalla Rajdepur, Ghazipur

(d) Madarsah Azimul Uloom, Machhli Mohal, Chandauli, Mughal Sarai

(e) Jamia Arabia Ahle Sunnat Muzaffarul Uloom, Bargadwa Saif, Sidharath Nagar

It is evident that the Modernization Scheme having been introduced in a hurry is half-baked. It has however served one useful purpose. It has eroded the initial resistance to the introduction of modern subjects. Now is the time for launching a full-fledged scheme after removing the defects and deficiencies. The scheme will acquire full credibility only when a proper organization for coordination, evaluation and monitoring is created and teachers are reasonably remunerated and teachers' training receives focused attention.

Tables

Modernization of Madarsah Education

(Amount in lakhs)

		Year			
Name of the State/UT	*1998-99*		*1999-2000*		
	Amount Released	No. of Madarsahs	Amount Released	No. of Madarsahs	
01. Uttar Pradesh	249.52	690	264.60	735	
02. Madhya Pradesh	96.84	189	..	..	
03. Haryana	..	..	..	..	
04. Kerala	..	..	..	..	
05. Tripura	79.25	127	..	..	
06. West Bengal	..	..	..	..	
07. Assam	156.24	217	..	..	
08. Tamil Nadu	..	..	..	..	
09. Rajasthan	17.85	619 (for estab of book bank)	..	..	
10. Sikkim	72.00	01	..	..	
11. Delhi	..	..	..	..	
12. Andhra Pradesh	30.24	68	14.22	26	
13. Bihar	..	..	47.45	136	
14. Chandigarh	..	..	44.00	01	
15. Maharashtra	2.16	06	2.16	06	
16. Karnataka	..	..	51.12	142	
17. Himachal Pradesh	..	..	..	..	
18. Orissa	..	..	81.12	111	
19. Dadar Nagar Haveli	72.00	01	72.00	01	
20. Goa	1.44	02	..	..	
Total	673.85	1354	460.76	1158	

Source: Evaluation Report on Modernization of the Madarsah Education Scheme (UP), Hamdard Education Society, New Delhi, 2003.

Ratio of Boys and Girls in
Aided/Un-aided/Independent Madarsahs in UP

Sex	Aided Madarsahs	Un-aided Madarsahs	Independent Madarsahs
Boys	8215	4005	3010
Girls	3025	2472	3929
Ratio	3:1	2:1	1:1

Source: *Evaluation Report on Modernization of the Madarsah Education Scheme (UP)*, Hamdard Education Society, New Delhi, 2003.

Number of Students in Different Classes and
Percentage of 'Boys' and 'Girls' in UP

(as on 1998-99)

Classes	Number of Students Enrolled		
	Boys	Girls	Total
Tahtania (I to V)	12,920 (60.79)	8,333 (39.21)	21,253 (100.0)
Fauqania (VI to VIII)	2,310 (67.88)	1,093 (32.12)	3,403 (100.0)
Munshi (IX-X)	4,192 (89.84)	474 (10.16)	4,666 (100.0)
Maulvi (IX-X)	280 (100.0)	Nil	280 (100.0)
Alim (Intermediate)	259 (100.0)	Nil	259 (100.0)
Kamil (B.A.)	185 (100.0)	Nil	185 (100.0)
Fazil (M.A.)	1345 (75.14)	445 (24.86)	1,790 (100.0)
Total	21491 (67.51)	10,345 (32.49)	31,836 (100.0)

Source: *Evaluation Report on Modernization of the Madarsah Education Scheme (UP)*, Hamdard Education Society, New Delhi, 2003.

Distribution of Teachers According to their Qualifications (UP)

Qualifications	Male	Female	Total
Intermediate (Science)	34 (87.18)	05 (12.82)	39 (100.0)
B.A.	07 (87.50)	01 (12.50)	08 (100.0)
B.Sc.	13 (92.86)	01 (17.14)	14 (100.0)
M.A.	04 (100.0)	Nil	04 (100.0)
M.Sc.	02 (66.67)	01 (33.33)	03 (100.0)
Trained: B.A., B.Ed/ B.Sc., B.Ed	03 (100.0)	Nil	03 (100.0)
Trained: M.Sc., M.Ed	01 (100.0)	Nil	01 (100.0)
TOTAL	64 (88.89)	08 (11.11)	72 (100.0)

Source: *Evaluation Report on Modernization of the Madarsah Education Scheme (UP)*, Hamdard Education Society, New Delhi, 2003.

Notes

1 The title of this paper is inspired by Harper Lee's timeless classic, *To Kill a Mockingbird*. The novel has become a metaphor for a misunderstanding of the 'other.' *Madarsahs* too, not only in India but also over the world, have been victims of misunderstanding and hate. Legend has it that the mockingbird was the giver of language; it taught other birds how to sing. *Madarsahs* have played a vital role in the field of education, so much so that, in the 10th century in Spain, talented young Christians were reading books in Arabic and were reported to "despise the Christian literature as unworthy of attention." Most scholars concur on the idea that it was the Muslim influence on Europe, through their seminaries, which brought about the Renaissance. (R.W. Southern, *Western Views of Islam in the Middle Ages*, Cambridge: Harvard University Press, 1962).

2 There are more than 8000 *Madarsahs*, big and small, in India from where hundreds of students graduate every year (M. Shoeb Ansari). According to other estimates, including the Home Ministry, the number of *Madarsahs* is now between thirty to forty thousand.

3 Since *Madarsahs* run on charity, they are often looked down upon by the Muslim elite. Affluent Muslims do not send their children to *Madarsahs*. As a result *Madarsahs* have become veritable orphanages. Syed Shahabuddin says, "Hunger for education is increasing and even poor families are investing in education. In Muslim areas, one sees private schools sprouting, as also private *Madarsahs*. They compete with each other. Naturally the well-to-do go to schools; *Madarsahs* care for the poor" (*Muslim India*, October 2001).

4 This mistrust goes back to the days of the British and more particularly to the setting up of the Wardha scheme of education. The latter probably ensured that Muslims would not trust government backed schools and their curricula. The Wardha scheme was taken as a rigid framework to propagate the ideas of a political party. The fact that the Wardha scheme also replaced Urdu with Hindustani made a number of people uneasy.

5 When the Afghan Taliban came into the international spotlight at the end of the twentieth century, no image was more central than what seemed to be their rigid and repressive control of individual behavior justified in the name of Islam. They set standards of dress and public behavior that were particularly extreme in relation to women, limiting their movement in public space and their employment outside the home. They enforced their decrees through public corporal punishment. Their image was

further damaged, particularly after the bombings of the East African American embassies in 1998, when they emerged as the "hosts" of Osama Bin Laden and other "Arab Afghans" associated with him. (*"Traditionalist" Islamic Activism: Deoband, Tablighis, and Talibs*, Barbara D. Metcalf, Professor of History, University of California, Davis).

6	The Taliban emerged as a local power in Afghanistan in 1994 because they were able to provide protection and stability in a context of warlordism, raping, and corruption. They found ready support from elements within the Pakistani state, which welcomed an ally likely to protect trade routes to Central Asia and to provide a friendly buffer on the frontier. Similarly, the Taliban also appeared in the mid 1990s to serve a range of U.S. interests, above all in securing a route for an oil pipeline to the Central Asian oilfields outside Iranian control. The United States' interest in the Taliban shifted away, however, first, because of what were seen as human rights abuses in relation to women, and second, because the East African embassy bombings in August 1998 were linked to the presence of terrorist activists within Taliban controlled areas, with Osama bin Laden as their most visible supporter. That alliance would, after the World Trade Center bombing of 11 September, 2001, be the Taliban's undoing. (Barbara D. Metcalf, *op. cit.*)

7	The word *Madarsah* is an Arabic word, which has originated from another Arabic word *Mudarris*, and this comes from another Arabic word *Dars. Dars* means "to tell something or "to teach something. So the word *Madris* means the "one who tells *Dars i.e.,* the one who tells or teaches something. Therefore, the word *Madarsah* means "the place where something is taught." The word school in English also carries a similar meaning, so the word *Madarsah* actually means "school." The *Madarsah* is similar to the church school. In both places religious education is taught and people go there for prayers and for studying religion. *Madarsahs* can also be referred to as *Deeni madaris* (religious schools).

8	Historically *Madarsahs* have contributed to the national cause. Graduates from the *Madarsahs* as well as the founders of some of the leading Muslim seminaries in India played an important role in the struggle against the British. Prominent *ulema* led uprisings against the British in the 1857 revolt, and, for decades after, the reformist *ulema* kept aloft the banner of defiance in the Pathan borderlands till the British forcibly put them down. *Madarsah* teachers and students, such as Maulana Obaidullah Sindhi and Maulana Barkatullah Khan Bhopali were among the first Indians to demand complete freedom for India, at a time when Hindu and Muslim communalist groups were supporting the British. It is a fact, lost to those in the Hindutva crusade as well as the larger populace, that most *Madarsahs* vehemently opposed the Muslim League and its two-nation theory, insisting on a united India where people of different faiths could live in harmony.

9	The dichotomy between *Deen* and *Duniya* is stark and clear where the *Madarsah* vision is concerned. *Deen* stands for religious discourse, while *Duniya* is in the political power domain. The *Madarsah* teacher or the student goes to a *Madarsah* to reinforce his *Deen* and to pick up tools to work for his religion, he has little interest in the *Duniya* when he is at the *Madarsah*.

10	Most critics of the *Madarsahs* have probably never visited a *Madarsah*, and so much of what is said is pure hearsay. Yet, it may indeed be true that in some *Madarsahs*, students are taught to see all non-Muslims as *kafirs*, rebels against God doomed to perdition in Hell and so on. This understanding of the 'other' is actually something that they share with Hindutva militants, whose image of Muslims is no less lurid.

11	A study commissioned by the British government after the ethnic riots of Oldham and Burnby in March 2001 came out with some startling findings. It said Hindus in Britain are four times less likely to be unemployed than Pakistani and Bangladeshi Muslims. Muslim men of Pakistani and Bangladeshi background are disproportionately unemployed as compared to Hindus in Britain. This 220-page report says, "Among South Asians, Indian Muslims do better than Muslims from Pakistan or Bangladeshi background". Though the report warns against concluding that religion necessarily causes economic disadvantage, it notes "odds of being unemployed do vary significantly with religion". Religion, including the influence of Islam, seems to be one of the "unidentified factors which need to be considered" by the British government in dealing with race relations (quoted from *The Times*, London, by *The Statesman*, Calcutta, February 21, 2002).

12   Pakistan's President Pervez Musharraf addressing the Science and Technology Conference at Karachi on February 18, 2002 said: "Today we are the poorest, the most illiterate, the most backward, the most unhealthy, the most unenlightened, the most deprived and the weakest of all human race. The time has come for Islamic nations to take part in self-criticism".

13   "There were rival Islamic reformist schools in the quest for true Islamic practice. One group, the Ahl-i Hadith, for example, in their extreme opposition to such practices as visiting the Prophet's grave, rivaled that of the Arabians typically labeled "Wahabi. " The "Wahabis" were followers of an iconoclastic late 18th century reform movement associated with tribal unification who were to find renewed vigor in internal political competition within Arabia in the 1920s. From colonial times until today, it is worth noting, the label "Wahhabi" is often used to discredit any reformist or politically active Islamic group. Another group that emerged in these same years was popularly known as "Barelvi," and although engaged in the same process of measuring current practice against *hadith*, was more open to many customary practices. They called the others "Wahhabi." These orientations —"Deobandi," "Barelvi" or "Ahl-i Hadith" — would come to define sectarian divisions among Sunni Muslims of South Asian background to the present. Thus, *ulema*, mosques, and a wide range of political, educational, and missionary movements were known by these labels at the end of the twentieth century, both within the South Asian countries of India, Pakistan, and Bangladesh, as well as in places like Britain where South Asian populations settled." (Barbara D. Metcalf, *op. cit.*)

14   The Qadyanis, a sect of Muslims, have attained cent per cent literacy levels. Their Khalifa has declared education to be a compulsory element of their faith and life.

15   For detailed comments see Manzoor Ahmed, *Islamic Education*.

16   Imam Ghazali (1058-1111 AD) said that the first condition for the development of the active mind is the purity of faith and firmness of *iman*. Therefore, he said, primary education should be in accordance with religious beliefs and religious requirements. However, it should not be limited to these spheres alone. Therefore, Ghazali also emphasized imparting of technical and industrial knowledge along with religious education (Dr. Salamatullah, *Hindustan me Musalmano ki taleem*).

17   This is in contravention to the early reference to the segregation of religious and secular streams of knowledge. Most Muslim scholars maintain that the segregation of religious and temporal subjects in *Madarsahs* is a colonial invention.

18   Although the power of the *'ulema* among the Muslims of South Asia is today substantial, it is interesting to note that early Muslim history knew no such separate class of clerics as the *'ulema* or of an institution of specialized religious training as the *Madarsah*. Islam is probably unique among the world's religions in its radical disavowal of any intermediaries between God and ordinary believers. The *Qur'anic* assertion that Muslims could approach God directly obviated the need for a professional class of priests. Every Muslim was seen as, in a sense, his own priest. Prayers could be led by any believer, for God was believed to be equally accessible to all Muslims. Further undermining the institution of priesthood, acquiring knowledge of the scriptural tradition was seen as a duty binding on all Muslims, men as well as women, and not as the prerogative of a special class. While some people were recognized as more learned or pious than others, early Islamic history saw no professional class of *'ulema* as religious specialists. Islamic knowledge could be had by all, generally provided freely in mosques and, later, in Sufi lodges.

19   The system of *Madarsahs* came into existence towards the end of the tenth century. Before that, education was imparted in mosques or teachers taught at their own houses.

20   The contribution of Andulus (Islamic Spain) is very well known. Its universities at Grenada and Qurtaba (Cardova) made rich and ever lasting contribution in the fields of social and natural sciences, humanities, traditional sciences, *etc.* Hundreds of students from all parts of Europe flocked to these universities to seek knowledge about the sciences and Greek thought and philosophy. Thus the European Renaissance remains indebted to these Islamic institutions.

21   According to Dr. Salamatullah, there was no government control on the education system during the rule of Muslim kings in India. Education was free of government controls.

However, sometimes rulers and members of the rich class donated grants to educational institutions. The credit for governmental interest in education goes to Akbar in whose reign the government took some steps in the realm of education for the first time. A department of education was established which provided education to the masses without discrimination between the communities. Both Hindus and Muslims studied in the same institution, albeit their syllabi were different save for common subjects such as mathematics and sciences.

22   Interestingly, the descendents of the Firangi Mahal ulema are trying to revive the original *Madarsah* there.

23   Metcalf offers a different view on the history of *Madarsahs*: "The *Madarsah* does not appear to have been a major institution in the pre-colonial period. Instead, those who wished to be specialists in the great classic disciplines studied through Arabic - Qur'an, Qur'anic recitation and interpretation, *hadith*, jurisprudential reasoning based on these holy sources, and ancillary sciences like logic, rhetoric, and grammar - would sit at the feet of one or more teachers, traveling often from place to place, seeking not a degree but a certificate of completion of particular books and studies. The modern *Madarsah*, in contrast, as a formal institution, organized by classes, offering a sequential curriculum, staffed by a paid faculty, and supported by charitable campaigns, was a product of the colonial period and the result of familiarity with European educational institutions. The founders of the school gained support by utilizing all manner of new technologies from printing presses to the post office to railroads as they turned from reliance on increasingly-constrained princely patronage to popularly based contributions" (Barbara D. Metcalf, *op. cit.*)

24   "The surge in the number of *Madarsahs* in the 1980s coincided with the influx of some three million Afghan refugees, for whose boys the *Madarsahs* located along the frontier frequently provided the only available education. One school in particular, the *Madarsah* Haqqaniya, in Akora Kathak near Peshawar, trained many of the top Taliban leaders. These sometime students (*talib*; plural, *taliban*) were shaped by many of the core Deobandi reformist causes, all of which were further encouraged by Arab volunteers in Afghanistan. These causes, as noted above, included rigorous concern with fulfilling rituals; opposition to custom laden ceremonies like weddings and pilgrimage to shrines, along with practices associated with the Shi`a minority; and a focus on seclusion of women as a central symbol of a morally ordered society. Theirs was, according to Ahmed Rashid, a long time observer, "an extreme form of Deobandism, which was being preached by Pakistani Islamic parties in Afghan refugee camps in Pakistan." This focus on a fairly narrow range of *shari'a* law, which emphasized personal behavior and ritual, was something the Taliban shared with other Deobandi movements, even while the severity of the Taliban approach made them unique." (Barbara D. Metcalf, *op. cit.*)

25   Many of the Taliban had, indeed, studied in Deobandi schools, but one spokesman for the movement in its final months went so far as to declare "Every Afghan is a Deobandi." (Barbara Metcalf)

26   The influence of the *ulema* seems to have declined with each passing year in the last decade. The power of the Shahi Imam of Jama Masjid, Delhi, whose voice seemed to speak for the Indian Muslims, has declined to naught.

27   M. V. Kamath, What should we do with mushrooming *Madarsahs*? Should they be allowed to spread hatred? *Free Press Journal*, July 25, 2002, *http://www.samachar.com/ features/250702-fpj.html.*

28   Interestingly, about 100 Hindu children are enrolled in *Madarsahs* across Bihar. Hindu parents — both upper caste Brahmins and lower caste Dalits — are now increasingly sending their children to *Madarsahs*, *http://www.bihareducation.net/local/frmnews.htm*

29   Anand Mohan Sahay, "In Bihar, even non-Muslims prefer *Madarsahs*", *http:// www.rediff.com/news/2003/feb/22bihar.htm.*

30   Their exact number is not known although, according to President Pervez Musharraf, they total 10,000 — an understated figure that fails to take into account the number of mosques offering the same religious education, say observers. ("Myth and reality of a Pakistani *Madarsah*," *Rediff.com*)

31   "Twin advantage: Bangladesh and Pakistan join hands to spread terror in the northeast," *The Week*, Jan 5, 2003.

32   B. Prashad, *The Progress of Science in India during the Past Twenty-five Years*, Indian Science Congress Association, Calcutta, 1938, pp vii-viii.

33   *Muslim India*, October 21, 2001.

34   Dr. Rahat Abrar and Dr. M. Qamar Ishaque, "Introduction," in *Directory of Muslim Educational Institutions in India*.

35   Dr. Fahimuddin, "Globalization and Growth of *Madarsahs* In India", *http://www.bsos.umd.edu/socy/conference/newpapers/uddin.txt*.

36   There are about 3,500 *Madarsahs* in Bihar, including 1,100 state-run Islamic schools where the teaching and non-teaching staff get their salaries from the government. The remaining 2,500 *Madarsahs* are affiliated to the board. The Bihar government was one of the first in India to give a clean chit to *Madarsahs* and laud them for doing commendable work last year. It also said it had no information about any objectionable or anti-national activities in *Madarsahs*. ("RSS plans 40,000 schools to counter 'Madarsahs' along borders", Imran Khan, *Indo-Asian News Service*, Patna, Feb 27)

37   A curriculum is a means to achieve the objectives of education. It can be defined as the planned experiences provided by the school to assist pupils in attaining the designated learning outcomes to the best of their abilities. A syllabus on the other hand would down its scope to the various details to be studied in the subjects included in the curriculum.

38   See the chapter "An Appraisal of Islamic Curricula in India," in *Islamic Education* (47-48 pp.)

39   In South India, students are also taught regional languages.

40   Syed Shahabuddin: "...I would like to see the *Madarsah* syllabus, which has for long been in a process of change, to have a certain element of general education as well, so that the *Madarsah* products, while being good *ulema*, are not men who live in a sociological vacuum. And this process has begun in several *Madarsahs* all over the country. But I think we should let the *Madarsahs* decide how to go about this. It is up to them to decide what they need. They should remain primarily attuned to their actual purpose, the training of religious specialists, and at the same time help train students who will go on to become aware and responsible citizens of the country. The *Madarsahs* are continuously interacting with the broader community, because it is from the community and not from the state that they get their funds, and so they do respond to the demands that the community places on them," http://www.islamicvoice.com/february.2000/interview.htm.

41   For the detailed syllabus, see *Nisab-e Taleem*, by Dr. Ghulam Yahya Anjum, Jamia Hamdard, 2001.

42   See the observations of M. Shoeb Ansari in the preface to his book, *Education in Dini Madaris*.

43   According to Pakistani President Gen. Pervez Musharraf in an interview with CNN, "actually those who know what is going on in *Madarsahs* would support this point that I'm going to tell you, that this is the biggest welfare organization anywhere in the world operated today—about 600,000 to 700,000 children of the poor get free board and lodge, and they get free education (Amanpour, CNN)

44   In West Bengal up to 1977 there were 238 official *Madarsahs*. During the LF rule from 1977 onwards, so far additional 269 new *Madarsahs* have been opened. The budget allocation for *Madarsah* education was Rs 5.06 lakh in 1977. In the 2000-2001 budget, it was Rs 115 crore.

45   The Union Minister of State for Home, Ch. Vidyasagar Rao, has urged the State Governments to be vigilant while registering *Madarsahs*. He has said his appeal follows a study by a group of Ministers, which found that *Madarsahs* were proliferating in the country with 11,453 existing in 12 States bordering the country. The Centre has only one legislation — *the Religions Institutions (Prevention of Misuse) Act of 1988* — to deal with

the problem, provided a religious institution runs the *Madarsah*, whereas their registration and regulation is the responsibility of State Governments. (*The Hindu*, May 19, 2002), http://www.hindu.com/thehindu/2002/05/19/stories 2002051901361000.htm)

46 Well-known *Madarsahs* including the three at Deoband, Lucknow and Saharanpur which are recognized by the community, have refused to accept government aid since 1947, though they had played a major role in mobilizing Muslims for anti-British freedom struggle.

47 The Union Minister of State for Home, Ch. Vidyasagar Rao said religious institutions in the country were receiving nearly Rs. 4,000 crores under FRCA with Tamil Nadu, Delhi, Andhra Pradesh, Kerala and Maharashtra being the top five recipients (*The Hindu*, May 19, 2002).

48 The "Wahhabis" were followers of an iconoclastic late 18th century reform movement associated with tribal unification, who were to find renewed vigor in internal political competition within Arabia in the 1920s. From colonial times until today, it is worth noting, the label "Wahhabi" is often used to discredit any reformist or politically active Islamic group. (Barbara D. Metcalf, *op. cit.*)

49 M. Shoeb Ansari, *Education in Dini Madaris.*

50 Syed Shahabuddin on *Madarsah* reforms: "I personally feel that the question of reforms in the *Madarsahs* should be left to them. I would not like to inflict two systems of education —the *Madarsah* and the school syllabus—on them. That has been done in Bihar with fatal results—the products of those *Madarsahs* are neither good *maulvis* nor good graduates. They are neither here nor there. I feel that every mosque should have a *Madarsah* attached to it, where essential Islamic education is provided to every Muslim child till the age of five to seven. The children of a locality should attend this *Madarsah* as well as the regular school. But the community also needs some people who are experts in the *Quran*, the Traditions of the Prophet [*hadith*] and Islamic law [*fiqh*]. And so, some students should go in for higher Islamic education as well in order to become *ulema*. I would prefer it if the number of *Madarsahs* could be restricted to certain standardized institutions all over the country which would provide students with education right up to the research level. There should not be a glut in the market. Today, we have graduates of Deoband, the largest *Madarsah* in India, with no place to go. Not all of them can become *imams* in mosques, so many of them are forced to set up their own little shops or petty businesses to make a living." http://www.islamicvoice.com/february.2000/interview.htm

51 After going through the curricula in vogue in important *Madarsahs* like Darul-uloom Deoband, Darul-uloom Nadwat-ul-ulema, Lucknow, Jamiatul-falah, Balaria Gunj, Jamiatul-Islah at Saraimeer and Jamia salafiah at Varanasi, all in Uttar Pradesh, one has to confess that the charges of stagnation and statusquoism against *Madarsahs* in India are primarily a result of the sad state of education in the country as a whole. *Madarsahs* by and large follow the same pattern followed by government run primary schools and teach using the same old syllabi and outdated texts.

52 In contrast to this kind of reform, a Pakistani scholar has a different line of reform as a suggestion; "In Pakistan even the modern educational system is like the *Madarsahs* as far as the curriculum is concerned. The only way out is to radically change and reform the curriculum and introduce the teaching of social sciences. Instead of doing this, our government is focusing on the introduction of the natural sciences in the *Madarsah* syllabus and is also providing them computers. I think this is a useless exercise. It is the social sciences that make people to think and helps them open their minds, not the natural sciences." (Mubarak Ali is a leading Pakistani scholar and activist; he said this in an interview to Yogendra Sikand.)

53 Asghar Ali Engineer's views on curricular reforms are as follows: "I have been critical of the *dars-i-nizami*, the syllabus which is used in most of the Indian *Madarsahs*. This syllabus is, in my view, outdated and needs to be revised. *Madarsahs* still teach subjects like ancient Greek philosophy and Ptolemian astronomy, which they wrongly consider to be somehow part of the Islamic tradition. At a certain stage in history perhaps these

subjects were useful, but are no longer so and so should be done away with. I am not alone in saying this- many *'ulema* hold the same position. In place of the old and outdated 'rational sciences' (*ma'qulat*), modern social and natural sciences and humanities should be taught, as well as comparative religions. In this way, the graduates of the *Madarsahs* would be better informed about the conditions of the modern world and hence would be in a better position to give their legal opinions (*fatawa*) on matters related to Islamic jurisprudence. Christian seminaries are doing this today. Catholic priests are studying, besides their own religion, subjects like history, economics, sociology, political science and comparative religions, and so are better equipped to handle the challenges that modernity places before us all. In medieval times, leading Muslim *'ulema* did likewise. Faced with the challenge of Greek philosophy, they mastered it, and medieval *Madarsahs* produced leading Muslim philosophers, scientists, logicians and mathematicians, who were also pious Muslims themselves. So, there is no reason why the *'ulema* of today shouldn't do the same, and learn modern subjects. Instead of blindly opposing the *Madarsahs*, I feel one should think of ways to creatively work with them for reform. After all, for many Muslims, especially the poor, *Madarsahs* serve a valuable function of providing free education and literacy."

54 "I don't know what the international community can do except encourage national governments to change the system of education. There is a lot of change which is taking place in many countries around the world in the old system of *Madarsah* education. In our own country, in India I am aware of the fact that now *Madarsahs* are taking to information technology, they are using computers to train their students in a totally different kind of environment, and I think that is a kind of sustained effort which we need to pursue not only with regard to *Madarsah* education but with regard to all education which is based on religion," India's Foreign Minister, Yashwant Sinha in an interview, *http://www.brook.edu/dybdocroot/comm/events/20020910.pdf*.

55 Syed Shabuddin sees it in a different light: "In India, there has been a systematic campaign to vilify the *Madarsahs* as dens of the ISI and as shelters for the terrorists and the militants over the last few years. Out of this distrust and suspicion, came the Central Scheme for the Modernization of *Madarsahs* Education."

56 For further details, see Evaluation Report on Modernization of the *Madarsah* Education Scheme (UP), Hamdard Education Society, New Delhi, 2003.

57 See Syed Shahabuddin's article "Throttling the *Madarsahs* in the name of security", *http://www.milligazette.com/Archives/01072001/16.htm*.

58 It is learnt that the relevant Working Group for the Ninth Five Year Plan had recommended a provision of Rs. 91.65 crores for the modernization scheme. The amount actually provided was Rs. 48 crore. The total amount released does not exceed Rs. 16 crore, *Hamdard Education Society Report*, 2000.

59 Syed Hamid, "Deeni Madaris aur Asri Uloom," in the book, *Deeni Madaris aur unke masayal*, Seminar papers, February 1988, Idara-e Ilmia, Jamiat ul Falah, Azamgarh.

60 This case study is by Amir Ullah Khan and Zafar H. Anjum.

61 We visited the Jamia Arabia Shamsul Uloom on Sunday, April 6, 2003.

62 Dr. Abida Samiuddin, *Radiance*, New Delhi, 9-15 February, 1997.

References

Ahmed, Manzoor, *Islamic Education*, Genuine Publications, New Delhi, 1990.

Anjum, Ghulam Yahya, *Nisab-e Taleem*, Jamia Hamdard, New Delhi, 2001.

Ansari, M. Shoyeb, *Education in Deeni Madaris*, Institute of Objective Studies, New Delhi, 1997.

Fahimuddin, Dr., "Globalization and Growth of Madarsahs in India", Seminar paper, *http://www.bsos.umd.edu/socy/conference/newpapers/uddin.txt*.

Farooqui, Ammadul Hasan Azad, *Hindustan me Islami Uloom o Adabyat*, Maktabsa Jamia, New Delhi, 1986.

Hamid, Syed, "Deeni Madaris aur Asri Uloom," in the book, *Deeni Madaris aur unke masayal*, Seminar papers, February 1988, Idara-e Ilmia, Jamiat ul Falah, Azamgarh.

Institute of Objective Studies, *Directory of Muslim Educational Institutions in India*, New Delhi, 2002.

Hamdard Education Society, *Evaluation Report on Modernization of the Madarsah Education Scheme (UP)*, New Delhi, 2003.

Kamath, M. V., "What should we do with mushrooming Madarsahs? Should they be allowed to spread hatred?" *Free Press Journal*, July 25, 2002, *http://www.samachar.com/features/250702-fpj.html*.

Metcalf, Barbara D., "Traditionalist" Islamic Activism: Deoband, Tablighis, and Talibs, *http://www.ssrc.org/sept11/essays/metcalf.htm*.

Salamatullah, Dr., *Hindustan me Musalmanon ki Taleem*, Maktabsa Jamia, New Delhi, 1990.

Shahabuddin, Syed, "Throttling the Madarsahs in the name of security," *Milli Gazette*, New Delhi, *http://www.milligazette.com/Archives/01072001/16.htm*).

6

The Muslim Educational Problem and the Urdu Dimension

SALMAN KHURSHID

Educational problems of Muslims are obviously very complex. Our policy makers have not given enough serious thought to them. To begin with, we will have to address the following.

In general, Muslims are economically backward and do not have resources to send their wards to English medium private schools. Despite general acceptability of the excellent and commercial value of English medium education, the State cannot for Constitutional and political reasons, transform the State education system into an English-medium one. State Governments provide education in their respective regional languages. Hence, adequate facilities of teaching their own languages are assured. Urdu does not have that benefit.

Urdu, as cultural heritage, is part of Indian Muslim sensibility. It is also coincidentally the medium of religious education. In all the North Indian States, the prevailing education system has forced Muslims to abandon the language of their cultural identity. As a result, people who want to learn Urdu need either to make their own private arrangements or seek admission in *madarsahs*, basically set up to impart religious education. Part-time arrangements are not a feasible proposition in general, because the economic condition of an average Urdu-speaking person does not allow this. However, one can hope that the 86th Constitutional Amendment that provides a fundamental right to education up to the age of 14 years will facilitate arrangements for Urdu education, as well for Urdu speaking children.

In post-partition India, Urdu's fate was sealed with its ouster from the secular education curriculum. Unfortunately *madarsahs* remained the only places where Urdu was available and they became repositories of Urdu. But *madarsah* education is intimately associated with religious identity. These *madarsahs* impart education primarily in Urdu medium. To an extent, they represent those who emphasize upon a separate religious identity. A large number of students come from a very poor economic background and cannot afford education elsewhere. *Madarsahs* depend entirely on donations by the Muslim community, and students do not have to pay for their education. Religion is definitely an important part of their life, but *madarsah* education is certainly not their conscious free choice. Only a few of them take up higher education in the *madarsah* system as a career. The question remains: how do we improve the poor students' economic condition and social status to provide real access to the attributes of modern life? For this, education of contemporary subjects, as well as technical education, should become a compulsory part of the curriculum of the *madarsah* system. But the authorities of the *madarsah* system have to be first convinced. Government interference, even in 'advisory capacity' in the name of introduction of modern secular subjects could prove counter productive. However, non-government organizations working among Muslims and local educated people can play a significant role in introducing *madarsah* managements to subjects aimed at jobs-skills and enhancing the earning capacity of students. In view of the very disappointing result of the *madarsah* modernization scheme, it should be substituted with something more reasonable and effective. Regretfully, in the present political atmosphere and controversies raging on school curricula, people feel that if the ruling BJP government is showing interest in Urdu and *madarsahs*, it must be with the intention of eventually harming them.

On the other hand, despite the Constitutional affirmation of status of Urdu as a National Language, efforts have been made in the past to drive it out from the social sphere by atavists. Earlier, they could have been dismissed as an aberration, but now these forces are in power. After Independence, as a consequence of partition, Urdu was undermined by the decision of its exclusion from the education curriculum. Much water has flown down the river since then. Efforts such as by left-wing intellectuals like Daniel Latifi towards the end of the last century have been made, but the agenda for Urdu's revival remains ineffective.

Over a period, Muslims have realized that the revival of Urdu education in the secular curriculum is imperative because isolationist *madarsah* education is inadequate to ensure social status and economic growth. In the whole of Uttar Pradesh, where at least twenty million Urdu speaking people reside, there is hardly any Urdu medium primary school. This is so, despite the Constitutional directive (under Article 350-A) for education in the mother tongue. Even more surprisingly, the North Indian States, particularly UP, do not have provision for Urdu even as an elective subject, and offer Sanskrit as a modern Indian language, making it compulsory up to the 12th standard, under the Three Language formula.

So what can be done for Urdu medium education for those who claim Urdu as their language and want to teach it to their children? Most of them are under-privileged and unable to get education in English medium schools. A simple formulation is that for government schools situated in Urdu speaking localities, Urdu should be the medium of education up to 5th class. Hindi should be introduced from class III and English from class VI, so that the students can easily switch to Hindi medium schools at secondary level and learn English gradually. In the Northern parts of India, at present Hindi is exclusively the medium of education and Sanskrit is taught from class III upwards as a modern Indian language. English is introduced from class VI. From class VI, a combined course of Hindi and Sanskrit is taught up to class XII. In a nutshell, out of 300 marks for languages, 134 go to Sanskrit, 66 to Hindi and 100 to English. Urdu gets nothing! This situation must change and that will not be possible unless there is a strong political will, backed by a mass movement.

This grating injustice suffered by Urdu speaking people has also posed a threat to the very survival of their language. The community has therefore begun to equate the survival of Urdu and revival of Urdu education with the well being of Muslims as a political, cultural and religious entity. A debate on this issue has begun. It remains to be seen whether this will lead to a real political awakening. Political will and educational empowerment is desperately needed to revive this language and in turn for the language to bolster empowerment.

The eventual solution to the diverse problems of Muslims will be found in political power augmented by the community's will to organize itself and harness that political power. Here we focus on the educational problems of the Muslims, which need urgent political intervention.

Urdu language remains perhaps the most important dimension of Muslim sensibility. According to the Census figures of 1991, India has 4.3 crores (43.3 million) Urdu speakers – despite the feeling that Census records of North Indian States may have recorded Hindi as the mother-tongue of many Urdu speaking people. These 43.3 million people will have a substantive role in political developments in the days to come. Given in the trend of population growth in our country, this figure will increase in the Census of 2001. Technically speaking, Urdu is the mother tongue of most of the North Indian Muslims. It is the language whish fulfills the religious needs, and besides Arabic, it has the largest number of books on religion. Naturally, many Muslims of the Hindi region consider Urdu a part of their religious and cultural identity.

Due to its roots in Muslim identity, Urdu has incurred the distaste of majoritarian communalists, although some of them learnt the language in undivided India. A campaign to undermine Urdu has been a prominent part of the policies of some groups. Political parties have failed Urdu, due to their fear of losing popular support.

In fairness, since partition, our intelligentsia has been sympathetic towards Urdu, but somewhat ineffectively. Few intellectuals have supported the cause of Urdu through their writings. The situation is so dismal that one can hardly find any academic writing in the field of social sciences focussing on the problems of Urdu. Research scholars pay scant attention to its problems. As a result, we have no academic inputs for policy planning. The government policy concentrates only on Urdu literature and culture- promoting *mushairas*, fiction and criticism *etc*. Government assignments for Urdu textbooks are routinely given to Urdu poets, littérateurs and so-called literary critics. Nobody – including Urduwallahs – have spoken against this shortsighted treatment meted out to the education of a language. Urdu is either unavailable, or else captive of mediocre syllabi - thus compelling low-income group Urdu speakers to put their children through alternative Hindi medium education. In States like Maharashtra where education is provided, the standard of books is very low in comparison to those of the regional languages. Serious thought has not been given to re-evaluating these substandard books, which include NCERT books. The trend of assigning projects for preparing the syllabus for Urdu medium students to poets and critics was established by NCERT. Though our academia, having great command of history, is shaping sensibilities of citizen and promptly reacted against saffornisation, it is sad that they remain ignorant of the problems faced by Urdu speaking people. The result of leaving the future of Urdu education entirely to poets and writes is that we have to put up with an esoteric and impractical syllabus up to the university level.

Our aim here is threefold - to undertake a realistic reappraisal of Urdu language in the formal system of education in contemporary India; to address the representation of Urdu and the community of its speakers; and to explore the possibility of Urdu as a first and compulsory language for Urdu speakers under the three language formula. Urdu has been deprived of its rightful place in the curriculum of secular education.

Our conviction is that Urdu cannot survive as a language of cultural expression unless it is included as a subject in the curriculum from the primary to the secondary level.

As a language of cultural heritage, Urdu can be accessed as an optional subject by students studying in English or in a regional medium. In those parts of northern India where Urdu speaking people are in substantial number, Urdu can be offered as a medium of instruction at primary level – up to the age of 14 years. Afterwards, students can learn it is a first, second or third language up to 12th standard, depending upon the available system and their informed preferences.

We should of course teach foreign languages, at least after class X. For that purpose, we must have more advanced systems. For those who wish to opt for a European language, a combined course with English could be introduced. An advanced course of Hindi and Sanskrit must be provided as an option for those who want to continue the study of Hindi and Sanskrit at the senior secondary level.

With these observations, I emphasize:

1. Inclusion of Urdu in the secular curriculum from primary level as a medium of instruction in central government schools and schools affiliated to the State Governments or State Boards up

to the age of 14 years. For those who declare Urdu as their mother tongue, primary Urdu medium schools must be provided in localities that meet the national norm of 300 Urdu speakers.

2. From VI to XII standard, under the Three-Language Formula, Urdu must be taught as a first language (exclusively the mother tongue) to Urdu speaking children.

3. Hindi may be introduced as the principal [compulsory] State Language from class IV and English as the third language from class VI to XII.

4. From class VI onwards, Hindi should become the medium of instruction in North India in Government-run schools, as well as in schools that receive grant-in-aid from the Government. In these schools, Urdu should be included as first and compulsory language, along with Hindi as second compulsory language and English as third language. From class VIII, there should be a composite course of Hindi and Sanskrit. Wherever the people declaring Urdu as their mother tongue comprise 300 houses in one or more than one locality, Urdu medium primary schools should be opened for their children.

Unless Urdu is included in the school curriculum, no efforts for its revival will succeed. Survival of Urdu will bolster the survival of our secular values and democratic tradition. If secular values are at stake, the future of all linguistic minorities will become bleak because anti-secular forces purport to deny democratic space to every other identity besides their own. So it is high time for Muslims and other religious and linguistic minorities to unite with the secular and democratic forces for preservation of our rich diversity. Unless Muslims give up the tendency of looking toward others to take up battle for their rights, they will remain marginalized. They have to join the fight for secular and democratic space and their social and educational empowerment – if they want to be seen as more than passive vote banks. To get secular education is their Constitutional right, and they should legitimately demand schools and facilities in their mother tongue.

As in any other dynamic society, changes are taking place in India. The 86th Amendment of the Constitution of India notified on 13

December, 2002, gave the fundamental right of education up to the age of 14 years. Those children must get this education in their mother tongue - in case of the Urdu linguistic minority, in Urdu. We should not oppose English medium education *per se*. But education in private institutions with English as the medium of instruction is a costly affair and cannot be a substitute for our own languages. Hence, every possible step must be taken to improve the system of education in Indian languages.

7

India, 1947-2003: The Dangers of Communalism and Urdu Education

BIKRAMJIT DE

Society in India is still perceived to be static. The predominance of the caste system and the stranglehold it exercises over the modes of production as well as the distribution of labour are cited as example of an immutable social structure, despite the beneficial aspects of colonial interaction between Europe and its others. Such a conservative view considers the predominance of Sanskrit and the languages that emerged from it, for example Hindi and the other North Indian languages, to be the main medium of communication. Sanskrit is accorded the status of the *de facto* official language in India.[1] The existence of languages in which the minorities, such as Muslims speak, for instance Urdu, is considered to be marginal to the necessity for the framing of a constructive language policy at the centre, through which the Indian state is enabled to grant equal status to all Indian languages. Urdu, which is primarily a spoken language, is the mother tongue of most of the Indian Muslims. It is spoken in vast segments of North and West India, as well as in Hyderabad.[2]

Introduction

The Idea of India was, following the initial years of Independence, a reaffirmation of the principles governing the structures of a composite culture. Admittedly, it derived its origins from the historical conjuncture of the shaping of the framework of European de-colonization following the termination of the Second World War, the defeat of fascist regimes and their satellite states in Europe, and the demise of the obverse side of a similar urge for territorial expansion, British imperialism, along with the emerging principles of liberal western democracies.[3] The Indian constitution, enshrining the features of this culture, was indeed based on a wide range of European constitutions, most notably the Irish and British, as well as the American Charter of Independence. The preliminary draft of the constitution was framed and passed as the *Government of India Act,* 1935, under the tutelage of British policy-makers operating from Whitehall and Delhi. The arrival of the first blue print for the modern Indian nation state can also be attributed to the early years of the establishment of the British Dependency in India in the nineteenth century, when the new Anglo-Indian administrators were still in the process of acclimatizing themselves to the institutions of governance. Through the establishment of an efficient network of officials recruited to gather and disseminate knowledge at the level of informers belonging to the indigenous society, the Raj managed to create, indeed by default, a sense of unity among its Indian subjects. Even though the initial intention of the British masters revealed a tendency to view the emergence of the new group of Indian nationalists as subjects of their ingenious 'safety valve' theory, the Congress under the moderates in the period between 1885-1915, succeeded in building an independent platform for the expression of their legitimate grievances, which can be rightly considered to have offered the first seeds of Indian nationalism.[4]

Contemporary Indian consciousness was also characterized by transference of political authority from its exercise at diverse levels of local governance, based on traditional modes of economy to a single sovereign state at the centre. The new Indian state was entrusted with manifold responsibilities, such as the maintenance of its territorial boundaries, a legacy bequeathed to them by the British, preservation of domestic authority and the protection of physical security and social opportunities and the welfare of its citizens, as well as the new task of creating a dynamic situation for economic development, especially increase in the scope of gainful employment.[5] That the respective central governments from 1950 made the effort to adopt these new measures rapidly indicates that transformation in the premises and postulates of policy, after the completion of the process of transfer of power from British to Indian hands, had begun in right earnest. There still remained questions regarding the speed and spread of reforms, and the methods of implementation of the programmes. Ironically, the inheritance of the edifices of the Raj, such as the Indian Civil Services [ICS], and its mere renaming into the Indian Administrative Services [IAS], prevented the guardians of the modern Indian state, still standing in the shaft of sunlight, from improvising new forms of administration necessary for the management of complex issues of development at the level of the village councils and the *panchayats*.[6]

The attempt to establish a firm structure of democracy in India has indeed been a success story, although there remains the necessity to re-evaluate the scale of the spread of democratic values at the grassroots level. It is indeed a matter of considerable pride for all Indians that set against the backdrop of certain traditional forms of exploitation, for instance the existence of the caste system, and the interpolation of imperial and authoritarian state systems from the west into pre-colonial modes of economy and governance, the present set of policy-makers and intellectuals have succeeded in retaining the edifices of democracy and the utilization of principles of choice in India. Despite the depths of poverty and illiteracy the Indians inherited from the British in 1947, the state has continued to hold elections at regular intervals. The Idea of India, as Gandhi and Nehru conceived it, has lived up to the expectations of its citizens. Our western mindset must not be viewed as an example of the inability of the liberal minded Indian civil servants, the oriental versions of the framers of modern state centric policy, to free the Indian people from the shackles of a colonial ideological orientation. The speed of reforms has been uneven, but it has been barely half a century since independence, and the progress the country has made, especially in the field of communication and the acquisition of knowledge has indeed been staggering. Macaulay once commented that India is "the strangest of all political anomalies". Despite its vastness, and numerous contradictions, after fifty years of independence, India still retains its democratic institutions, and has the distinction of holding regular elections on a scale, which is unprecedented even in Europe. In its democratic experiment, the Indian government has succeeded in combining the power of political regimes and institutions designed for the requirements of the modern nation state, with the force of human will. The evolving of democratic norms and practices in India was indigenous in character and automatic.[7]

The form of democracy that has been in practice in colonial societies and their successor states, for instance in India, was not the immutable contribution of the British. It developed out of a necessity felt by the Indians to modernize themselves. The new set of policy-makers realized that they had to assist the Indians to chart an independent course from the existing structures of administration, discarded by the British, which were tied in subtle knots of excessive bureaucratization. The framers also believed that pre-colonial modes of governance, which relied on a modicum of proof of consultative and deliberative forms of political institutions, had become outmoded in the context of the rapid strides made in the conceptualization of democracy by the developed nations in the twentieth century. Indeed, rulers in pre-British India did not make any perceptible effort to install an adequately representative mode of government, nor did they allow the emergence of popular movements to effectively challenge their form of despotism. But democracy was preserved in the diverse and disjointed nature of sub-continental politics: through a system of checks and balances protected through the absence of a single superpower in the peninsula, but bearing the same social and political institutions for the management of their communities. It was conceived and maintained in the semi-autonomous village societies, through the empowerment of the *jati*, which functioned through the agency of the *varna*. Other similarities between the diverse ethnic groups, which allowed democracy to flourish in the subcontinent, included the continuance of a single thread representing common aesthetic and architectural styles, myths, and ritual motifs. Thus the origins of representative forms of governance rest in the ideological mechanisms of which can be considered to have held the subcontinent together before the arrival of the British. Indeed, the roots of this form of ideology were to be traced to Brahminical forms of education despite its brand of oppressive economic production.[8]

A value system based on western liberalism envisaged the establishment of the institutions of modernity, which was however, fraught with inner contradictions from the inception of the modern nation state in India. Nehru's drive towards the building of the pillars of the movement for the maintenance of universal history, which was rooted in attempts to explore historical processes from the dimension of a scientific enquiry imbedded in the existing conditions of the present, was an expression of a significant characteristic of the project of conceiving India. The codification of a mongrel language, spoken by a minority of British and a few Indian officials in the civil services for the purpose of revenue collection and property laws, created a status of inferiority for the members of the colony. It was not granted equal status to the use of Queen's English.[9] This presented difficulties to the visionaries from breaking new intellectual ground from their British counterparts. An early academic example of segments of the governing elites' tendency to view Indian history from the perspective of the exigencies of building political icons was the tendency to compare modern Indian Hindu leaders with rulers belonging to the ancient period, such as Emperor Asoka, and Muslim rulers in the medieval period, such as Emperor Akbar. Both these kings have been lionized as upholders of brief interludes when secularism became acceptable within the structures of the elites in almost the whole of the subcontinent. They have been accorded the status of role models for Indian political leaders functioning within the framework offered by diverse forms of western democracies.[10] Obversely, the structures of governance would have benefited more had the visionaries been able to properly identify the requirements of associating India's present with the West's current political destiny.[11]

One of the adverse consequences of the aggressive advocacy of the two-nation theory, which can be considered to have been utilized by fundamentalist elements evident in the Muslim League and the Hindu Mahasabha alike, as well as the ranks of the British policy-makers as a tool against the popularity of Indian nationalism, was the institutionalization of communal animosity between the Hindus and Muslims. The conflict over the question of the acceptance of the Hindi-Urdu script in the pre-independence period was utilized as one of the principal arenas of communal mobilization by political leaders, belonging to the old and new élite and popular segments of the Muslim community, aiming to sharply communalize the nationalist framework of politics.[12] Even though there have been several instances of incendiary communal clashes over the last fifty years, the scale of rioting has markedly increased in the last one decade. The 1990s has had the unique distinction of witnessing the emergence of a deep-seated response of large segments of conservative Hindu opinion to what they inappropriately consider to be the 'appeasement' of the

Muslim community since independence. The ire of the Hindu Nationalist politicians, about whom very little was known at the time of the General Election of 1989, both moderate and reactionary, had been aimed especially at the role played by the Muslim leadership in the Shah Bano case. The Supreme Court's decision, in the Danial Latifi vs. Supreme Court case, not to allow the husband of a Muslim lady called Shah Bano to not pay her any compensation after abandoning his wife [which he had justified by Muslim law] was reversed by the central government. Recently the decision of the present political leadership of the country has been guided by segments of the powerful conservative Muslim opinion to overturn the earlier decision of the Supreme Court. This move has been perceived as a victory for the traditionalist Muslims who have been successful in utilizing the tools of parliamentary legislation to bend aspects of the rule of law, originally designed to protect the interests of the Muslim community. The subversion of the judgment passed by Latifi at the time of the initiation of the case by the existing ruling Hindu Nationalist regime, is an example of aspects of the hidden agenda of the BJP to indulge in opportunistic forms of politics to garner the support of fundamentalist elements of the Muslim community.

This created a public mood, which was portrayed, as hostile to the government. The nature of reportage in the national newspapers also emphasized the failure of the central government to protect the rights of the Muslim married women in the event of a divorce. This decision was perceived as a prime example of the ruling party's attempt to capture votes in elections. The role of a segment of the Muslim leadership, who advised the Prime Minister of India to reverse the decision of the Supreme Court, has been held to be a principal cause for the swift rise of Hindu Nationalism in India in the following years. 'Appeasement' was a policy, which was not only supposed to have been followed by the Congress governments [even before, and since Independence], but also by the Janata Dal regime under the leadership of Prime Minister Vishwanath Pratap Singh, who declared the Prophet's birthday as a national holiday in his Red Fort speech in 1990.[13] The opening of the lock of the Babri Masjid for the Muslim community has contributed in equal measure to pandering to the political demands placed by the advocates of both Hindu and Muslim fundamentalists on government policies.

The second pillar of strength on which the rise of unbridled demonstration of hostility towards the Muslim community and an increase in unwarranted levels of religiosity was the emergence of 'investigative' journalism by the middle of the 1980s – this interestingly petered out by the middle of the following decade. This was supported by a determined opposition bent on the sole aim of dismantling of the existing edifices of government at the centre. The then united opposition, a phenomenon which has since not been emulated, failed to provide a viable alternative for governance to the one offered and indeed practiced with some measure of success by the Indian National Congress [INC] in both Delhi and the states. Once again this resulted in the swift emergence of majoritarian *Hindutva*, which temporarily occupied the void created by the sudden disappearance of a responsible party with officials and members fully experienced in the modes of governance. The consequent analyses and criticisms of the so-called 'elitist' Nehruvian political rhetoric expressed an unprecedented rejection of liberal values, protected until then by successive Congress Prime Ministers from 1947-89, with a minor break of one and half years.[14]

In addition, on the international stage, the collapse of the USSR, and the decline of communism, and the consequent arrival of a period of political and economic disintegration in the Commonwealth of Independent States [CIS] assisted the champions of an unattractive breed of conservative nationalism to incorrectly identify the existing ruling party, the INC and by default its supporters and beneficiaries of its policies, as the upholder of values and systems with which the Soviet Union was identified. The almost total rejection of the time-tested principles of Non-Alignment in the country's foreign policy was yet another indicator of the rightward shift of the political and social climate of a system, which has, is, and will indeed continue to be identified in international diplomatic circles with the universal principles of tolerance preached by Mahatma Gandhi. The champions of Hindu nationalism gained from the demise of a powerful anti-imperialist and anti-racist movement, which was given vital leadership by the member states of the South within the arena of North-South economic confrontation. The BJP has also considerably benefited from the altered circumstances of the international economic system.[15] The current ruling party has succeeded in disengaging India from the movement. India was the leading country, in the period between 1950-1990, to have assisted the other member states of the non-aligned movement to expand and institutionalize the structures of the administrative and confidence-building apparatus of the movement.[15] Amongst some of his significant achievements, Prime Minister Rajiv Gandhi had been successful in reviving the Non-Aligned Movement [NAM] by reviewing its objectives, which were based on liberal principles. Nuclear disarmament, promotion of the idea of G-15 and the identification of India as a major world power were principles, which were swiftly either discarded or appropriated by rival parties for the purpose of building their own electoral agendas.[16]

One of the principal factors, which can be considered to have fanned communal hostility on a national scale in the 1980s, was the failure of the members of the public services, for instance the civil servants, politicians and the intelligentsia, to contain the adverse impact arising from the rampant political opportunism in the political system. The origins of opportunistic politics can be traced back to the 1960s, which can perhaps be considered to have been the most volatile decade in history of post-independence India – this was the period after the years following the Independence when the first strains of dissent became evident within the internal politics of the Congress. The marrying of religion with politics, and the tendency of an undetermined liberal and left-wing intelligentsia to retreat in the face of a right-wing communal onslaught resulted not surprisingly in the politics of compromise. The tendency to enter into short-term political alliances with obviously communalized forces hindered the development of what has now come to be recognized as the world's greatest democracy. The alliance of both the Congress and the communists with the Muslim League in Kerala in the 1960s, and the socialists and the secular political combinations with the Jan Sangh for the purpose of seat adjustments immensely damaged the prospects of a fledgling democracy. More damaging was the association between Jayaprakash Narayan and the Rashtriya Sayamsevak Sangh [RSS], the Jan Sangh and the Jamaat-e-Islami in 1974-75, with the sole objective of removing the Congress government from power. Finally, the forces of divisive politics once again became evident when the Janata Dal willingly entered into an electoral alliance with the Bharatiya Janata Party [BJP] in 1989. Such a laxity in an erstwhile firmly value-oriented political system, with an intellectual ancestry dating back to the origins of the Bengal Renaissance, allowed the loosening of the state apparatuses. The branch of the public service, which was most adversely affected by the rise of opportunism, was the police, whose members not only failed to comprehend and contain the nature of communal tension, often leading to skirmishes and riots, but participated in the communalization of the polity. The central and state administrations have indeed remained, in the last one decade, unsuccessful in acting against the incidence of riots, which have continued to increase with every electoral defeat of the Bharatiya Janata Party [BJP], as well as deal effectively with the inflammatory propaganda carried out by rabidly communalized segments of the information media.[17]

Since independence, the successive central governments have also remained unsuccessful in according the languages of the single largest religious minority the status of a major Indian language. One of the immediate results of the rise of Hindu chauvinism has been the tendency to view the principal languages of the Muslim community as irrelevant to the development of a coherent and improved language policy in India. Urdu, which is spoken by more than 10 per cent of the nation's population, is not an exception in this regard. In fact, the importance of other West Asian languages, such as Persian, to the study of Medieval Indian history ought to remain at the forefront of any historical enquiry of the middle ages. No full study, including proper academic articles or indeed full-length books, has been carried out on the development or even the causes for the decline of Urdu in India. The little academic output that has taken place has been casual in mentioning the centrality of the role of the language as a medium of communication at the level of scholarly research in India and abroad, as well as daily communication. I will address the existing problems and prospects of Urdu in India, between 1947-2002. I have used secondary literature, mostly short articles published in journals and a few books on related themes. This paper does not claim to have been based on primary archival research.

Through a survey of the course taken by Urdu over the last two centuries, this paper will enquire the attitudes of the official agencies to the development of the language in India. One of the principal themes of investigation will be the guidelines for the framing of a new language policy both at the state and the central levels for the promotion of Urdu as a parallel language. It will address whether Urdu ought to be taught in schools and colleges as the first language, with the potential of filling the void created by the decline of Hindustani, which is a combination of Hindi and Urdu, due to the adoption of a new brand of excessively Sanskritised form of Hindi. I will deal with the relationship between Urdu and English, which has remained the principal official medium of communication in the country in the last fifty-five years. The imperatives faced by the policy-makers responsible for the promotion of Urdu with regard to the possibility of increasing the language's popularity in English-speaking groups is another topic of discussion here. I will briefly mention the relationship between Urdu and *Madarsah* education, and the role of Urdu outside the ambit of the *Madarsahs*.

The Decline of Urdu as an Official Medium of Communication

The term 'Urdu' is found to have been used for the first time by the poet Mir Taqi Mir in 1752. Mir gave it the name *Urdu-e-mu'allah*, which means courtly language. The Emperor Shah Alam II, who took up residence in the Red Fort in Delhi in 1772, accorded it the status of a language of power by actively patronizing it.[18] The authors of *Hobson Jobson* cite a reference, dating back to 1560, which reveals the use of the word Urdu Bazar [camp market].[19] The word, which has a Turkish origin [*Ordu* or of the *orda* or camp of the horde], was originally used to refer to the language spoken by army officers and in camps. It was also considered to have started as a 'courtly language' that was treated as a medium of everyday communication by elites, owing allegiance to the Mughal Empire. The name was derived from the term *zaban-e-urdu-e-mu'allah-e-Shajahanabad*, which indicated the language spoken in the exalted city/court of Shajahanabad or Delhi. Soon this term was abridged to *zaban-e-urdu* and eventually to just Urdu.[20]

At the time of its inception, Urdu and Hindi were almost totally indistinguishable, but by 1600 A.D. they began to diverge from each other. But over the next four centuries they continued to remain linguistically identical.[21] Urdu, also heavily absorbed words from Persian and Arabic. Loan words, syntactic terms of phrases, borrowed sounds, such as 'q', 'z', and 'gh' were examples of the contributions made by the other two Islamic languages. Two centuries ago, the closeness between Hindi and Urdu was evidenced in the their common origins in the Indo-European family of languages. They are the variants of the same language form. Both evolved from *Khari Boli*, a branch of western Hindi, which was spoken in Haryana, Delhi and Meerut. But Urdu was written in a modified version of the Persian script, which itself had originally derived in the medieval period from Arabic, while Hindi was written in Devanagari. In the course of time, the spheres of influence of the two languages also varied – Urdu was spoken exclusively in Delhi, Awadh and Hyderabad, while Hindustani along with regional languages, in the rest of the country.[22] It is a misconception of the non-Urdu speakers that Urdu is a foreign language in the subcontinent. It represents the fruitful development of a local language.[23]

The background to the emergence of Urdu and Persian as a medium of communication in India, especially the United Provinces, Bihar and Bengal can be traced back to the establishment of the Calcutta *Madarsah* in 1781. Urdu was supposed to have evolved as an assertive medium of communication, for the use of Muslims and all other communities, overriding religious barriers. The other two seats of learning, which had been established by the British for the purpose of the spread of the language, were the Fort William College [1780] and the Hindu College [1817], which was later renamed Presidency College [1856]. Both these institutions were established in Calcutta. The *Sadr Diwani Adalat* and the *Sadr Nizamat Adalat* in Calcutta were also responsible for the employment and the education of *Maulvis* and *Pundits* for the purpose of the interpretation of Muslim and Hindu laws. In addition, British officials established the Calcutta School Book Society and Calcutta School Society in 1817 and 1818 respectively.[24] The starting of a number of newspapers in Urdu and Bengali, their brief progress and eventual closing down, and the reception of these newspapers in Bengal, as well as among government circles, were some of the measures taken by Muslims and Hindus to promote Urdu education. From 28 March, 1822, an Urdu weekly journal, entitled *Jami-Jahan Numa*, was published. Interestingly, its publisher was a Hindu called Harihar Dutta, a writer in the Account's Office in the Military Department of the East India Company's government.[25] After the publication of the sixth number of the journal, it was stated in an editorial of the *Calcutta Journal* that Hindoostanee, the language adopted by the journal, was too colloquial and popular, although well received in the polite and highly informed circles. To make it more accessible to the 'natives', dual use of Persian was recommended, since the learning of Persian, the Mughal official language, was considered to be a "necessary part of the education of every person who has any pretensions to respectability."[26] Apart from the growing distance between Urdu and Hindi, clearly a clash also emerged between the readers of Persian and Urdu. In the next couple of years, the popular demand for the publication of an Urdu newspaper did not show any perceptible increase, and soon the management of *Jami-Jahan Numa* had to discontinue its Urdu section, reverting to publication in Persian. Another weekly journal, entitled *Mirat-ul Akhbar*, was founded in April 1822 by Rammohan Ray, later given the title of Raja by Akbar III, the second last Mughal Emperor. Its medium of instruction was Persian from the beginning. The first signal of the rejection of Urdu by even the Muslim community had started to become evident. In addition, in Bengal, the Urdu-speakers had to contend with the existence of Bengali as another medium of communication for the Muslims. The impetus for the advance of secondary and higher education benefited the Bengali language immensely.[27] However, the conflict between Urdu and the other languages did not assume serious proportions since it was still early days for the development of the language. In the first half of the nineteenth century Urdu was still in the process of being received by a newly informed readership. It was adopted as a new genre of communication and transmission of Islamic culture by an emerging indigenous intelligentsia, comprising academicians, litterateurs and journalists. In the early nineteenth century it demonstrated the ability to supplement the role of Persian, which continued to remain as the principal language of the governing and cosmopolitan classes. It emerged as a modern prose language. Like many other regional languages, it also underwent considerable structural transition meant to enrich the content and usage of the language, which contributed to the close relationship between the individual and his society. The influence of Urdu extended to almost all fields of Islamic learning, such as translation of Quranic verses and the practice of traditional forms of medicine.[28]

It was in the post-Mutiny period that the Hindi-Urdu-Persian conflict began to sharpen. The decision of the British to introduce Urdu in the Perso-Arabic script as the main medium of communication in courts and administrative offices, especially in the North Western Frontier Provinces [NWFP], heightened the sense of competition felt by Hindi, Urdu and Persian speakers *vis-à-vis* each other. In addition, in 1864, Urdu was mandated as the spoken language of army officers and ordinary soldiers. Despite the popularity of Hindi and its script, the colonial officials devised Hindustani at the level of the common people, a term the British coined, to connote the use of Hindi and Urdu words, as the *lingua franca* of the entire country.[29] The status of Urdu started to decline considerably towards the end of the nineteenth century in the directly ruled provinces, such as the United Provinces, which was until then dominated by Urdu-speaking élites, as well as in Bengal. The policies of the British officials which can be attributed to the waning popularity of Urdu, included the gradual assertion of power and patronage by bureaucrats, both British and Indian, and commercial men at the expense of the local landed magnates, who predominantly spoke in the language.

Prominent literary personalities, such as Bharatendu Harishchandra contributed to the process of the decline of Urdu as well. Harishchandra believed that Hindi ought to be accorded more importance than Urdu due to its perceived 'moral' and 'religious' superiority. In vulgar and savage satires he mocked the death of the Urdu Begum, whose mourners included Arabic, Persian, Pushto, and Punjabi, all of whom had committed a crime by sharing a 'foreign' script. He clearly stated his position on the necessity to denigrate Urdu in an address to the Education Commission in 1882, "The use of Persian letters in offices is not only an injustice to Hindus, but it is a cause of annoyance and inconvenience to the majority of the local subjects of the Her Imperial Majesty".[30] Harishchandra's sense of grievance, although exaggerated, against the Urdu speaking elites was not entirely unjustified. The Hindi speakers in North India believed that Urdu was not their mother tongue, and in order to excel in the language they were expected to learn Urdu better than the Muslims. Firaq Gorakhpuri [1896-1984], commented as late as in 1945, "what is needed is for him [Hindus] to grasp firmly in his hands the inner veins of that language in the same way that Urdu, or western Hindi was grasped by Mir, Ghalib, Anis, Atash and Dagh'.[31]

The emerging group of British Indian civil servants, who represented the new professions, assumed control of networks of communication, for example local posts, roads, railways [mostly administered by the British] and the police. The British reformed the bureaucracy, which introduced the use of English in government offices, at the expense of Urdu. The nascent bourgeoisie, on the other hand, took advantage of the immense development of the networks of communication and successfully expanded the scope of their trade. They also resorted to cash cropping, and bought large tracts of land. In addition, the spread of western education, as well as the encouragement of the vernacular languages of eastern India, threatened the continued exertion of influence by the Urdu-speaking landed gentry. Other factors that contributed to the decline of Urdu as the principal mode of communication lay in the arena of local self-government. The hereditary landlords were exempted from participating in elective politics, which further reduced the scope of control exercised by Urdu in the towns.[32] Over the next one hundred years, it was the Muslim élites who themselves deliberately neglected the development of Urdu because of a misconception that "the language was a dimension of the two-nation theory".[33]

The British administrators were never interested in allowing Urdu to be promoted at the expense of what they considered to be the development of the rich traditions of Sanskrit. A British policy-maker commented, "We are far more interested in [encouraging] a Hindu predominance than in [encouraging] a Mahomedan predominance, which, in the nature of things, must be hostile to us."[34] The British actively participated in the sanctification of Devas, from which originated the Devanagari script, and accorded more importance to the imparting of Sanskrit, which they believed was akin to Latin.[35] In addition, they tried to impose the use of the Roman script for the use of the Indian army. The British displayed an inability to configure without the utilization of Roman diacritics, many important Urdu words and their exact phonetic implications. Garcin de Tassy reported that the critics of Urdu had been "blinded by prejudice", and the impact on Urdu of the successful imposition of the Roman script "would be extremely unfortunate".[36]

The colonial period can also be treated as the watershed mark in the history of Urdu, when the language was restricted for the use of only Muslims. Initially, it was spoken by North Indian Hindus as well, but the colonial administrators reckoned that by irreparably separating the two languages, they would be able to not only compartmentalize the communities speaking in them, but also strengthen the influence of the structures of Hindu and Muslim patriarchies, basing their notions of hegemony within their respective communities on the Nietzschean conception of fear of castration from nowhere. At one stroke, the British were successful in terminating for a considerable length of time the possibility of any radical movement of one segment of the society on the other, as such an advance would be considered to be external to the influences of the internal forms of authority.[37]

In the twentieth century a complex of political, economic and social factors continued to hamper the development of the language. The role of the nationalist politicians can be considered to have been that of mute spectators to the steady decline of the language. After the end of the First World War [1914-18], the dismemberment of the Ottoman Empire, and the economic disparity between the Muslim and Hindu communities – the Hindus were relatively better educated and more prosperous – resulted in the loss of a sense of identity of the Indian Muslims. This had an adverse impact on the prestige of Urdu.[38] The sense of alienation of the Indian Muslims was evident in the poetry of Mohammad Iqbal. Iqbal, who received his doctorate in Europe, was arguably the most accomplished representative of the Muslim community to have aired his sense of disenchantment with the emerging forms of Indian nationalism. Even though his views were later appropriated by sections of the Muslim intelligentsia, including the Muslim League in their quest to conceive the idea of Pakistan, Iqbal was considered to have been the poet of all South Asian Muslims. He was the author of the lines, "Of all the countries of the world, the best is our Hindustan" ["*Sarey Jahan Se Achcha, Hindustan Hamara*"], which one hears every 15 August, even to this day. Yet, he was the first Muslim writer to demand an autonomous Muslim territoriality for all Muslims, which gave evidence of his sense of contradiction, as well as detachment with his perception of 'Congress' brand of 'majoritarian' pan-Indian nationalism. His contempt for the Hindus was evidenced in his poem *Shikwa* ['Complaint'] recited in 1909 at a meeting of the Anjuman-i-Himayat-i-Islam in Lahore, where he complained that in the Hindu temples the idols boasted that the guardians of the Kaaba had been forced to withdraw from India. In 1913, in his recitation of *Jawab-i-Shikwa* ['Answer'] at a gathering held at Mochi Gate in Lahore, he lamented that the Muslims in India had been infected by western values and the ways of the Brahmins.[39]

In the post-Partition period, the officials of the modern Indian state demonstrated a brazen indifference to the utilization of the language as an official medium. It is a matter of disgrace to all Indians that the motion recommending the adoption of Hindustani as the national language in the Indian Constituent Assembly, which was brought by Gandhi and Nehru, lost by one vote. Within the Congress, Nehru was once again defeated in voting, which was held to decide whether Hindustani should become India's national language by a much larger margin of 63-32.[40] Article 351 of the Indian Constitution ignored the relevance of Persian and only highlighted the role of Sanskrit in the new nation-building project. Despite the minority status of Hindi as the language of merely 38 per cent of the population of the country, and its diverse character due to the existence of a dozen dialects, with distinctive character, Hindi was accorded more importance than Urdu. Even though the Radhakrishnan Commission on University Education stated that Hindi did "not possess any advantages, literary or historical, over other modern languages" and "is a statist and not a nationalist one, if nation is conceived in inclusive and egalitarian terms", it continued to be treated as the principle link language of the country.[41] With the increasing dissemination of information technology in India through the successful launching of radio in the 1950s and television in the 1960s, in the absence of Hindustani, the paths taken by Urdu and Hindi tended to diverge radically. Hindi became increasingly dominated by the use of words borrowed from Sanskrit, which was interestingly considered to have suddenly become fashionable in sections of the élite Indian middle classes.[42] Urdu, which was adopted by the Pakistani state at the time of its independence as its national language, was made almost unintelligible to the Indian Hindus. While Nehru himself expressed dissatisfaction with the alienation of the Urdu speaking population from the national mainstream – he spoke the language fluently – officials posted lower down the ranks of the Indian bureaucracy demonstrated scant regard for his views.[43] He repeatedly pled on behalf of the granting of equal status to Urdu and Hindi. Urdu was "essentially an Indian language", and was widely spoken in North India. Urdu newspapers owned and published by members of the Hindu Mahasabha in Delhi, enjoyed larger circulation than their Hindi counterparts. In addition, he admitted that Urdu even acted as a strengthening element in the composition and spread of Hindi.[44] In 1958, in a Press note issued by the Government of India, it was bluntly admitted that the Indian government had failed to implement its policy on Urdu. It also indicated the specific areas, such as Delhi, Punjab, Uttar Pradesh and Bihar, where Urdu had to be given equal status to Hindi.[45] In certain journalistic and literary circles an effort was made in 1969 to revive the reading and appreciation of Urdu. Khushwant Singh, as the Editor of the *Illustrated Weekly of India* reintroduced the publication of Urdu prose and poetry, especially the poems of Iqbal, to redress a measure of grievances of the Muslim community. Singh wrote in 1981: "The chief reason why I chose to re-start with Iqbal was that he not only handled the language with exquisite skill but also made it a medium for expressing the hopes and aspirations of Indian Muslims of my generation."[46]

However, by the beginning of 1972, after the formation of Bangladesh, the popularity of the language was clearly once again on the wane in official circles. The language policy-makers in Delhi demonstrated firstly, a lack of comprehension and secondly, a state of confusion regarding the guidelines necessary for injecting new life into the framework necessary for the development of the language. They did try to offer a set of guidelines for the regeneration of the language, but an absence of full grasp of the scale of its usage in the whole country and the sentiments of large segments of the Indian population attached to the well-being of the language resulted in a half-hearted effort made by the central government officials. The Government of India introduced a three-language formula "to enable a child at the primary level to gain knowledge of the other important and necessary languages, along with the parallel language."[47] It was enunciated in the *Resolution on National Policy on Education* to benefit those who opted to read in the mother tongue at the school level. In 1975, the Gujral Committee, under the Chairmanship of Inder Kumar Gujral, amended this policy. No room was spared for the inclusion of Urdu in the formula, which had three clauses: firstly, the adoption of a regional language, which meant that Hindi was accepted as the mother tongue. Hindi had been granted the status of a regional language much earlier. Secondly, the provinces were encouraged to include a language from the Eight Schedule of the Constitution. The Chief Ministers of the North Indian states accorded more importance to Sanskrit, a classical language, rejecting Urdu. An annual outlay of Rs. 50 crores was set aside by the University Grants Commission [UGC] for the promotion of Sanskrit. Finally, English was adopted as the third language, which was stated to be an important medium of communication. At that time, apart from the South Indian states, West Bengal, which had a Congress government led by Siddhartha Shankar Ray, had refused to implement this formula. Tamil Nadu adopted a two-language policy, which included Tamil and English as the main mediums of instructions. Unfortunately, Urdu came to be identified with the imposition of Hindi on the South Indian population.[48] Also, Urdu was accorded maximum publicity by the Gujral committee for 25 years, merely for electoral purposes, but was unceremoniously rejected after the victory of the United Front government in 1997.[49]

The irony lies in the nature of rejection of the very principles for which Nehru stood within ten years of his demise. The cause of secularism, for which more than one generation of highly trained professionals and intellectuals stood, could not have been more damaged than by the neglect of a language which could have acted as one of the pillars of the Indian democracy. The acceptance of the principal language of the single largest minority in the national mainstream is an example of upholding of democratic values. Even though Indira Gandhi supported the cause of the promotion of Urdu, there was very little achieved by the central government to redress this injustice. In the following decades, two successive committees were established by the Government of India, in 1979 and 1983, and one more in 1990, headed by Ali Sardar Jafri, under the Prime Ministership of Vishwanath Pratap Singh. The third one reported that ninety five per cent of the recommendations made by the Gujral Committee were not implemented. As a belated act of clemency shown towards the language, first Bihar and then Uttar Pradesh recognized Urdu as an official language, but the process of implementation has not yet been fully carried out.[50] On 6 October, 1989, the UP legislature passed an amendment of the *UP Official*

Languages Act 28 of 1989, incorporating a new section 3 to the Act. On paper this amendment allowed the state government to treat Urdu as the second official language in UP. However, from its initiation, obstacles were placed before the passage of the bill: the necessity to enact it was challenged by UP Hindi Sammelan in a *PIL Writ Petition No.10313 of 1989* filed in the Lucknow Branch of the Allahabad High Court. The petitioners demanded that since Hindi had been declared an official language, no other language could be accorded the same status. They also insisted that substantial segments of the population in the UP did not speak in Urdu.[51]

The role of the Urdu-speaking elites in contributing to the decline of the language in the nineteenth and twentieth centuries cannot be ignored. If the nineteenth centuries witnessed the establishment of patterns of decay, the twentieth century oversaw the dismantling of the structures of dominance as well as popularity enjoyed by Urdu. The hostility of the Hindi speaking intelligentsia did not assist the development of Urdu. Cultural personalities, such as Harishchandra actively and intentionally took steps to denigrate the language, in order to promote Hindi. In the latter half of the century, the political leaders and their advisers demonstrated a tendency to overlook the collateral damages caused to the state of the language by their indifference to Urdu. The left wing intelligentsia too has remained unsuccessful in campaigning for the promotion of the language. Urdu has not been given the status it deserves in social science research. Also, the National Council of Education and Research Training (NCERT) has been misused by the present government to accelerate the decline and saffronise the language. The NCERT has almost totally abandoned its earlier policy of assigning its projects for the preparation of a syllabus for the education of Urdu-medium students to poets and critics of the language.[52]

Proposals for the Promotion of Urdu in the Twenty-First Century

The future of Urdu education and the language has to be situated in attempts made by the Muslims to respond favourably to the establishment of a pluralistic Indian society. For a reaffirmation of the values associated with a secular polity, severely undermined by the more chauvinist or fundamentalist champions of Sanskrit education,

Muslims will have to be encouraged to demand from the Indian State complete access to all avenues of elementary education in their mother tongue. Indian citizens belonging to all other religious groups, also interested in a rich language, replete with the heritage of India's composite culture ought to be able to avail of the same avenues for education in their respective mother tongues. Also, Urdu ought to be offered as an elective subject to members of non-Muslim communities who express the intention to learn the language.[53] It is indeed unfortunate that in a cross-section of states, ranging from West Bengal, Bihar, Andhra Pradesh to Maharashtra, no non-Muslim student is enrolled to take Urdu as an optional subject in primary or secondary schools, or opt for the language as the main medium of instruction. Nor have the official agencies, such as the respective state governments or the central government, or Non-Governmental Organisations [NGOs], collaborating with the administrations, made any serious attempt to write a comprehensive report bearing information gathered on the ground describing the state of apathy regarding the adoption of Urdu as one of the important languages in these states. The absence of importance attached to Urdu is evident from the harsh reality that it is accorded the status of an optional subject from the sixth standard or in some schools from the tenth standard. This, despite a provision in Uttar Pradesh, which states that Urdu has to be necessarily taught from the sixth to the eighth standards. Ideally, it should be taught from the third or fourth standard, a policy that is followed in only a handful of local Urdu schools in Uttar Pradesh.

The revival of Urdu can be achieved through the efficient implementation of the policy of Reversing Language Shift [RLS]. The prospects of saving the language can be found in the encouragement of self-reliance, and by the Urdu speakers' utilization of their own educational and economic resources. The defenders of Urdu will have to stress that the RLS programme lies in a tradition of linguistic pluralism. This programme will have to be intergenerational in nature and begin with pre-school children along with their other family members. An extensive framework of nine stages of development has been quoted as an alternative method of carrying out the RLS programme. The stages are: [i] 'Reconstruction' [vernacularising] of the language and the acquisition of Urdu by the adult members of the families under consideration, [ii] community-based cultural interaction, in Urdu, among the members of the older generations, [iii] composition of intergenerational and demographically centred home-family-neighborhood on the basis of mother tongue transmission, and [iv] the acquisition of school for the purpose of spreading literacy among the old and the young, independent of compulsory education. The other imperatives for ensuring the success of the programme are [v] the promotion of own schools and own curricular and staffing control instead of compulsory education, [vi] offering encouragement to public schools to start courses in Urdu under the stewardship of non-Muslim curricular and staff control, [vii] utilization of Urdu in local and regional work spheres or non-neighborhoods, [viii] compulsory use of the language in the local and regional mass media and government services, and finally, [ix] its use in education as a medium of instruction, in work spheres, mass media and governmental operations at the national level.[54] The other plank of the RLS programme is the necessity to combat the serious menace of English, which is considered to be the most serious threat to the survival of Urdu. It is also considered to be a hindrance to the dissemination of the more enlightened features of Islamic values.[55]

The policy-makers will have to take into consideration the possibility of Urdu in the secular curriculum from the primary level to the age of 14 years as a chief medium of instruction in all government aided schools and the state governments and state board schools. Under the 93rd Amendment of the Indian Constitution, the Government of India is obliged, under the 'Directive Principals of State Policy' to provide compulsory education as a fundamental right to every child until he/she attains 14 years of age.[56] Under the Three-Language Formula, Urdu must be adopted as a compulsory first language for Urdu-speaking students studying in standards 6 to 12. Hindi can be introduced as a principal [compulsory] state language from standard 4 and English as the third and compulsory language from standards 6 to 12. Also, Hindi should be taken as the main medium of instruction for the Hindi speaking students from class 6.[57]

Ideally, the upliftment of Urdu should involve an alteration in the perception of the language amongst the members of the English and Hindi speaking populations, and vice versa, which would assist Urdu to be included in the national mainstream. One of the foremost imperatives of a pro-Urdu policy in education is to ensure that the language does not remain restricted to the *Madarsahs*. Just as Urdu ought to be introduced in the school syllabi, English will also have to be simultaneously introduced as a second or third language to the students of the *Madarsahs*, in order to prepare them for higher learning, which is still dominated by English. Also, Urdu will have to be made more accessible to those Indians who are more adept at speaking in their respective vernacular languages, such as Bengali, Marathi and Tamil, the other three major regional languages in the country. The government should pay more attention to the immediate necessity of increasing the funding for the establishment of schools in urban areas as well as in district towns that have a significant percentage of Muslims. The medium of instruction in these schools should be Urdu, which can be taught as the first and compulsory language up to standard V, after which English can be taken as the main medium of instruction.[58] Such a strategy of mixed medium instruction effectively integrates the benefits of both English and Urdu. The other measure, which is crucially required for the promotion of the language, is the spread of Urdu-language newspapers, journals and news programmes on private channels as well as Doordarshan. It is through the regular dissemination and correct utilization of the language at the level of the educated groups that the language is likely to gain acceptance.[59]

The failure of the guardians of the Muslim community to promote Urdu also lies in the absence of an adequate and scientific vocabulary. The language has until now been restricted to the imparting of social science disciplines, such as history and geography, two subjects which have demonstrated a perceptible decline in their levels of popularity among students. To make matters worse, in most Urdu medium schools of the country, subjects such as the different branches of the sciences, and mathematics are imparted in English, or sometimes even other Indian languages, for example Hindi. After independence, in Hyderabad, Urdu was abolished as a medium of instruction ostensibly to contain the ill effects arising from the spread of communal violence associated with the Partition. As a consequence, books published by the *Darul-Tarjuma*, an institution established for the translation of technical books into Urdu, were burnt by misguided sections of the Indian state.[60]

The prospect for the improvement of Urdu and the educational institutions responsible for imparting and managing the language would naturally make it more acceptable not only to Indian Muslims, but also to the Hindus and members of other religious minorities. To favorably view the language, Urdu has to be integrated in the national mainstream of Indian languages. There are three main imperatives for Urdu's speedy improvement: endowment of Islamic educational institutions, such as the *Madarsahs*, with financial resources generated by the management of the *Madarsahs* themselves. The future of Urdu education clearly lies in the principle that "funding of religious instruction at the expense of [the] public exchequer is undesirable and unconstitutional."[61] The same resolution adopted by the International Conference organized by the Dr. Zakir Husain Study Circle from 8-11 February, 2002, went on to recommend that the management of the *Madarsah* system, which is solely meant to serve the objective of "instructing Muslim children in the basic tenets of Islam and of producing religious functionaries needed by the community and of maintaining the continuity of religious scholarship", should be entrusted to the respective communities benefiting from the survival of these religious schools. The resolution further stated, "the *Madarsah* system contributes only marginally to the development of education among Muslims".[62] *Madarsah* education tends to become the sole patron of Urdu if the language is omitted from the secular syllabus. The primary aim of *Madarsah* education is not to promote Urdu, but to use it as a medium of communication. Persian and Arabic are the other two equally powerful contenders for the status of the main medium of instruction in the *Madarsahs*. Also, the teaching of the *Quran*, which is the chief exercise of the *Madarsah* educationists, is less taught in Urdu than in Arabic. In states where there is a strong regional bias in the use of languages, the vernacular tongue became the medium of instruction in the *Madarsahs*. Thus in West Bengal, the teaching of precepts of Islam was mostly carried out in Bengali. In Assam, Tamil Nadu and Kerala, Urdu was ignored. In Kerala, Malayalam became the medium of instruction.[63]

The Urdu elites, considered to be *Sarkari Muslamans* and *Sarkari Urduwallahs*, have not made any effort to contribute to the development of the language. They pretend not to have been aware of this lacuna in the state syllabus. Nor are the privileged Urdu speaking elites interested in addressing the dangers of state sponsored homogenization of the language in lieu of channeling funds in to a handful of Non-

Governmental Organizations [NGOs] owned by them. This exclusive group of Muslims has allowed themselves to become tools in the hands of the present government to further the Hindu Nationalists' fascist and now increasingly open agenda.[64] The government has misutilized the Jamia-e Urdu, consisting of Urdu intellectuals to further its hidden agenda of subverting the use of the language. Some leaders have, since independence, used the language as a necessary tool for accruing of political benefits of an only a small minority of urban Muslims. It is an irony that the existing Urdu speaking elites have acquiesced in the BJP's project of overhauling the framework of Urdu education for the purpose of safeguarding their political and professional interests. Ather Farouqui considers the Islamisation of non-scheduled languages as a dangerous development for Urdu.[65] He suggests that the Urdu chauvinists themselves have been guilty of "Islamisation ... by ... choosing Urdu as their linguistic identity",[66] just as the Hindiwallahs demonstrated a tendency to monopolize languages such as Awadhi, Magadhi, Maithili, Brij and Bhojpuri. Their failure to form a united front, comprising speakers of other marginalized language groups, has contributed in no small measure to their state of helplessness in the face of a cultural onslaught led by the BJP, which has used this weakness to drive the Urduwallahs into a corner. The absence of an efficient network of voluntary organizations is responsible for the plight of the existing Urdu speaking people. Also, the Urdu speaking community in North India will have to be made aware that primary education in Urdu is a fundamental right under Article 350 [A] of the Constitution of India. There is a necessity to encourage the Hindu backward castes to participate constructively in the campaign for the promotion of Urdu. Through an alliance between the victims of upper caste exploitation and the majority of the Urdu speakers can a movement for the application of the principals of social justice be adequately carried forward.[67] Farouqui calls for the "total withdrawal of official patronage and facilities for education in Urdu".

The question still remains whether a parallel language ought to be accepted as a spoken one in India. The case for Urdu is a strong one. In the late 1980s and early 1990s, when the Hindu Nationalists started to emerge as an alternative to the Congress at the centre, the *lingua franca* of large majority of families in Northern India was suddenly altered, albeit in an insidious manner. Television newsreaders, who were heard in almost every urban home, overnight started to use highly specialized Sanskrit words in their bulletins. All other news programmes were telecast in English. A special Urdu news bulletin was introduced on Doordarshan. Urdu-speakers, not used to hearing any other language, were thus handed down a separate news programme, telecast in the post-lunch session, which is not prime time for television audiences. Alienation of Muslims was being institutionalized at the domestic level through the exclusion of the community from the daily news. The BJP's Goebbelsian technique of erasing the use of Hindustani as a daily medium of communication by people who could not speak in any other language was evidenced not only in the Hindi one heard on the small screen, but also in Hindi films. The dialogues in the Bombay movies, produced from the time of their inception to the beginning of the 1990s, were always interlaced with Urdu or at least Hindustani words. The new generation of Hindi movies in the last one decade demonstrated an increasing shift towards the social and family dramas. For example, the emergence of 'feel good' movies, such as *Kuch Kuch Hota Hai*, and *Hum Dil De Chukey Sanam* made hardly any secret of the entertainment industry's preference for films which emphasized the virtues of male dominated Hindu joint families. Fewer Urdu couplets were interspersed in the dialogues of the modern Hindi films.

There never was a single language of communication in India. When I was young, we conversed in a combination of languages consisting of English, the vernacular [in my case Bengali], and Hindi, which I took as my third language in school. Large segments of the Indian population still speak predominantly in their respective mother tongues. Suddenly, a highly sophisticated but extremely arid form of Hindi was beamed across the country, impressing on us the polemicised view that Sanskritised Hindi alone retains the right to become our mother tongue. The RLS programme suggested by some scholars may not be able to offer a complete solution to the problem of re-admitting Urdu in the national mainstream either. But it can serve the purpose of initiating the process of assimilation of Urdu in the mainstream. It is entirely fair that the Indian government cannot and must not adopt the national language of Pakistan as its national language. Apart from a theocracy, which goes against the grain of a secular India, the Pakistani government has and is most likely to continue to demonstrate unbridled hostility towards all Indians, irrespective of their caste or creed. Over the next one hundred years, Urdu is likely to acquire the status of a classical language, just as Sanskrit or Latin did in the nineteenth centuries. One wonders if it is not appropriate at this juncture for the Government of India to treat Urdu as a classical language instead of shunting it aside. The existing formula suggested by the RLS can be modified to the extent of mentioning that Urdu could be treated as a parallel language rather than use the word 'national'. How many national languages can we accommodate in one country? We will have to adopt a national language, which will consist of words drawn from all major and preferably minor languages of the country, thus giving representation to the maximum number of religious and ethnic groups. Hindustani does possess the potential to emerge as the link language, since it is a combination of two or more different languages. The purist quality in Hindi, on the other hand, can be reduced to make it more accessible to those large segments of the Indian population, both Hindu and Muslim, which find the use of archaic words difficult to understand. Since English will continue to occupy the status of official language, due to the predominance of the Internet, which makes English the language of the international community, a language, which is both colloquial and representative of the sentiments of all the religious communities ought to be given the status of the national language.

The future of Urdu lies in the acceptance of the language as a main medium of instruction for the Muslims living in the Muslim dominated regions. The RLS can be viewed as a tool in the promotion of the language. Urdu-speaking élites will also have to be encouraged to overcome their tendency to collaborate with the respective governments in relegating the language to the margins of the subcontinent's language policy. Also, it needs stressing that the demand for the acceptance of Urdu as a mainstream language was not responsible for the Partition, even though the adversaries of the promotion of the language have long held this view.

Conclusion

The Idea of India will remain incomplete without an adequate application of principles, such as the protection of the languages of the minorities, especially Urdu, guaranteed under the Constitution of India. India does posses the potential to emerge as a major power in the global community. But the willful suppression of the fundamental right of education and freedom of expression of the single largest minority in the country will not only hurt the country's image as a secular nation on par with the European and Anglo-American powers, but also deprive us of the benefits accruing from the newly emerging knowledge industry. India has been officially described as a 'powerhouse' of knowledge. The uniqueness of our culture lies in its composite character which accords equal status to all languages. India has five major languages according to the percentage of people conversing in it and the influence they wield over the size of the territories. They are Hindi, Bengali, Marathi, Tamil and Urdu. The deletion or marginalisation of any one of these languages, or indeed any other language scheduled in the Constitution, will not only imply the erosion of goodwill we enjoy in the international community, but also the freedom with which we can now gainfully utilize all of them.

The case for Urdu demonstrates that while there have been adequate conceptual efforts to retain the edifices of modernity which was envisaged by the Nehruvian civil servants in language policy, internal contradictions pulling in different directions have continued to undermine the best efforts of the policy-makers in the post-independence period. The scale of decline of Urdu may not have increased in the Nehru years, but official attitude to the language underwent radical alterations. Compared to the officials in the British periods, the civil servants in the post-1947 years demonstrated irreverence to the language. While segments of the intelligentsia and the civil services have indicated their cultural preference for the many uses of the language, its abuses have multiplied in manifold ways in independent India. If development has to be identified with the granting of freedom to all South Asians, it has to be necessarily viewed as a framework, which should include the languages of the second largest religious and cultural community in the country. The use of the term 'minorities' is entirely inappropriate in a discussion on the scale of neglect shown towards Urdu, since it was the spoken language of not only the Muslims in the pre-independence era, but Hindus too. For instance, I find it easier to understand and use Urdu words when listening to it and converse in Hindi. I had the opportunity to be informed in Hindustani words by family members, who were trained to speak in the language through the 1940s' Calcutta. Most Indians belonging to the generation benefiting from the departure of the British from the subcontinent did. Indeed, the disappearance of an exquisitely crafted language can be considered to be one of the most expensive prices of freedom that we, the members of a sovereign, secular, democratic, republic are being compelled to pay.

Whatever the contours of a new language policy, it must be well grounded in the principle of devising Urdu as a parallel language that will possess the potential to benefit all Indians, not just the Muslims. India is, and will indeed remain, a union of states, as envisaged by the founding fathers, and the place of Urdu must remain secure in that framework. This paper does not intend to use terms such as 'pluralism' for rhetorical purposes. Nor does the future of India, and its main languages, such as Sanskrit, Urdu, and Hindi, lie in the indigenisation of noble principles, such as the melting pot theory, which have western connotations. The proper spread of Urdu does possess the potential to knit together the disparate cultural regions in the country that is absolutely necessary to reaffirm the principle of unity in diversity. To keep India intact, dangers that lie within, will have be contested first. One such peril to India's unity is manifested in the tendency towards the failure to frame or persist with a coherent language policy. Through a qualified acceptance of the RLS, keeping in mind the region-specific necessities governing the promotion of Urdu, we can begin the lengthy and time consuming process of steering clear of value-based education which is aimed at the subversion of the language, which is perceived in Hindu Nationalist circles as the language of the communication of segments of the governing classes. It is not the intention of this paper to suggest that any other classical Indian language ought to be removed from the national curriculum of Indian languages in order to accommodate Urdu in the mainstream. But the vice versa must not be allowed to occur.

There is a clear and present danger of grievous bodily harm being done to the overall fabric of independent India. The indifference shown towards Urdu represents that mood. A pro-active policy of involving committed political and social activists, and all other like-minded Indians, in the country and outside, has become the vital need of the hour to launch a vigorous campaign to fight communal and fascist forces. The principles upheld by champions of Urdu, by eminent personalities such as Danial Latifi, closely tie in with the policy of launching a campaign for the protection of Urdu. A consistent rejection of religious obscurantism is another plank of this struggle.

Notes

1 Robert D. King, *Nehru and the Language Politics of India*, Delhi, 1998.

2 Ralph Russell, "Urdu in India since Independence", in *Economic and Political Weekly* [hereinafter *EPW*], 9 January, 1999, p.45.

3 Bikramjit Dé, "British Policy in Bengal, 1939-1945", unpublished D.Phil. thesis, University of Oxford, Trinity Term, 2002, p.18.

4 Christopher Bayly, *Empire and Information: Intelligence Gathering and Social Communication in India, 1780-1870*, Cambridge, 1996.

5 Sunil Khilnani, *The Idea of India*, Penguin Books, 1997, pp.3-4.

6 Judith Brown, *Nehru*, London, 1999.

7 Khilnani, *The Idea of India*, p.16-17.

8 *Ibid*, pp.17-19.

9 *Ibid*, p.22.

10 Romila Thapar, *Asoka and the Decline of the Mauryas*, Delhi, 1963.

11 Khilnani, *Idea of India*, p.8.

12 Sumit Sarkar, *Modern India*, Delhi, 1983, p.79; see also Pratyush Chandra, *Defining Urdu Politics in Post-Colonial India – Towards a Counter-Hegemonic Agenda*, unpublished article, p.1.

13 Bipan Chandra, *et al*, *India After Independence, 1947-2000*, Delhi, 1999, p.439.

14 *Ibid*, pp.281-84.

15 Jayantanuja Bandopadhyaya, *The Making of India's Foreign Policy: Determinants, Institutions, Processes and Personalities*, New Delhi, 1970, p.109.

15 *Ibid*.

16 Jayantanuja Bandopadhyaya, "The Non-aligned Movement and International Relations", *India Quarterly*, New Delhi, October-December 1974.

17 *Ibid*.

18 Vasudha Dalmia, *The Nationalisation of Hindu Traditions: Bharatendu Harishchandra and Nineteenth Century Benaras*, New Delhi, 1997.

19 Shamsur Rahman Faruqi, *Early Urdu: Literary Culture and History*, Oxford, 2001, pp.25.

20 *Ibid*, *Early Urdu*, p.22.

21 Hasan Abdullah, 'International Urdu Conference – A Review', in *Mainstream*, Vol. XL, No.29, 22 June 2002, p.29.

22 Robert D.King, *Nehru and the Language Politics of India*, Delhi, 1998.

23 Abdullah, 'International Urdu Conference', p.29.

24 A.F. Salahuddin Ahmed, *India, Pakistan, Bangladesh: Perspectives on History, Society and Politics*, Calcutta, 2001, p.128.

25 *Ibid*, p.129.

26 *Calcutta Journal*, Calcutta, 8 May, 1822.

27 *Friend of India* [Serampur], Quarterly Series, 1820, I, 1, 122, cited in Ahmed, *India, Pakistan, Bangladesh*.

28 Abdullah, 'International Urdu Conference', p.29.

29 King, *Nehru and the Language Politics*, p.80.

30 Sagaree Sengupta, 'Krsna the Cruel Beloved: Harishchandra and Urdu', in *Annual of Urdu Studies*, Madison, WI, 9, 1994, pp.133-52.

31 Firaq Gorakhpuri, 'Answer to a Letter', Firaq Gorakhpuri Foundation, *Souvenir* [issued on the occasion of the celebration held for the presentation of the Firaq Award to Balraj Komal in 1996], pp.40-41. Originally published in the fortnightly *Ajkal*, Delhi, 15 August, 1945; reprinted in the monthly *Ajkal*, Delhi, August 1996.

32 Francis Robinson, *Separatism Among Indian Muslims: The Politics of the United Provinces Muslims, 1860-1923*, Delhi, 1997, pp.33-34.

33 Salman Khurshid, 'Religion and Modernity', in *Daily Pioneer*, Saturday, 22 June, 2002.

34 Alok Rai, *Hindi Nationalism*, Orient Longman, 2000.

35 Chandra, p.1.

36 Farman Fathpuri, *Urdu Imta Aur Rasm ul-Khat*, Lahore, 1977, pp.10-44.

37 Ibid, p.2.

38 King, *Nehru and the Language Politics*, pp.80-81.

39 Mohammad Iqbal, '*Shikwa* and *Jawab-i-Shikwa*' [Complaint and Answer, Iqbal's Dialogue with Allah], Delhi, 1981, pp.42, 59.

40 Kerrin Ditmer, 'The Hindi-Urdu Controversy and the Constituent Assembly', *Indian Journal of Politics*, VI, 1 January-June 1972, pp.13-22.

41 Abdullah, 'International Urdu Conference, p.26.

42 A.R. Kelkar, *Studies in Hindi – Urdu* Poona, 1968, pp.6-7; J. Das Gupta and J.J. Gumperz, 'Language Communication and Control in North India', in J.A. Fishman and J. Das Gupta [eds.], *Language Problems of Developing Nations* New York, 1968, pp.151-66.

43 King, *Nehru and the Language Politics of India*, pp.77-78.

44 *Times of India*, 6 January, 1955, 26 October, 1956, in Noorani, *The Muslims of India*, pp.307-08, 315.

45 *Times of India*, 15 July, 1958, in Noorani, *The Muslims of India*, pp.323-24.

46 Khushwant Singh, 'Preface', in Iqbal, *Shikwa and Jawab-i-Shikwa*, p.15.

47 Ather Farouqui, 'Urdu Education in India: Four Representative States', in *EPW*, Vol. XXIX, No.14, April 2, 1994, p.783.

48 *Ibid*, pp. 783-784.

49 Danial Latifi, 'Urdu in UP', in *EPW*, 17 February, 2001.

50 Russell, 'Urdu in India since Independence', p.44.

51 Latifi, 'Urdu in UP', in *EPW*, pp.533-34.

52 Salman Khurshid, 'Welcome Address' to International Conference on Minorities, Education and Language in Twenty-First Century Indian Democracy – the Case of Urdu with Special Reference to Dr. Zakir Husain, Late President of India, sponsored by the Dr. Zakir Husain Study Circle [ZHSC], and Modern Education Foundation, 8-11 February, 2002, p.557.

53 *Ibid.*

54 Theodore P. Wright, Jr., 'Urdu in India, Strategies for Survival of Formerly Dominant Languages', in *EPW*, Vol. XXXVII, No.2, January, 12-18, 2002, pp.109-110.

55 Joshua A. Fishman, *Reversing Language Shift*, Clevedon, 1991, p.315.

56 Syed Shahabuddin, 'Urdu in India, Education and Muslims – a Trinity without a Church', in *Mainstream*, Vol. XL, No.28, New Delhi, June 29, 2002, p.22.

57 Khurshid, 'Welcome Address', p.558.

58 Ather Farouqui, 'Urdu Education in India', in *EPW*, 12 January, 2000, p.106.

59 Fishman, 'Reversing Language Shift', p.315; Wright, 'Urdu in India', p.110.

60 Farouqui, 'Urdu Education in India', p.782.

61 Khurshid, 'Religion and Modernity', op-ed page.

62 *Ibid.*

63 Imtiaz Ahmad, 'Urdu and Madrasa Education', in *EPW*, Vol. XXXVII, No.24, June 15, 2002, p.2286.

64 Ather Farouqui, 'Urdu Should be Brought into Mainstream Secular Education', in *Mainstream*, New Delhi, 22 June, 2002, Vol. XL, No.27, p.26.

65 Ather Farouqui, 'Re-defining Islamic Thought', in *The Pioneer*, New Delhi, 27 August, 2002.

66 Ather Farouqui, 'Urdu Movement Has Still Far to Go' in *The Pioneer*, New Delhi, 7 February, 2003.

67 Ather Farouqui, 'Education Among Muslims: Quality Urdu as Counter to Madrasas', in *The Times of India*, New Delhi, 7 February, 2003.

References

Newspapers

Calcutta Journal, (1822), Calcutta.

Hindustan Times, (2003), Kolkata.

The Pioneer, (2002-2003), New Delhi.

Times of India, (2003), New Delhi.

Quami Awaz, (2003), New Delhi, April 22.

Books/Papers

Abdullah, Hasan, (2002), 'International Urdu Conference – A Review', in *Mainstream*, Vol. XL, No.29, June 22.

Ahmed, A.F. Salahuddin, (2001), *India, Pakistan, Bangladesh: Perspectives on History, Society and Politics*, Calcutta.

Ahmad, Imtiaz, (2002), 'Urdu and Madrasa Education', in *Economic and Political Weekly*, Vol. XXXVII, No.24, June 15.

Ara, Arjumand, (2003), 'Madrasas and the Making of Muslim Identity', in *Correspondence*, [a monthly journal of the Indian Institute of Marxist Studies], New Delhi, May.

Bandopadhyaya, Jayantanuja, (1970), *The Making of India's Foreign Policy: Determinants, Institutions, Processes and Personalities*, New Delhi.

Bayly, Christopher, (1996), *Empire and Information: Intelligence Gathering and Social Communication in India, 1780-1870*, Cambridge.

Brass, Paul, (1995), *The Politics of Urdu since Independence*, New Delhi.

Brown, Judith, *Nehru*, London.

Chandra, Bipan, et al., (1999), *India After Independence, 1947-2000*, Delhi.

Dalmia, Vasudha, (1997), *The Nationalisation of Hindu Traditions: Bharatendu Harishchandra and Nineteenth Century Benaras*, New Delhi.

Dé, Bikramjit, (2002), 'British Policy in Bengal, 1939-1945', unpublished D.Phil. thesis, University of Oxford, Trinity Term.

Ditmer, Kerrin, (1972) 'The Hindi-Urdu Controversy and the Constituent Assembly', *Indian Journal of Politics*, VI, 1, January-June.

Faruqi, Shamsur Rahman, (2001), *Early Urdu: Literary Culture and History*, Oxford.

Farouqui, Ather, (1994), 'Urdu Education in India: Four Representative States', in *Economic and Political Weekly*, Vol. XXIX, No.14, April 2.

'Urdu Should be Brought into Mainstream Secular Education', in *Mainstream*, New Delhi, 22 June, 2002, Vol. XL, No.27.

Fishman, Joshua A., (1991), *Reversing Language Shift*, Clevedon.

Fishman, Joshua A. and J. Das Gupta [eds.], (1968), *Language Problems of Developing Nations* New York.

Gandhi, Sonia, (2002), 'Our National Obligation: Revival of Urdu as a Living Heritage', in *Mainstream*, New Delhi, June 22, Vol.XL, No.27.

Iqbal, Mohammad, '*Shikwa* and *Jawab-i-Shikwa*' (1981) [Complaint and Answer, Iqbal's Dialogue with Allah], Delhi.

Kelkar, A.R., (1968), *Studies in Hindi – Urdu*, Poona.

Khilnani, Sunil, (1997), *The Idea of India*, Penguin Books.

King, Robert, (1998), *Nehru and the Language Politics of India*, Delhi.

Khurshid, Salman, (2002), 'Urdu's Survival Linked to Survival of Secular Values', in *Mainstream*, New Delhi, June 22, Vol.XL, No.27.

'Welcome Address' to International Conference on Minorities, Education and Language in Twenty-First Century Indian Democracy – the Case of Urdu with Special Reference to Dr. Zakir Husain, Late President of India, sponsored by the Dr. Zakir Husain Study Circle [ZHSC], and Modern Education Foundation, 8-11 February, 2002.

Latifi, Danial, (2001), 'Urdu in UP', in *Economic and Political Weekly*, February 17.

'Linguistic Minorities' Guild's: Proposals to Venkatachalliah Commission', *Muslim India*, 230, February 2002.

Mathews, David, (2002), 'Urdu in India', in *The Annual of Urdu Studies*, No.17.

Noorani, A.G. [ed.], (2003) *The Muslims of India: A Documentary Record*, Oxford.

Pasha, Anwar, (2002), 'Urdu Education: Some Points Worth Repeating', in *Mainstream*, Vol. XL, No.28, New Delhi, June 29.

Premchand, (1983), *Sahitya ka Uddeshya*, Allahabad.

Rai, Alok, (2000), *Hindi Nationalism*, Orient Longman.

Robinson, Francis, (1997), *Separatism Among Indian Muslims: The Politics of the United Provinces Muslims, 1860-1923*, Delhi.

Russell, Ralph, (1999), 'Urdu in India since Independence', in *Economic and Political Weekly*, 9 January.

Sengupta, Sagaree, (1994), 'Krsna the Cruel Beloved: Harishchandra and Urdu', in *Annual of Urdu Studies*, [Madison, WI], 9.

Shahabuddin, Syed, (2002), 'Urdu in India, Education and Muslims – a Trinity without a Church', in *Mainstream*, Vol. XL, No.28, New Delhi, June 29.

Thapar, Romila, (1953), *Asoka and the Decline of the Mauryas*, Delhi.

Wright, Jr., Theodore P., (2002), 'Urdu in India, Strategies for Survival of Formerly Dominant Languages', in *Economic and Political Weekly*, Vol. XXXVII, No.2, January, 12-18.

8

The Indian Media and the Idea of India

A Patchy Democratisation

SAGARIKA GHOSE

The sheer size, diversity and fragmentation of the media necessarily means that it reflects competing ideas of India. The media today is incorrigibly diverse, in many ways crucially influential, in other ways a byword for that cultural epidemic known as 'dumbing down'. Yet if there is one truth that can be safely advanced about the media today is that in its dizzying variety, it reflects a hectic if patchy democratization of the public space.

In 1950 there were 214 daily newspapers with 44 in English and the rest in regional languages. By 1990 the number of daily newspapers had grown to 2,856 with 209 in English and 2,647 in indigenous languages. Today, there are massive multi-edition newspapers like *the Times of India, the Hindustan Times, the Indian Express* and *the Ananda Bazaar Patrika* group. There are also giant language papers such as *Malayala Manorama, Dainik Jagran, Punjab Kesri*. Most importantly, there are the television channels. A dozen regional channels, four 24-hour news channels as well as a plethora of news-based shows, talk shows and interactive programmes.

The so-called golden age of Indian journalism of 1920s to 1950s is considered to be the age of the great editors like Chelapathy Rao, Frank Moraes, Devdas Gandhi *et al* who treated advertising managers with contempt, treated local news with disdain and believed that the written world should be loftily concerned with the grave issues not only of India but also of the world. Yet this old India was a rarefied genteel world, quite ill at ease with the mass aspiration society that exists today. That old world has been destroyed by big business, by the PR executive and by the advertiser, pushing up budgets and turning media into businesses. Television companies, requiring vast amounts of capital investment must attract advertisements in order to become viable. According to Mckann Erickson, global advertising alone will amount to almost 200 trillion dollars by 2020. Returns are a must, so sales drives, distribution strategies, event management and sponsorships, naked ladies and the glamorous parties are all pressed into service to secure higher and higher circulation figures and TRPs demanded by the advertiser. All sorts of marketing wisdom are churning around every newspaper office and TV studio. The English-speaking viewer's choices, the Hindi-speaking viewer's preferences. The young only want entertainment. Women only want fashion. Bollywood is the only thing that really sells.

There is the phenomenon known as Page Three. While the written word dominated until a decade ago, this is the age of television, the age of marketing, the age of the advertiser and the age of the PR executive. There are political alliances. There are local mafias between journalist and politician. There are sponsored features. There are managed events to popularize brands. They are the demons who dominate the media arena and who have, according to the lamenting pundits, sounded the death knell of all seriousness.

But has the death knell of seriousness been sounded? Are all newspapers dead because of the onslaught of television? There are tremendous fears about advertising. There are fears that the citizen has been replaced by the consumer. That the individual is no longer capable of walking into the wilderness for the sake of a principle, or going to jail because freedoms are at stake, because all principles have been compromised by a shallow, complacent affluence-seeking society. The Graviera Man or the Raymond Man, the high consuming "winner" who is known primarily by what he consumes, rather than the beliefs he holds, is the new role model. The beautiful home, high-speed car, the trophy wife and two beautiful kids has becomes the Mark of a Man. There are other fears. The role of media mafias at the local levels means that dailies are often used for settling private scores, vendettas and criminal activity. In this case, the media becomes a participant in local politics and relays conflicting and biased reports.

However it is my argument here that these fears are to some extent, unfounded. In fact, the notion that the India project in itself is being derailed by a conspicuously consuming compromising media, which is busy bartering away the national interest, cannot really be sustained across the board if one looks at the range of publications and electronic images on offer today. While there is certainly strong evidence to suggest that standards are falling, that language is being degraded, that the colour supplements often look like soft pornography, yet taken as a whole, the media today is very much a symbol of the evolving democratisation of India.

Written before the television revolution, in a book entitled *India's Newspaper Revolution*, Robin Jeffrey wrote, "the overall thrust of news gathering and dissemination was to propagate subliminal ideas about the existence and legitimacy of an Indian state and an Indian nation. The daily consumption of a newspaper seemed to affirm the existence of other people of the same nationality who, newspapers reminded readers every day, were also reading their newspapers. The fact that I read mine in Telegu in Renigunta while a fellow Indian read hers in Gujarati in Rajkot was less important than that both our newspapers told us about what was happening in our state and our locality. Part of this process of affirmation of an Indian identity was unconscious; proprietors and the people they employed as editors and reporters took the Indian state as a given and desirable." In fact television also powerfully promotes the idea of nationhood by relaying images from every part of the country as part of a single news bulletin and part therefore of a single national life. The public consciousness is also stirred by debates, discussions and question-answer sessions with those in authority. So while the media may be fragmented along the lines of language, that is in terms of numbers a vastly smaller percentage would consume national English-language media products than those in regional languages, yet it is also true that the media is fostering, in spite of the naked ladies and Page Three culture, indeed coterminous with it, a certain public mindedness, increased engagement with the news and strong stances on policy issues (however patchily informed those stances may be).

There is even the emergence of the 'news junkie' among affluent sections, those who apparently only consume soaps and fashion magazines. If the TRPs of news programmes are anything to go by, many of these metropolitan segments watch and follow the news and develop fascinations with news anchors who are seen to possess as much "star quality" as film stars. The fact that individual television "brands" are increasingly used as marketing devices, on street corner hoardings and billboards, suggest that the news reading personality is a valuable asset to a large public. Television news is thus seductive and has willy-nilly created a questioning public minded class in different regional languages and centres. The notion of the "Indian public", or of the single entity known as "Indian public opinion", has certainly received a fillip from the constant presence of the media during every national question or crisis.

Additionally, there are no clear signs yet that television is killing the written word. In fact media critic Sevanti Ninan in a study in Chennai found that the more people watched TV, the more they returned hungrily to print in order to delve into issues more deeply. English-language newspapers may have stopped growing. But what about regional language newspapers? In the year 2000 about 60 per cent adults were literate in their own mother tongues, a class of potential newspaper readers numbering close to 500 million. Indians buy 50 million newspapers every day. Only 6 million of those newspapers, less than 15 per cent, are in English. 40 million newspapers every day are printed in regional languages. India is reading, but increasingly in regional languages, in spite of the exponential growth of TV. In fact media critics have pointed to the complementarity of TV and print, the more TV people watch, the more they are driven to print as their excitement with issues is awakened.

The disappearance of crucial institutions like the editor-in-chief and his replacement by a brand manager was seen as the nail in the coffin of respectable journalism, but the fact is that after 9/11, the second Gulf war, the declared war on terrorism in India and the momentous political developments of our times, have in spite of smart marketing, put the news agenda back on course. It can also be argued that as long as there are serious issues in the world, there will be a serious media and the future of seriousness is not as bleak as we sometimes tend to think it is. The *India Today* group puts actress Aishwarya Rai on its cover and at the same time holds a conclave on the development of Indian states. *The Times Of India*'s sponsorships of the Miss World and Miss Universe pageants attracts scorn and derision, but the Old Lady of Boribunder, whose management is notoriously famous for its disdain for journalism, has still has not thought it fit to entirely scrap its editorial page as the management once vowed to do. And if seriousness was finished, then what explains the fact that the biggest media story last year, the Tehelka expose, was about a serious subject of corruption? *The Indian Express* expose of the scam of petrol pump allotments, the media's stance on Gujarat, the media's reportage of Kargil, were all massive public issues proving the point that as long as serious issues exist, there will also be a serious media.

Sure, parts of the media are in alliance with the government. There is certainly a 'manufactured consensus' because journalists remain dependent on politicians and bureaucrats for news and client-patron relations undoubtedly develop between politicians and journalists. But while some media is in permanent alliance, others are in permanent opposition.

The death of the opposition and the rise of the media-as-opposition is a new trend noted in UK, US as well as in India. With the NDA government, a permanent clash between opposing ideas of India along Hindutva and secular lines is clear. In this, the India idea is a severely contested one, with the media taking sharp stands on one or the other issue. In Gujarat for example, even though this is supposed to be a non-ideological age, the media became ideologically polarized.

In fact the surfeit of politics has had an unfortunate fallout. National interest and patriotism are located invariably in politics. Media choices on the front page govern what are the ideas of the national interest. The relegation of health, environment, crime and local news to the role of the "soft", as opposed to the pre-occupation with "hard" politics, in turn creates a politicized society where ideas of India are built around political issues rather than on health, lifestyle, architecture or cultural tastes. The kind of search for the political truth that the media is undertaking is not matched by a similarly intense search for a cultural truth or an equally intense search for the truth of an Indian arts identity, or an identity in music or literature or even the environment. This is undoubtedly a sad skewing of priorities.

But then again these are partial truths. *HT City*, the color supplement of *the Hindustan Times*, may provide only empty glamour, but *Hastkshep*, formerly the Sunday magazine of the *Rashtriya Sahara* provided sharp political and exciting comment. Periodicals like *Seminar* and *Economic and Political Weekly* coexist with *India Today Plus* and *Cosmopolitan*. Take the example of Aaj Tak: a truly catch-all Indian channel unabashedly tabloid in the way that it treats news. Yet on the day that it provides summer fashion, it also provides the *India Today* conclave on the state of the states. The reports on Abu Salem's incarceration in Portugal may have been slugged "Shikanje Mein Don" with an ostentatious musical lead-in, but the "serious" content of the news in Aaj Tak is maintained through detailed ground level reports and investigative features.

Old style newspapers tended to rely on national and international stories translated from English, which were devoid of personality and style. Circulation-building newspapers on the other hand have to develop styles that ordinary people can easily read and write about affairs that interest ordinary folk. The Tamil daily *Dina Thanthi* is dismissed as a paper for rickshaw drivers. But although cinema and crime may be its staple, but it still provides a huge amount of politics. There is also no doubt there has been a degradation of language. M.T. Vasudevan Nair, editor of the 'serious' *Malayalam Mathrubhumi Weekly*, echoes views from Maharashtra to Bengal when he says, "Readers for serious publications have dwindled. The younger generation is not reading Malayalam."

Actually, as Jeffrey says, they are reading Malayalam, but not Vasudevan Nair's preferred Malayalam. In the mid-90s two popular story magazines *Manorama Weekly* and *Mangalam* sold 2 million copies a week. The sober and cultured *Mathrubhumi Weekly* sold only 60,000 copies and had fallen by 40,000 in the previous five years. It's the same story with periodicals like *Desh, Seminar, Biblio,* all cultured and refined products experiencing a dwindling in their numbers. However I would argue that the scope for inserting serious articles and think pieces into high circulating magazines, as seen in *Vanity Fair* or *Playboy,* remains an important possibility and in the future this may be a trend. Indians may not buy a serious product, but they will buy non-serious products and read them from cover to cover. The scope of enlarging the ambit of the 'non-serious' in a positive sense thus remains huge. The fact that newspapers are adopting a tabloid form and introducing screaming headlines on the front pages and society columns in the back pages does not mean that the editorials have been scrapped and all debate has ceased.

The marketing wisdom is that India's youth or Generation Next is entirely caught up in MTV, fun food and fornication. Yet this unjust myth has been exposed by many young people themselves. In a notable article in an online magazine *The Hoot*, a student Shivam Vij writes, "If we seem so hopeless why was there a reduction in the use of firecrackers last Diwali? Why did the youth on Independence Day distribute and wear white ribbons in protest against communal violence? Walk into any school with a decent teaching faculty and ask them who Gandhiji was or what the Quit India movement represented, and they will all have answers. You have not only misrepresented youth but also assumed that you know us better than we do."

Be it advertising or journalism or cinema or the Ekta Kapoor serials, the media is loath to represent the young as real people with real concerns. News channels are peddling Pretty Young Things. But if it was true that teens only wanted non-serious content then would *Teens Today*, which had all the elements of yuppie culture which apparently is the prevailing culture today, be forced to shut down? According to NRS 2002 (National Readership Survey) India's largest selling magazine is *Saras Salil* of the Delhi Press Publications. *Saras Salil* is a B-grade Hindi magazine which costs Rs 4. Of course there is sex, but there is also politics, there is the budget, there is corruption and there are comments on society. *Saras Salil* with its huge circulation, cannot simply be written off as a non-serious magazine. According to IRS 2002, the top circulating daily today is *Dainik Bhaskar* with a readership of 136 lakh. Anyone who's read the *Dainik Bhaskar* will see that it is a broadsheet in the truest senses and although it has now brought in a Page Three, there are furious political and social debates in its editorial pages and sharply written news stories. It is the same with *Dainik Jagran*, which has a circulation of 135 lakh. It is only the example of the *Times of India* (circulation 61 lakh) that has sent the alarm bells ringing about the death of the media.

And in many ways the destruction of the post of the editor, the establishment of the corporate director as controller of news, has had far reaching affects on the media. Certain structural constraints may be mentioned here. *The TOI*'s freedom to "dumb down" and lower its price has everything to do with its leviathan-like status in the English-language newspaper market. The monopolistic role that *the TOI* plays will be greatly reduced if FDI is introduced in the print media and other smaller papers are allowed to flourish better. But suffice to say that even with *the TOI* being a behemoth, the repackaged *Sunday Express* was able to gain some ground without compromising on *the Express* brand of hard hitting exposes. The success of *Outlook*, at a time when *India Today* reigned supreme and the magazine market was thought to be dead, is also a mark of the fact that the market is not necessarily inimical to anything that verges on the "serious".

When Kargil occurred, *the Times Of India* forgot to dumb down and rose to the hour. Every newspaper sent reporters to the front and carried serious stories. The same *TOI*, criticized for being dumb and trivial, rose to the occasion in Gujarat as well and *the TOI* played a stellar role in its reportage of the riots. During the Emergency, when newspapers were battling for survival, once again the broadsheets emerged as political and intelligent voices. During the Iraq war, every newspaper was marked by long articles on the war. The press has created a "public sphere" or what is known as a "democratic public realm" based on cafes, footpath chatter. Newspapers reflect an evolving discussion on public moral and political issues. In fact politics and the media are crucially dependent on each other. The consumption of media opens up new avenues in politics. There is a demand to know, a demand to be heard. The dozens of Public Interest Litigations, public interest actions undertaken by dozens of groups, all work in alliance with the media. Certainly the mass-circulating consumption-oriented press may retard the citizenship aspect of the media, but I would argue that the very politicised nature of Indian society ensures that serious media will always be at hand to feed off and create political excitement.

Nowhere is this better exemplified than in the rise of the media as an opposition. After the Gujarat results, whom did the politicians attack most gleefully? Not their own opposition, but the media. The media has lost, roared Jayalalitha. Time for the media to apologize, gloated Narendra Modi. In fact after Gujarat and during the riots, it seemed as if it was the media, and specifically certain TV channels and newspapers that had set themselves up as the secular critics of Hindutva Modi far more trenchantly than the political opposition. Whether on scandals, politics or corruption, the media does to some extent take on an oppositional role. The media's massive reach, the sheer decibel level of the morning headline, clever visuals and sound bytes can make it a powerful adversary of the government of the day and can even, such as during the Kandahar hijacking, force the government's hand on policies. Thus the trivialization of the media may be undeniable, but there is also no doubt also of its serious participatory functions. In other situations, the media is an ally, whether of the parents of the Uphaar Cinema fire tragedy victims or the crashed MiG pilots or the parents of murdered sons. The relentless media pressure simply cannot be ignored and even provides succor to the grief-stricken.

To conclude, I would say, that the contemporary media remains intrinsic to the idea of modern India because it is in the media that conflicting ideas are played out, subliminal choices are made and opinions are formed. The pressure to build circulation may have led to tabloidisation, but the pressure to be locally answerable has also led to local stories and an emphasis on health, environment, crime and civic facilities. A tabloid media is also an immediate intimate media and the time of the thoughtful and the patrician Frank Moraes has undoubtedly given way to a shrieking reporter standing in front of a fire. Yet the rise of Indian "individuality", as well as Indian "public", is spurred by the media. The increased attention on localities and cities has popularized issues of "common" concern. No doubt advertising spending and cash flows into the media will increase exponentially in the coming years, but the influence of the market, I feel, is a challenge rather than a reason for hand-wringing outrage. Market forces may spur media products of a certain kind, but the very raw material of the media industry, life itself, death, invasion, illness and terrorism, will ensure that the entirety of media can never become hopelessly trivial, however far the trappings of triviality are taken.

What might the Indian media look like in 2020? Might foreign direct investment lift the standards of the print media? Will television become more tabloid, or turn serious again? Will India become a post-literate society through the media, jumping straight from illiteracy to the television age, with newspapers becoming extinct? Will the massive growth of advertising render news irrelevant? My prognosis is that there will be fragmentation, smaller media will cater to niche groups, but in order to survive and satisfy an increasingly literate public, media will be forced to become more intelligent. Ten years ago, there was talk that *the Times Of India* would scrap the edit page completely: until today, it has still not happened. In the last decade of journalism, there have certainly been huge changes, but there have not been any tectonic shifts. Newspapers still exist, more being born every day. Issues are still discussed. Television dominates, but has not killed the editorial. 24-hour television has, I would argue, spurred an engaged Indian citizenship rather than simply dumb everybody down. Sure there is the pap and the rubbish that is played out, but the kernel of seriousness doesn't look as if it is dying. On the face of it, the scantily clad women and the parties seem to dominate, but the signed article in the old format still captures imaginations. Television is tabloid, but rough and ready, and it is getting down and dirty. The cameras are everywhere and they are constantly on: take away the dross and chaff and you'll get reports on UP schools, Laloo Prasad Yadav, filthy hospitals, ghastly mental homes, abandoned babies, corruption and sex scandals. In fact, in the contemporary Indian media today, there is a hectic democracy at work, which is not pretty, which is flawed, but which exists and which is growing.

9

Re-Appraising the Idea of India

VINOD SAIGHAL

The 'Idea of India' has been variously commented upon by several persons, many of them well known, from the perspective of their own background, whether they be writers, expatriates, political scientists, constitutional experts, philosophers and the like. Almost invariably the discipline or the academic background of the person putting forward the ideas has manifested itself in the views expressed, perhaps naturally so. This point is mentioned because the diversity of views of the idea of India can be seen to be as abundant as the idea of India itself. On the academic plane, *i.e.* from the perspective of persons who are able to put across their views to a larger audience through their writings or discourses, the 'Idea' has been regarded, or at times discredited as one or the other label, most notably cultural, civilisational, political or an amalgam of complexities, too difficult to discern with any degree of clarity. As if these complexities were not enough, the present dialogue on the idea of India has been overwhelmingly coloured by the controversy raging over secular and non-secular debates that have taken place or are taking shape at the very moment when the world itself is being buffeted by contradictions that it thought it had wound down for a century or more.

To a lay person standing aside from the debate on the Idea of India, which itself is a subliminal thrust towards a perceived ideal for the person informing the debate, the idea *per se* becomes a super-imposition of the beliefs or prejudices of the person concerned. Standing back, at some remove from a direct involvement, it should be possible for any objective observer to anticipate with a reasonable degree of accuracy the position that would be likely to be taken by a well known person putting across his or her Idea of India. This statement should not be construed as a criticism of a given mindset of the Idea of India, which in several cases would be seen to conform to the ideal of the person formulating the Idea of India. The digression at the start of the paper is made to show that the very subjectivity attached to the Idea of India makes it an imperfect ideal for being accepted as such – in case it is meant to be so – by the majority of the people who go through the humdrum of Indian existence without trying to look for anything beyond the travails of their existence. To that extent, the debate remains esoteric.

The amorphous nature of the idea of the 'Idea of India' allows for as many interpretations as there are people pondering over it as an intellectual exercise. There are so many ways of looking at a country whose civilisational base goes back to the dawn of civilization itself. An individual, or groups of individuals, who in their remoteness remain steeped in the traditions patterned on the lives of their forefathers since time immemorial, do not have to delve into aspects that are of analytical, philosophical or historical interest to writers and savants, who debate these issues. They **live** the tradition. It is part of their very being. It is the continuum that in their mind was without beginning, flows effortlessly into the present, and by their reckoning, moves as easily into the future. It is a faith and an understanding untrammeled by self-doubt or doubt about the tradition in which they are steeped.

There are others, comprising the bulk of the people of India, living in India, who may share the attitudes of their brethren, although the pre-modern type of existence would appear to be an anachronism to many people who have stepped into the modern world. Here again, by and large the new lifestyle adopted by them – by some as recently as the last 30 or 40 years – need not lead to questioning of their civilisational past or their idea of what that past was and how it is to be lived in the present. Therefore, in a statistical sense, it would be only a small percentage of Indians who would be grappling with the question of what the Idea of India represents to them or for them.

A re-worked Idea of India, shaped at the beginning of the new century through the dizzying scientific breakthroughs taking place at a myriad points on the scientific horizon, must take into account the externalities that will have a major effect on the thinking of the Indian nation, of all nations, for that matter. True, that in a country like India, the external impulses are felt most keenly, in the first instance, by the power elites and the globalized elites in the metropolitan cities most receptive to them. On the face of it, they do not directly buffet the minds of people in communities still steeped in the ways of their forefathers. Although the trickle down effect is slower, much slower, it cannot be escaped altogether, even by people living in remote regions of the country, cocooned in their time warp due to their relative inaccessibility. Nevertheless, since the policies being enacted by the governing elites are directly influenced - or imposed upon - by the prime movers of globalization, they will, over a period of time, have an effect on the lives of most people; whether it would be to a lesser or greater degree will be determined by the distance of the communities from the centers of globalization. Naturally, there will be other determinants as well.

The India, which now situates itself at the dawn of the third millennium after Christ, must take into account the political aspect. Modern India, after attaining its independence in 1947 has been shaped, reshaped or become misshapen by the parliamentary form of government that the founding fathers of post-Independent India chose for it in the belief that it represented the best ideal for 'their' Idea of India; for transforming it after centuries of subjugation into a strong healthy society. Therefore, the country's political identity is based on its commitment to certain fundamental principles, namely justice, liberty, equality, fraternity and the dignity of the individual. Fundamental Rights institutionalize, respect and protect the individual's dignity and freedom. The Directive Principles go further in that they have a strong egalitarian thrust. After 50 years of what many would call national decline, at least in the realm of governance, blame is being put upon the Constitution, which India gave itself on achieving Independence. Rightly or wrongly, whether condemning it outright or picking holes in it from time to time, it remains undeniable that the people at the helm of affairs who guided India's destiny through that turbulent period of the partition of India must have based their actions upon **their** Idea of India. Something akin to what is being attempted now; except that in the present case the projections remain academic and possibly idealistic, without the compelling burden of transforming those ideas into actions that could shape the country's future for the next 50 years or more, as was the case with the decisions that followed the ideation of the founding fathers of that earlier era.

It would be futile to keep harping on the rightness or otherwise of the decisions taken at that time by the leaders of the country, whose stature and idealism as well as the sacrifices made by them during the freedom struggle, conferred upon them an aura and mystique that few leaders can hope to achieve in the present day. Their stature as leaders beloved of their people reverberated beyond the confines of India's geographic boundary. It cannot be a matter of satisfaction that charismatic leaders of yesteryears, who rode as colossi on the national as well as global arenas, have almost disappeared from the face of the earth, yielding place to pygmies who lead their people through autocratic dispensations or the vagaries of the ballot box. In the latter case, often coming to power for reasons far removed from their ability to lead their people.

Whether the Constitution failed India or the people who were in the ascendant over the years as educators, intellectuals, governing elites as well as the haves, failed the Constitution and the country, is a debate that is not likely to die down any time soon. Nor is it likely that the Constitution, which for all its failings – real or imaginary - has become reasonably well embedded, can be displaced or turned over in the foreseeable future. Fed up with the state of affairs, public ferment is bound to lead to changes, mostly for the good of the people as well as the country. Whether intellectuals and the educated elite, both within the country and the expatriates, will play a significant role as harbingers of salutary changes remains an open question. In the earlier centuries, men of letters influenced the thinking of their countrymen, or even the world, over long periods of time. In some cases, the movement of ideas would be considered to have been glacial by present reckoning. This is where the most significant change has come for the men of letters, the shapers of ideas, in the form of information technology. Hence, the ivory tower appellation of rarefied intellectual debates need not apply any longer, or at least not to the same extent. Diffusion and dissemination can take place very fast, with lightning speed if the mediums of transmission and diffusion happen to be receptive to the idea.

The political shape of the nation is bound to play an over-sized part – overwhelmingly larger, when compared to other factors that determine the future of the country. Ignoring this fact, building an ideal that does not take into account the ground reality in which India is anchored in the opening years of the 21st century, or mired as some others might like to word it, would make the idea devoid of substance.

Two major streams that dominate the intellectual as well as political discourse of the country today relate to the place of religion in modern India and the relevance of the philosophy and ideals of Mahatma Gandhi. Coming first to religion, it was denied sufficient space in the political mainstream - as well as by officialdom - due to the political philosophy and the thinking of Pandit Jawaharlal Nehru, the first Prime Minister of India, and the Congress Party that played an overarching role in the country's affairs in the opening decades after Independence. Moreover, it might have been a conscious effort on the part of all concerned to exorcise the ghosts of the violent partition of India. Whether the post-secular society that India became in the last decades of the 20th century was inevitable on account of the transformations taking place in neighboring countries and their influence on the two largest religious communities in India, is a question that could be taken up by future historians. Whatever be the case, religion, in its more assertive and virulent form, came upfront in many parts of the world. India was no exception. Even if externalities had not impinged upon India, the country would have reached the same point, almost inevitably so, by a different route. If interdenominational clashes between the two main communities had not come to the fore earlier, this was also on account of the firm governance that obtained in the first few decades after Independence, due as much to the latent stability resulting from over one century of strong, well regulated centralized authority in India. It was this latent stability, added to the competence and commitment of the leaders and civil servants who governed the country in the period immediately after Independence, that kept a lid on many of the ills seen raising their ugly heads today in the country. Matters, of course, came to a head during the emergency. The post-emergency decline in almost all spheres of governance and in almost all strata of society, has led the country to the state that it finds itself in at the beginning of the new century. That this is not a happy state of affairs, hardly needs reiteration.

The second important aspect relates to the philosophy of Gandhi. Although Gandhi continues to form an important part of the ongoing political and economic discourse taking place in the country, and elsewhere in the world, for that matter, it has to be mentioned that in spite of the ideals of the Mahatma quoted with reverence at most forums discussing the future course of the country, his economic and political philosophy has not really found acceptance in the country, in so far as their practical application goes. And at the end it is difficult to think of an Idea of India that completely dissociates itself from the maxims of the Mahatma, whether they relate to governance, sustainable development, harmony in pluralistic societies or for the conduct of nations in the global arena. It is not surprising that Gandhi continues to attract the attention of so many people around the world, both as the man and the ideals that he stood for. Unfortunately, the debate around the Mahatma rages, especially in India, around elements that were never put into practice in the land where they took birth.

Looking back on the events of the 20th century, both pre and post-Independence in India, one cannot fail to get the impression that although he did not lose hope or his faith in his ideals, Gandhi might have died a disillusioned man. If not disillusioned, certainly heartsick at the turn of the events. Did the bloodletting that took place at the time of partition in the land where for over four decades he had preached *ahimsa*, indicate that his philosophy had failed? Amongst others, this was the land of Mahavira and Buddha. It did not end with partition. The bloodletting continues to this day, in every part of the subcontinent where the father of the nation traveled. If present indications are anything to go by, it could continue till well into the future, seeing the current trends across national divides in all directions in the subcontinent. Hence, it can be seen that the ground reality is almost diametrically opposed to the Gandhian tradition that so many Indians continue to extol in public forums, be they intellectuals, social workers, politicians or economists. The ordinary Indian too continues to revere the memory of the Mahatma. When the state of affairs threatens to get out of hand, people still go to Rajghat in ever increasing numbers to take a pledge at the *samadhi* of the Mahatma.

The increasing hiatus between Gandhianism and the policies followed by Gandhi's successors in India, regardless of their political leanings, raises fundamental questions for the Idea of India. For the people of India, and for people around the world there can be no perception of India, real or imagined, where the ideals of the Mahatma do not loom large. How is this contradiction to be reconciled?

Because, if it is not addressed and is merely glossed over at every public place within the country and without, where the name of Gandhi is taken, India will not be able to emerge unscathed from this troubling dissonance between the precept and its practice.

Seeing that India itself has veered so far away from the Gandhian mould, it should have been possible to reject Gandhi's philosophy out of hand and move forward without a backward glance at an ideal that was considered impractical; or could not be put into effect in a land were shallowness, hypocrisy and untruthfulness have become the order of the day, at least in public life. In which case, getting rid of the baggage of Gandhianism and getting on with the governance of the country in the non-Gandhian mould that it has adapted, should have been easy.

This has not been the case. At the same time that untruthfulness and venality are in full cry, the very leaders who have propelled the country in that direction have not been able to dispense with the trumpeting of Gandhi's legacy, because of a lurking fear that should it be discarded, India would not only have lost its way, it would have lost its soul. Then there would be no turning back. The thought of that final break, even shedding the pretence that is, troubles these people. They know that without the pretence, they would not be able to face their countrymen, not at the hustings, not in public, possibly not even in private. At a deeper level they are not unaware that a final abandonment of Gandhianism would be tantamount to condemning themselves to a *karmic* descent too horrid to contemplate. For, no matter how immoral the lot that governs the nation, in their heart of hearts they are deeply religious, albeit in a very warped sense of what their understanding of being religious should be. They also know that in India the vast majority of their countrymen revere the Mahatma and in spite of their poverty, deprivation and misery, still closely adhere to the thoughts and ideals of Gandhiji. For they are the ideals of Vivekananda, Sri Aurobindo and so many other sages and seers who moulded the character and destiny of India through the ages. That destiny that awaited India at midnight of 15th August, 1947 has still eluded the country. Beneath the despair and turmoil that afflicts the land, that destiny still awaits India. India will yet produce the leaders who will take India to the pinnacle that the Mahatma and the sages before him dreamed of. And therefore, the ideal cannot be lost sight off. The ideal of Mahatma Gandhi is far too important for the redemption of India, if it is to find its feet and its true destiny. For the very same reason, it is important for the world as well.

It is necessary to go a step further. The reasons as to why when the majority of Indians believe in it and the political leaders profess to believe in it, Gandhianism has not prevailed in the country of its origin have to be gone into. The main reason could be the difficulty of transplanting the Gandhian ideal of the early 20th century. Under an alien dispensation that ruled the country, and because of it being alien, it started uniting the country ideologically in the earlier decades before Independence. The circumstances that obtained post-Independence, after the partition of India, are not the same. And as the years went by, leading ultimately to the dominant market capitalist economy model pervading the world in the 21st century, the implementation of those ideas became even more difficult. Firstly, as mentioned earlier, the conditions had altered radically, and secondly, having moved so far away from the Gandhian philosophy and its economic derivatives, it became increasingly difficult to retrace the steps taken. Having said that, the attempts at strengthening *panchayati raj* and the adherence to the principle, if not the practice, of sustainable development would qualify as a bow in the direction of Gandhianism.

Meanwhile, a fundamental change has taken place in the make up of the people of India - and the world as well. More than fifty years after Gandhi's death, the capitalist model – and the morality that goes with it - has become the norm. Even countries most staunchly opposed to it earlier, have embraced it whole-heartedly, notably Russia and China. Could people of those days when Gandhi was popularizing the *charka* have anything in common with Deng Xiao Peng's famous exhortation to his countrymen that, 'it is glorious to be rich'. If it is glorious to be rich, then there is nothing left of the Gandhian philosophy. If not the masses, at least the political class and the elites of modern India, have embraced Deng's dictum as fervently as the Chinese in Beijing, Shanghai and Guangdong, in most cases as strongly as the American themselves. Whatever be the reason for this departure from socialism to capitalism, it is undeniable that going back to the economic idealism contained in Gandhi's writings would relegate India to an economic abyss from which there would be no recovery in the world of today. May be, when consumerism that is fast overtaking the globe makes life itself unsustainable on the planet, people across the world will start reappraising the economic philosophy of Gandhi. That is why the world is not going to forget Mahatma Gandhi. By association, India, rightly or wrongly, will benefit from that grand reversal, whenever it takes place on a global scale. If India is to remain as part of the global economy, without completely shedding some of the desirable aspects of its socialist past, it must start its own reappraisal for benefiting from the vision of Gandhi, wherever it is possible to transform that vision on the ground under the prevailing conditions in the country and the world. If the world has to save itself from self-destruction, Gandhian non-violence must become the leitmotif of a globalized world, and a reformed UN structure that allows non-violence between states must become the norm for the 21st century.

It was possibly Mahatma Gandhi who said: "for my worldly needs my village is my world; for my spiritual needs the world is my village".

The Indian diaspora is playing a much bigger role in moulding India's selfhood than it did before the 1990s. There could be several reasons for the renewed interest and what is more, the new activism of the Indian expatriate community, which is now far more affluent and self-assured than their counterparts who left India to seek their fortunes in other lands before and after India's partition. The self-assurance and higher incomes have allowed people of Indian origin from around the world to participate more directly in India's development. The pace at which the interaction is taking place could have, over the ensuing decades, a positive effect far out of proportion to the strength of the Indian diaspora that is actively engaged in the exercise to move India forward. More importantly, the Indian diaspora is making itself heard in safeguarding the country's interest in the corridors of power in USA and elsewhere. The Idea of India of the expatriates is in many ways distinct from that of their fellow Indians, **in** India. It is born out of their need for self-assertion in their adopted countries in a world where civilizations appear to be actually clashing - with the attendant uncertainties that such clashes generate for non-local persons.

The image of India for consumption in the West, notably America, as well as for home consumption in India, is also being shaped by

Indian expatriates who now number in tens of millions and whose wealth has grown into tens of billions of dollars. Their writings, actions and interactions have left an indelible impression on India's image abroad. The new lot of expatriates that went to find their fortunes in the West **after** the information technology revolution, represented a different breed from those that had gone earlier. The latter-day emigrants being largely the products of prestigious Indian institutes, started off at higher base income levels and quickly rose to prominence in several fields. For the same reason, they were far more self-assured, articulate and conscious of the need to rebuild India, as well as to refurbish its image. Their common institutional backgrounds allowed them to network far more effectively than their predecessors. Networking allowed them to form pressure groups for influencing policy and thinking about India in the countries of their adoption. This cohesion did not go unnoticed in India, by the government of India, the political parties, the states, as well as the Indian media. In-country networking led to inter-country networking. As their self-confidence grows, along with their ability to influence developments in India, the Indian diaspora will continue to play a significant role in the years ahead in remoulding India's image. Over a period of time, this interaction between India and Indian expatriate communities is bound to enrich India in several ways.

When one speaks of global projection of the Idea of India, there is a dual purpose attached to the Idea of India. First, it refers to the idea, which harmonizes with the idea that the Indian diaspora have formed and are propagating. It has to be dynamic. It cannot be something that is congealed in some hoary past and frozen at a given point in time, to be resurrected for showing India in a better light than the situation in the country at the dawn of the new millennium would warrant. Similarly, an Idea of India that is superlatively formulated to show India as the repository of all earthly wisdom from time immemorial, to the exclusion of the contribution made by other civilizations, would be at variance with the true spirit of the very wisdom that is being extolled. Arrogance, be it intellectual or on account of a great heritage, would not go down well with other components of the human mosaic of the 21st century. Therefore, the other aspect of the image that India wishes to transmit to the world must bring out the harmonizing effect of the ancient message that traveled from India to many parts of the world before many of the world's religions in the ascendant today had come into being.

India will not be able to find its true identity or realistically arrive at an idea of itself, which the country can live comfortably with, as also make it a worthwhile idea for global projection, unless the internal contradictions that are coming up are first addressed.

No set of people can really live in isolation or remain indifferent to the cross-currents being generated in the globalized world. The advance of technology will soon invade every remote niche that remains in the world, be it spatial, in the geographical sense, or the privacy of the human mind, in the metaphysical sense. Hence, seeing the pervasiveness of the processes that are being mobilized for invading the last bastions of the human as well as the natural environment, it would be appropriate to look around the world to see whether there is any country whose society can be seen, or can be deemed to be progressing towards the ideal state that a conclave of this nature would be attempting to interpret, or define, even if it were to remain a process of mere intellectualization, at some remove from the practicality of the ideal sought.

Who shapes the national - and international - dialogue? This is an important question, because it is those people who have gathered unto themselves the instruments for shaping the dominant discourse of today, who are leading the world into the cul-de-sac of negativism and violence. When scanning the global horizon in pursuit of seeking out societies that my be headed toward an idea of an ideal state that comes nearest to the global ideal of the 21st century, one finds that wherever one looks, be it USA, Russia, China, the countries of Latin America, Africa, Asia or Europe, it is seen that almost all these societies have developed into systems that have been unable by and large to maintain or improve upon the social cohesion of societies, which is fast breaking down in most parts of the world. There are many factors that are leading to the fragmentation of stable or relatively stable systems - and societies - that had enjoyed a greater measure of peace and harmony than they do now. Whether the state of churning or flux has been brought on by the post-World War II, followed by the post-Cold War re-ordering of the world order, or whether it is a by-product of rapid modernization and globalization, is a question that can be debated at length. Whatever be the case, the ambient condition today within societies - and between nations - is far from harmonious. Nor, on the face of it, does it seem to be heading in a direction that could bring comfort to people or nations.

The questions that would be uppermost in one's mind when contemplating India's future must take into account some, if not all, of the aspects that are listed below: -

- Has the political self-assertion, or the attempt at self-assertion by some of the deprived segments of Indian society now finding political representation ameliorated the condition of these classes as a whole or has it merely enabled the new leaders of the backward classes to exploit the situation for their own aggrandizement at the cost of their communities, without bringing any real benefits to the latter? Carrying this thought process further, "will these new leaders be co-opted into the governing elites once the process of self-aggrandizement has reached levels that allow them to emulate the sections that they were agitating against"?

- What will be the outcome a few years hence of the metropolitan elites around the world consciously collaborating with the forces of globalization? These forces might have started from America. However, they are no longer limited to that country.

- Leaders of political struggles, revolutionaries, upholders of public morality, social scientists and many others in similar categories have sought to describe their struggle or movement as one of liberation. It can be argued that the phrase 'struggle for liberation' has fallen into disuse, or become hackneyed. Nonetheless, it may become necessary to have another look at these clichés. Since they served their purpose admirably in the past, are they still relevant or do they sound hollow? Hollowness can result from overuse or misuse or it can be the result of the quality or worth of the people who use these slogans for purposes that may be far removed from the ideology that they proffer. At the end of it all, when applying the term liberation to India, some clarity must obtain as to where the process of liberation would lead *i.e.*, liberation from or liberation to? What the people are being liberated from has been variously described as hunger, want, deprivation, marginalisation, humiliation and all the ills that are visited upon the proverbial have-nots anywhere in the world. 'Liberation to' in its ideal sense can best be described in Tagore's immortal poem, which reads:

> *"Where the mind is without fear*
> *and the head is held high,*
> *Where knowledge is free,*
> *Where the world has not been broken*
> *Up into fragments by narrow domestic walls;*
> *Where words come out from the*
> *depth of truth;*
> *Where tireless striving stretches its*
> *arms towards perfection;*
> *Where the clear stream of reason*
> *has not lost its way*
> *into the dreary desert sand of dead habit;*
> *Where the mind is led forward*
> *by thee into ever-widening thought and action –*
> *into that heaven of freedom,*
> *my father, let my country awake."*

All countries have their religious practices, faiths and beliefs. The distinctiveness of India lies in the primacy attaching to the concept of self-abnegation and self-denial. In many ways, this goes deeper than similar tendencies that manifest themselves in many other religions and countries. It is for this reason that absolute poverty cannot be assigned a true statistical value in India. Because, at any given time, it is difficult to guess as to what percentage of the poor follow a lifestyle, which can be deemed to be below the poverty line due to circumstantial indigence, or the state of poverty being induced volitionally. It is practically impossible to fathom the number of mendicants who go around the country because they have chosen to adopt that particular way of life. Similarly, stories are still heard of well-to-do people giving up their wealth, finishing their duties as householders, and retiring to the banks of the Ganges to pass their remaining days in prayer, fasting, meditation and the like.

Most religions in the world, if not all of them, stress on the need for forgiveness, tolerance and compassion. In India compassion is extended to all living beings. Many followers of Jainism to this day go to great levels to ensure that no harm comes to other living creatures. Compassion for all beings must remain at the forefront of societal activity and, when the country is strong enough, even form part of India's relations with other nations.

When looking at the tragedy unfolding in the Middle East and the region on account of the unilateral US intervention, shedding at some stage even the fig leaf of justification for occupying Iraq, the supineness of the leaders of the countries opposed to the intervention has to be examined. This is especially so in the case of India. In spite of the widespread anger against the Anglo-American intervention, the government chose pragmatism as the state response to the tragic event. Although the government's response was in conformity with the response of practically all the governments in the world that chose to play it safe, the issue is raised in this discussion because it is in juxtaposition to the Idea of India, which leaders of India after Independence have been propagating to the world. Although the world has long become weary of the sermonizing coming from Indian shores, the message that came through was that India was a country that cherished the ideals of rightness of action and rightness of response. In abandoning its core values - the idea of an ancient civilization, steeped in wisdom and conscious of the difference between right and wrong - as a basis for conduct of foreign policy, the governmental elite of the country has vacated the space for basing international relations on the higher plane of moral principles to non-governmental entities or individuals who might command a measure of respect in public life. Needless to add that such abandonment of the path, or even the pretence, of right conduct, is in conformity with the prevailing norm across nations as the forces of globalization infuse the world with their non-virtues or the pleasure principle as the fulcrum of all actions.

To project or even propel India into a future which many people view with trepidation one must look over one's shoulder into the past. Not that remote past from which many people today want to draw their inspiration - more consciously than the ordinary consciousness that inheres in the minds of most Indians as to what that past might have been. That would be going too far back. Here, the past merely refers to the period after Independence, divided into those early years when many of today's Indians were very young, the

Republic of India even younger. How did people of that generation look at India at that time, as it was unfolding in the ever present and flowing into a future that beckoned enticingly, even enchantingly? Doubtless there were difficulties, trials and tribulations, which the nation was undergoing. Whatever may have been happening, dejection and despair were not in the ascendant to the same level that they are today. A few decades on, having journeyed with India into the new century, the same generation has a different vision of India. In spite of the remarkable progress made in many fields – and the achievements are certainly there for everyone to see – the spirit that pervades the nation seems to have lost the freshness and innocence, perhaps naiveté of those early years. What India has evolved into in the first decade of the new century is certainly not in keeping with the vision of what India should have evolved into, that goal people in the first decades after Independence cherished.

Here we come to the first dissonance. India has gained in many respects. In several other ways India has declined. How does one strike a balance between the gains and losses when the gains are in the material plane and the losses in planes other than material? Care is being taken to avoid the use of the word spiritual when chalking up the gains and the losses. For while efforts to resurrect the hoary past merge into the realm of the spiritual, the understanding of spirituality obtaining now in India - and perhaps the rest of the world - is not the same as it might have been when the great Vedic hymns to creation were being first sung on the banks of sacred rivers that now stand as polluted as the spirits of the souls that still ritualistically immerse themselves in these flows to seek salvation. Looking at it this way, the foremost image that leaps to the surface in the consciousness plane of the beings of today is a vast sea of pollution where the scum that rises to the surface represents, symbolically, the spiritual progress, even if it cannot be measured so as to be able to offset it against the material gains; represented almost exactly on the day of the discourse by a figure of 91 billion US dollars (the external reserves of the country).

Where does one go from here? Should the country pitch headlong into the globalizing mainstream and let the currents carry it in the direction of the new forms of *nirvana*, attained by the leaders of globalization - the USA and the West, ably followed by their counterparts in the extreme east, China and Japan. Following the leader, in the true spirit of globalization and the direction in which it is headed, will prevent people in India from falling between two stools, in this world and the next. The dilemma is very real. There are no easy answers. Having said that, answers have to be found. For it is not a question of black and white, of simply tossing a coin and then following the path indicated by the upward face of the coin, pointing towards the sky, the sun and the stars. It may be easier for other countries to do so, like China has done. India's manifest destiny does not lie in that direction. It lies in realms that can never be reached by true practitioners of globalization. Writing in *The Hindu* (October 1, 2002), Naresh Gupta aptly sums it up when he states: "the world of today has achieved much, but for all its declared love for humanity, it has based itself far more on hatred and violence than on the virtues that make man human".

There is a need to engage with those who belittle and condemn India, so that their varied and rich talent does not remain tied to an acerbic condemnation of their country – no matter how real their concern – in a language that can only be appreciated by the educated elite and foreigners who joyously lap up this condemnation and confer great honors upon the authors. Condemnation for the sake of condemnation, no matter how beautifully expressed, is not likely to lead to any real amelioration of the conditions that gave rise to the anger or the condemnation. Writing in *Young India* in 1929, Mahatma Gandhi said: "My mission is not merely brotherhood of Indian humanity... My patriotism is not an exclusive thing... The conception of my patriotism is nothing if it is not always, in every case without exception, consistent with the broadest good of humanity at large." Rabindranath Tagore said that while nationalism was often a blessing, too often it has been a curse. The Indian philosophy of *Vasudhaiva Kutumbam* promotes the feeling of 'one world'. Jawaharlal Nehru propounded the concept of *'Panchsheel'* as the basis of mutual relationship. The *Bhagavad Gita* and the *Isavasyopanishad* tell us that the *yogi* sees himself in all beings and all beings in himself. He sees the same in all. If one sees all living things as if they were in his body *i.e.* feels their joys and sorrows as his own, and sees the same Universal Spirit in all things, then there is no need for protecting oneself against others. When a man understands that all beings are, indeed, the all-pervading Spirit, then he realizes the oneness of all things.

Whatever be one's station in life - from those who are below the poverty line to those who are the wielders of power - all need to be reminded that the primary status of everyone in the country is first and foremost that of a citizen. In that respect, all are coequal. Similarly, the comity of nations will have to push towards a United Nations dispensation wherein from the most deprived nations barely existing as civilized structures owing to over-exploitation and marginalisation, to those mighty nations who decide what is good for the world, all must strive for the democratization of the UN. Therefore, in reshaping the Idea of India, its leaders have to recast their philosophy. They must resume engagement with all those who were being referred to as the 'third world' countries. The concept of the third world can be redefined to embrace all deprived nations whose primary impulse is towards global stability and harmony. In an over-exploited world, these are mostly nations who are struggling to simply find a place in the sun. The idea of leadership itself must undergo fundamental transformation. Traditionally, when talking of a leadership role amongst nations, the implication was to unite the group to confront other groups of nations seeking dominance in some form or the other. That remained the mindset of the post-colonial era after World War II, when the marginalized nations of the world were trying to position themselves as a third force between the two superpowers of the day.

The 21st century reality of the uni-polar world does not confer any leadership role upon India, should the country remain wedded to the prejudices of its earlier experience. If India wants to be heard, if it wants to strike out independently for charting a course that propels the world away from confrontation and the growing spiral of violence, it must adopt as a nation the values that enriched India in the past and continue to enrich mankind wherever those values take root. Simply put, those values relate to non-violence and self-abnegation. The aspect of non-violence has already been touched upon. The point at issue now is, as to whether self-abnegation or self-denial, the greatest of human virtues in an individual, can be extended to a nation. If the course of the history of violence since the last century, added to the proliferation of weapons of mass destruction is taken as a guide, the answer must be in the affirmative. There does not seem to be any other way. India is ideally positioned to take the lead. It must continue to make economic progress and strengthen itself internally and externally. However, having achieved these goals, it should deny itself a position at the top table. It should not hanker after a permanent seat in the United Nations Security Council, as that body is presently structured. India should categorically state that it remains anchored to the aspiration of all third world countries that are looking to change the lot of their people; be they mired in backwardness and poverty because they were the victims of exploitation in the colonial era, or on account of mis-governance. Having been a part of the third world, India must seek a collective betterment for all the nations who comprise the vast collectivity known as the developing nations. Either they all benefit from the new dispensation, even if it were to be so incrementally, over a given period of time, or they collectively hold out for a more just world order. India must assure them that it will not desert them, no matter how tempting the offers from the rich man's club. In reshaping the idea of India, the individual and national identity must aspire to march together for a better self and a better world.

When picking up a daily newspaper at random in any of the metropolitan cities, on any given day, the impression is likely to remain that India is an aggregation of dissonances.

The images that flicker across the reader's perceptual frame could include: unity in diversity in juxtaposition to increasing disunity - the more the diversity, the greater the disunity; national integration opposed by national dis-aggregation; cultural plurality yielding place to cultural segregation; multi-ethnicities leading to multitudinous divisions; and now at the beginning of the new century, the overarching intrusion of capitalism in full cry, which in developing countries like India translates into the accentuation of the divide between the haves and have-nots. It hardly needs to be stressed that for India to move ahead, it needs to rededicate itself to the ideas of social justice, equality, fraternity, individual liberty and human dignity that were so well set out in the preamble to the Constitution of India.

People who gather together to talk about the Idea of India or write about it, wherever they might happen to be, have to think about providing a set of guidelines, if not answers, for the new generation growing up at the beginning of the 21st century to shape the future of India. The questions that they would be grappling with would include, *inter alia*:

- How much has the globe impinged on India?
- How much is India impacting the world?
- What do the young people of India want?
- What questions are they posing?
- What is our response?
- **Do we have** a response (to their questions)?
- When we write about these matters or articulate them in different forums, in India and abroad, whom are we targeting?
- What audience is it actually reaching?
- In the land of tolerance, isn't it strange that discussion on tolerance has become one of the hottest issues?
- Role models. Who are they?
- Who or what represents the essence of India?
- For whom?
- India's conscience. Who are its minders and keepers?
- Do we really need minders and keepers?

Whatever the transformation in recent years and regardless of the polarization between religions and ethnic divides that is taking place, humaneness as the deeper instinct prevails more in Indian society than in many other societies. For example, the type of mass exterminations which were carried out during the Muslim invasions in many parts of Asia and during the era of the Christian colonization of the world, have never been attributed to Indian expansionism. Even the atrocities attributed to Indian security forces pale in comparison when compared to the scale of the atrocities committed by the armed forces of other nations. Any number of examples can be given: Pakistan, in East Bengal, where the Pakistan army slaughtered three million people and raped half a million women, all of them Pakistani citizens, since East Bengal was still a province of Pakistan when these atrocities were committed; the US excesses in Vietnam; the Chinese excesses in Xinjiang and Tibet; and so on.

At the dawn of the new millennium after Christ, when one looks around, it becomes abundantly clear that the spiral of violence within societies, and between nations, has reached self-energizing momentum that might only be stilled by a cataclysmic event, the likes of which has not been witnessed before in human experience.

Between societies and groupings that cohere to form nations, the ideal situation that must be worked towards would be one where the need for primacy does not arise. Non-violence appears to be the antithesis of the global reality in today's world. Nevertheless, the concept of non-violence which can be deemed to be the most profound contribution that ancient Indian thought made to the world, must regain its primacy, within India and without, if human society is to continue to live in a civilized form. That the essential harmony of all sentient beings, indeed sentience itself, as put forward by Mahavira, Gautama Buddha and many others, was made the basis for India's freedom struggle by Mahatma Gandhi should not be looked at in isolation, as a mere reiteration of non-violence. By introducing the ancient precept into the mainstream of the anti-colonial struggle in India, Gandhi may have been looking well beyond to the universal projection of his innate belief in the virtue of non-violence as a survival imperative for humanity, just when scientific breakthroughs were on the verge of putting immensely destructive capabilities into the hands of mankind.

10

Beyond Selfishness

GURCHARAN DAS[1]

"This is the use of memory:
For liberation—not less of love but expanding
Of love beyond desire, and so liberation
From the future as well as the past."

—T.S. Eliot, "Little Gidding" III, *The Four Quartets*

This paper falls between business, religion and philosophy, and it is quite likely in the end to leave all the three constituencies dissatisfied.

Having said that, my ambition does not lack for modesty. Just as Max Weber, the great German sociologist, took a religious idea from Calvinism and sought to explain the development of northern Europe and the United States a hundred years, so do I plan to take an idea from an ancient Sanskrit text and examine if it might yield contemporary significance, specifically if it might help to strengthen our fragile institutions in the 21st century. Just as Max Weber sought to explain the motivation of the Protestant entrepreneur through the notion of secular asceticism, so will I enquire if this ancient concept might help the Indian entrepreneur and manager to gain competitive advantage in today's global economy.[2]

I shall examine today if the central moral insight from *the Bhagavad Gita*, the celebrated notion of *nishkama karma* or disinterested action— to act for the sake of the action and not for its fruit—might be useful in our uncertain contemporary world.[3] I shall enquire if a person can, in fact, act when she or he is not driven by personal reward. Can this ancient Indian ideal promote ethical action in our corporations? Can it motivate excellence in the workplace, especially teamwork, which is seriously lacking in India? How can it serve others—for example, generals and lovers?

I approached this project with some diffidence and even skepticism. I am used to thinking historically about texts and did not wish to be guilty of wounding an ancient text or of trying to snatch an insight out of context. But I have felt somewhat reassured by the theologian, Paul Recour. 'St Paul's letters were written for me', he says, and goes on to speak about the 'surplus of meaning' in some texts. The *Gita* is one of these, I think—it contains an 'excess of meaning' in Recour's words, which is why every generation in India seems to want to interpret it for its own times, and that process has been going on for two thousand years. I must also confess that I am driven by a deeply personal agenda. Having worked for thirty years in six countries as a practicing manager, I have long despaired over the lack of cohesion and poor quality of teamwork in our companies and other institutions, and even wrote about this national deficit in my book, *India Unbound*. Since *nishkama karma* diminishes the ego, I have wondered, might it help improve teamwork? It would be a great pay-off if this was possible and if one could find a way to make it happen.

White Noise

Over the past hundred years *Bhagavad Gita* has acquired the status of a national text[4] somewhat like Cervantes' *Don Quixote* in Spain, but in the process it has become white noise. By this I mean that it is part of the background din of our lives in India, quoted platitudinously, and masking rather than provoking thought. The *Gita* is honoured more than read, and understood less than recited. Technically, white noise like white light contains all the frequencies and is used to hide other sounds—the way one uses a fan sometimes to shut out the noise of traffic in order to sleep. In the same way the *Gita*'s presence is imperceptible yet comforting, like the random sounds of a Hindi film song in the *bazaar*.

Arguably, the *Mahabharata* (and not the *Vedas*) is at the very centre of Hinduism; embedded in the heart of the *Mahabharata* is the *Bhagavad Gita*; and *nishkama karma* is core idea of the *Bhagavad Gita*. Hence, this concept (expressed famously in verse 47 Book II[5]) might unlock our understanding of the *Gita*, of the epic, and eventually of Hinduism. The setting of the philosophical poem is the battlefield of Kurukshetra, not far from Delhi, as a great war is about to begin between the virtuous *Pandavas* and their evil cousins, the *Kauravas*, who have usurped their kingdom. Nearly all the royal families on the Indo-Gangetic plain are ranged on one side or the other in this 'mother of all wars', and the opening lines announce famously that this is no ordinary battlefield—it is also a moral field (*dharmakshetra*) between good and evil within each of us and the state of our minds.

Arjuna's Dilemma

As the battle is about to begin, Arjuna, the *Pandava* prince and commander in chief, stands at the head of his troops. As Arjuna is about to lift his bow something goes wrong, and he speaks to his charioteer. (In setting the stage for my argument, I ask your indulgence to actually read some verses from Books I and II, which I hope will also remind you of the fine quality of the poetry, as well as the excellence of Barbara Stoler Miller's translation[6]):

> Krishna,
>
> halt my chariot
>
> between the armies!
>
> Far enough for me to see
>
> these men who lust for war
>
> ready to fight with me
>
> in the strain of battle.   (1. 21-22)

After Arjuna spoke, Krishna halted their splendid chariot between the armies, and

> Arjuna saw them standing there:
>
> fathers, grandfathers, teachers,
>
> uncles, brothers, sons,
>
> grandsons and friends.   (1.26)

As he surveys the field full of his kinsmen who want war, Arjuna gets dejected and is filled with strange pity and says:

> My limbs sink,
>
> my mouth is parched,
>
> my body trembles,
>
> the hair bristles on my flesh.

> The magic bow[7] slips
> from my hand, my skin burns,
> I cannot stand still,
> my mind reels.   (1.29-30)

He sees no good in killing his kinsmen in battle. All of us empathise with his dilemma, certainly, but this is also rich poetry, and it reminded me of the Greek poet, Sappho, who expressed similar sentiments in a poem about jealousy. Arjuna sees so many on the enemy side are blameless, for whom he has great affection, and with whom he played when he was young. In the ensuing war he will have to kill as many of them as possible. How can it be right to kill the ones you love?

> Saying this in the time of war
> Arjuna slumped into the chariot
> and laid down his bows and arrows,
> His mind tormented by grief.   (1.47)

Arjuna had hitherto been of the war party; hence Krishna is dumbfounded at this sudden *volte-face*, as indeed Eisenhower's driver might have thought it strange if her boss—the driver, I am told, was a woman—had dithered on the eve of Normandy landings.

> Arjuna sat dejected,
> filled with pity,
> his sad eyes blurred by tears.
> Krishna gave him counsel.   (II.1)

> Seeing him thus, Krishna asks,
> Why this cowardice
> in time of crisis, Arjuna?
> The coward is ignoble, shameful,
> foreign to the ways of heaven[8].   (II.2)

And Arjuna replies,

> It is better in this world
> to beg for scraps of food
> than to eat meals smeared
> with the blood of elders[9]   (II.5)

'I shall not fight,'
[and] he fell silent.   (II.9)

Arjuna does not doubt that his cause is just, the war is necessary, and his side will win given the relative strengths, not least his own skills as a general and a soldier. To avoid killing so many that he holds in affection, he suggests that perhaps he ought to give up the kingdom as the lesser of two evils. Although its ostensible purpose is to persuade him to fight in 700 fratricidal verses, the poem is also about the deepest questions of human action, about time and the relationship of man and God.

Nishkama Karma

Krishna offers many reasons for fighting, some more persuasive than others, but his dominant refrain is to fight because it is his duty as a soldier and when he acts for the sake of the action rather than for personal reward, he will not only be doing the right thing, he will, in fact, be successful. He calls it *nishkama karma*. 'Nish' means 'without' in Sanskrit; '*kama*' is desire, '*karma*' is action'—literally, 'desireless or disinterested action'. Krishna also calls it '*nishphala karma*' or an action performed without thinking of the fruit of the action, and expresses it famously in the 47th verse of Book II:

Karmanyevadikaru aste
Ma phaleshu kadachana!

Be intent on action,
not on the fruits of action

And then he explains the philosophy of *karma yoga* as the way to get there:

Perform actions, firm in discipline,
relinquishing attachment;
be impartial to failure and success—
this equanimity is called discipline[10]   (II.48)

What should Arjuna do?

In a practical sense it is clear what Arjuna should do. Throwing away his arrows would achieve nothing; the war would still go on; and there might in fact be more killing on his side than if he did fight; moreover, his just cause would be lost. So, he should fight.

But this practical sort of reasoning, which thinks about the consequences of his acts and the costs and benefits involved does not really solve his moral dilemma, as the distinguished philosopher Martha Nussbaum has recently pointed out.[11] Arjuna must choose: he can either be a dutiful soldier, fight this righteous war (*dharmayuddha*) and rid the world of truly wicked people; but in the process he will kill his family members and friends. Or he can be a non-violent human being, save the lives of his family and kin, but lose the kingdom that rightfully belongs to him and his brothers, and worse, allow the forces of evil to prevail. He must choose between these two courses. It is a tragic dilemma (*dharmasankat*) because either choice is bad; both choices involve serious wrongdoing, and in that sense there seems to be no right answer. There is often no right answer in the *Mahabharata*.

Krishna points to Arjuna's duty to fight irrespective of the consequences. It is a just cause, and as a warrior and as a general, he must obey his duty and take up arms. Krishna's advice assumes that intent matters more than consequences in judging the morality of an act, and he suggests the single-minded pursuit of duty without any thought for the unpleasant consequences, somewhat in the way the Stoics might have advised—to pay attention to motives in judging moral worth.

Nishkama karma was an innovative and a revolutionary idea in its time because it created obligation without reference to the consequences of the action. Till then, Indian ethics had been under the sway of the notion of *karma*, which of course is driven by consequences. You do good deeds because you will reap the rewards of your good actions; you don't do wrong because you will be punished in this or the next life.

Arjuna's position, on the other hand, is based precisely on thinking about the consequences of his actions, not unlike the Utilitarians, who judged moral worth based on the greatest good for the greatest number.[12] This line of reasoning, as we well know in recent times, has been high-jacked by supporters of 'welfare', who have demanded that you judge the morality of an action by its utility (as measured by its ability to produce happiness or fulfil desires), even though the act might be nasty or violate someone's personal liberty.

Who is right, Arjuna or Krishna?

Certainly, in the poem Krishna succeeds in persuading Arjuna and wins the argument. Whenever I have asked this question of Indian military leaders, their response uniformly is, 'Quite right, Arjuna should realize where his duty lies and he ought to get on with it without this fuss. We don't want officers to agonize self-indulgently; it's harmful and it weakens the resolve of the troops.' Historically, people in India have tended to identify with Krishna's position (not least because he is God) and the *Gita* has become one of the most influential texts in the history of philosophy. Even Mahatma Gandhi, the great apostle of non-violence in the 20th century, felt inspired by Krishna's words, even though Arjuna's duty is to fight and kill in a violent war. The poet, T.S. Eliot, also seemed to endorse Krishna's high deontological position in *the Four Quartets*, when he wrote in 'The Dry Salvages':

> And do not think of the fruit of action.
> Fare forward...
> So Krishna, as when he admonished Arjuna
> On the field of battle.
> Not fare well,
> But fare forward, voyagers.[13]

Arjuna too has a strong case, and some would argue that in many ways he is a better model of ethical deliberation than Krishna for he takes responsibility for the consequences of his actions and this ought to have moral value. In an insightful paper, Amartya Sen, the Nobel Prize winner, argues that 'Arjuna is bothered not merely by the fact that many will die if war were to take place, but also by the fact that he himself will be killing lots of people and by the further fact that many of the people to be killed are persons for whom he himself has affection.... Another observer who is uninvolved in these events need not attach any special importance to the fact that Arjuna (not he, but Arjuna) will be killing people, and that among the dead will be people for whom Arjuna (not he, but Arjuna) feels closeness and affection. Arjuna cannot reasonably take a similarly detached view of the consequences of his choice.'[14] Sen's position of agent sensitive evaluation is in contrast to the utilitarian formula that the evaluation must be independent of the evaluator; he believes that moral responsibility demands situated valuation by agents.

Martha Nussbaum also applauds Arjuna for being aware that his action is immoral. 'The recognition that one has "dirty hands" is not just self-indulgence: it has significance for future actions,' she says. 'It informs the chooser that he may owe reparations to the vanquished....When the recognition is public, it constitutes an acknowledgement of moral culpability'[15], about which, for example, Michael Walzer has written extensively in connection with Hiroshima. Nussbaum adds that a failure to recognize moral ties, as Sartre's Orestes does, and as many existentialists do, undeterred by remorse for the wrong they have done, is not the way that we would wish our soldiers, politicians, or ourselves to behave. Arjuna's tragic dilemma teaches us that moral choices are not merely private, but should be deliberated in public, and a sense of tragedy should inform decent moral human beings. 'We all know too many people who think that if they wring their hands enough they can do anything they like....[By raising this question], Arjuna has learned something about the difference between self-interest and moral commitment.'[16]

But What is my Duty?

G.W.F. Hegel, the German philosopher, tried to make sense of what *nishkama karma* might mean in two famous articles on the *Bhagavad Gita* in 1827. He wrote them as reviews of lectures delivered by Wilhelm von Humboldt in Berlin, who became upset thinking that they were personal attacks on him. While Hegel recognised in 'the moral obligation to do the good for the sake of the good only and duty only for duty's sake', he had a number of objections.[17] He thought that while this is 'great moral intention', there is the practical problem, 'namely to know what aim [the] action is to strive after, what duties it must fulfil or must respect.' especially if the action one is asked to perform is arbitrary. He added, however, that this is not merely a difficulty with this Indian notion, but it is generally a problem with contemporary European moral philosophy, especially that of Immanuel Kant—*nishkama karma* does not 'lead to anything, and from itself there cannot result any moral duties'.[18]

This objection is well founded. The problem is not so much that Krishna does not specify the agent's duties, but that the moral law of acting disinterestedly might result in immoral actions, such as killing one's kinsmen as we have just seen. To many, especially to pacifists, none of Krishna's answers to Arjuna's dilemma are morally satisfying, including his case for a just war. The principle of disinterested action might lead one to kill in a disinterested manner or be an '*nkk* serial killer'. In this sense Hegel is right: *nkk* as a moral principle does not provide content for my action or my duty.

Such problems beset other deontological theories, especially Kant's, who, for example, has been criticized on the grounds that being compelled to tell the truth (as a duty) to a murderer might force one to tell him where his potential victim is hiding. Ignoring the consequences is strength and weakness of deontological ethics, and because one does not look to consequences, it is possible that morally unacceptable consequences could result in extreme cases. However, if one removes the extreme cases, I think, *nishkama karma*, like other duty oriented ethics, might serve as a useful principle based on our normal intuitions of right and wrong, and it can guide our commonsense behaviour and judgment of moral worth. Acting unselfishly should normally result in doing the right thing, which is why I find that this principle resonates with 'mentally tough' business executives.[19]

The author of the *Gita* might defend himself against Hegel's objection by saying that he has specified at least 25 virtues, and although they might sound in the raw like a boy scout's creed, it is precisely their absolute nature that attracts millions to this text.[20] Secondly, the *Gita*'s author would argue that the human being is filled with desires and inclinations pressing for fulfillment and satisfaction. These desires are the product of three *gunas* or natural qualities within us, and the balance struck by them determines how we happen to act. A virtuous person has more of the higher and less of the lower *guna*, and the *dharma* texts offer detailed prescriptions on how to raise the balance.

These natural *gunas* are, in some ways, similar to Kant's inclinations and impulses generated in us by our bodily wants and needs as well as our socialized processes of learning and education. The principle of *nishkama karma* is meant to act as a constraint on our natural inclinations as defined by the *gunas*, in much the same manner as Kant's good will. As a constraint, it also creates a moral obligation and duty for all human beings. Just as Kant's good will is a will that acts from duty and not from inclination, and actions done from duty have moral worth,[21] so an action motivated by *nishkama* is done out of duty and can be said to have moral worth, irrespective of consequences.

Its historic influence on Indian society

I have dragged in poor Kant and Hegel into this discussion not for pedantic reasons but because I genuinely believe that moral philosophers can help us to better understand *nishkama karma*, especially when applying it as an actionable moral concept in the contemporary world. This then has been a preliminary sketch of the direction that my work is taking with regard to the normative side of this concept. Clearly much more needs to be done. I shall now briefly note the historic influence of this concept on Indian society, and then move onto *nishkama karma*'s performative role.

When defending the importance of action and of right action the author of the *Gita* treads a fine balance between the two reigning ideologies of his time, neither of which he seemed to like particularly but nor was willing to alienate. He strikes a fine balance of political correctness between the overzealous advocates of Vedic ritualism on the one hand and the heterodox renouncers and ascetics of Buddhism, Jainism, who believed that all acts in this world should be given up so as to avoid accumulating *karma*. The *Gita* says that one cannot help but act, but if one performs the action in the right attitude of *nishkama karma* then it will not accumulate *karma* and not result in rebirth. Thus, one does not have to renounce the world. In this revolutionary way the *Gita* makes action possible in the world.

At the same time, the text is conservative and it upholds the prevailing norms of social action, stating clearly that Arjuna's duty is to act according to his *swadharma*, his caste duty as a *kshatriya*. However, it soon undercuts the caste system by another revolutionary move—it offers the democratic path of *bhakti* or devotion, which is open to all irrespective of caste. And by the end of the poem it expresses a clear preference for the path of *bhakti* in comparison to the paths to action and knowledge. In this way, it goes around both the powerful brahminical forces supporting the stratified social order, as well as the strong pull exerted by the renouncers of the new religions, without overtly criticizing them.

Indians have always been fascinated by the renouncer (*sannyasi*), who stands tall and splendid, a theatrical figure in ochre robes. In a famous essay Louis Dumont wrote, 'the secret of Hinduism may be found in the dialogue between the renouncer and the man-in-the-world [*grihasti*]'[22] This ideal took a mesmerizing hold on the ordinary householder with the advent of Buddhism and Jainism, so much so that the *Manusmriti* had to forbid men to become renouncers until they had successfully fulfilled the previous three stages of life and discharged their debt to secular society.[23] To the humble householder *nishkama karma* offered a way to combine the best of both worlds—to live in the world but with the attitude of the renouncer. It told him that he could live authentically if he remained detached and self-possessed in the midst of worldly activity. It taught him how to live in the world: not to become a slave of worldly activity but live the life of self-discipline, avoiding the extremes of indulgence and asceticism.

Thus, *nishkama karma* gave new meaning to the ordered life of day to day action of the ordinary householder, who has to make a living, look after his family, live as a citizen in society, be a good friend and neighbour, discharge his caste responsibilities, and prepare for the next stage of his life. To him the *Gita* offered the solution of stoically living life by acting selflessly, acting for its own sake, and in the process it devalued the attractions of the rituals of the Brahmins and of the ascetic life of renunciation. It offered the ideal of a 'secular ascetic'.

Later, our medieval protestant movements took up this theme with gusto. They extolled the virtues of disciplined domesticity in the good life. Basava (c. 1125-1170), the founder of the Lingayat movement in the south, Nanak (1469-1538), the first of the Sikh gurus in the north, Vallabha (1479-1531) in the west, and Chaitanya (1485-1534), the popular mystic in the east were uniformly eulogistic of the householder's domestic, conjugal state and argued against renunciation.[24]

These medieval sects also embraced vigorously the *Gita*'s other big idea, that of *bhakti* and the possibility of direct experience of God through love and surrender.[25] They taught that the spirit of egolessness and disinterest of *nishkama karma* is better inculcated when one seeks refuge in the deity and is deeply devoted to it. This is also Krishna's message to Arjuna at the end of the *Gita*; Mahatma Gandhi believed the same—to act in an unmotivated, disciplined manner of *karma yoga*, he felt, one needed *bhakti*'s spirit of devotion and surrender.[26]

Thank God, it is Friday!

Being a practical sort of fellow, I should like to examine if *nishkama karma* has the potential to be a motivator of day-to-day human action, to promote excellence, and improve performance in the workplace. I shall relate it to my own experience in the managerial world. I shall examine the psychological conditions that make possible high performance in organizations in the same way that Max Weber explored the psychological conditions that motivated the Protestant entrepreneur (and made possible the development of capitalist civilization). My premise is that even if one does not believe in rebirth or in God, this notion can be a useful and attractive principle—as a way to freedom from human bondage based on the wonderful potential for perfection of ordinary human beings.

The truth is that most people hate their jobs and are bored at work. 'Thank God it's Friday' is a ubiquitous feature of modern work life, both in the West and in urban India. Work is seen as the unpleasant price that one pays in order to earn weekends and holidays, which are meant to be the main determinants of human happiness. Only a few seem to actually enjoy work, and most people when they retire end up feeling that their work lives have been wasted. Jack Nicholson recently portrayed this feeling poignantly in the film, *About Schmidt*. This is also why CEOs are constantly seeking after training programs to motivate their employees.

My other premise is the old Buddhist idea that the 'self' usually produces harmful thoughts of 'me and mine', selfish desires, craving, attachment, hatred, ill-will, conceit, pride, egotism, and many other problems, as we all know. It is also the source of much trouble in the world from personal conflicts to wars between nations. In our daily work life it often comes in the way of performance. Instead of focusing on the job, we get easily distracted and find it difficult to get absorbed. Hence, we brood and mostly about ourselves. Our thoughts stray too often to the size of our desk or to our room in comparison to our neighbour's, or 'why did I get smaller annual raise than Ravi'. Not only does this create negative energy but also boredom. When I was a middle manager a colleague of mine spent three miserable years ruminating over why his room was two inches smaller than mine, for it meant the terrible fate of being denied a sofa and appearing less considerable in the eyes of the world.

'Your work will succeed as long as you don't care who gets the credit'

Can the central insight of *nishkama karma*—not to act for the fruit of an action but for the sake of the action—help to make our work life more meaningful? What does it means in a practical sense to act in this way? What sort of action is it where the 'self' disappears? My own reaction is that when you remove the self out of the equation, you are left with the activity alone, and to be driven by the activity is to be driven by the excellence of the activity—a sort of Aristotelian take,[27] inimitably expressed by Harry Truman, the American president in a folksy way: 'your work will succeed as long as you don't care who gets the credit.'

Nishkama karma might teach us that the meaning in our lives comes from absorbing ourselves so deeply in the microcosm of our work that we forget ourselves, such that even the difference between subject and object disappears. We have all experienced this psychological state. When we are absorbed in an activity, our ego seems to disappear and time seems to get distorted. We find ourselves saying, 'It's already six o'clock. I thought it was three.' Our 'self' had disappeared for those three hours. We emerge from this state of selflessness feeling positive, a sense of having been in control of our life, of being masters of our fate. Donald Hall, the American poet says that Henry Moore, the sculptor, was perpetually in this state and his wife had to drag him home from his studio at midnight because he had forgotten lunch, dinner, and to send bills to his customers. Einstein was the same—when he died, they discovered lots of cheques that he had just forgotten to deposit. Athletes call this feeling as 'being in the zone'. Not only famous people, but my carpenter in Bombay used to be constantly in this state.

A number of psychologists have tried to describe this state of selfless absorption in the job. Maslow described such a person as 'problem centred rather than ego-centred' and he placed her at the stage of 'self-actualisation'[28] in an ascending hierarchy of human needs; his faith in the perfectibility of human beings fifty years ago brought a healthy antidote to the depressive determinism of Freud and B.F. Skinner. Chiksentmihaly calls it 'flow' or optimal experience, which he describes as 'something that we make happen' rather than something that happens to us, such as a passive moment of relaxed pleasure. It is 'when a person's body or mind is stretched to its limits in a voluntary effort to accomplish something difficult and worthwhile.'[29] David McClelland described such motivated persons as being more concerned with the job's achievement than the rewards of success, either money or praise. Money was only valuable as a measure of their performance, and the main claim to their attention was how to do the job better.[30]

David Reisman's old distinction between the inner and outer directed is also useful[31] in understanding this attitude. When we are outer-directed, we tend to be less in control of our feelings and our actions, and others set the standard or mark the card for us. We are judged. When inner driven we tend to set our own tasks and standards and when these are achieved we have a feeling of being empowered. It doesn't matter what others think; one happily ignores them. We can easily imagine artists and scientists as inner-directed, but can the ordinary person on the job act with a self-forgetting attitude? Can the distribution manager in the company, for example, behave in this manner? Can the employee of Northern Railways pick up the phone on the second ring rather than the fifteenth? In short, can we create conditions at the work place that will elicit this sort of response?

How to create conditions for self-forgetting behaviour?

I have found that in small, entrepreneurial start-ups it is more common to find this self-forgetting behavior. The reason is that there is a family feeling in the company and there is greater sense of ownership. Even in large companies where the leader delegates authority to the lowest practical level, employees tend to feel a sense of autonomy and this improves motivation and promotes selfless behavior. Employees seem to feel more valued and work towards goals rather than tasks. Studies suggest that when 'one feels in charge over even the smallest decision or detail', it tends to improve one's performance. Another condition for fostering *nishkama karma*, I expect, is trust and fairness. Where people trust each other and where they perceive a level of fairness in the organization's dealings within and without, they are likely to behave less selfishly.

In the end, I do not think people in any number will act outside of their own interests, and the art is to shape those interests in order to encourage unselfish behaviour. In the early nineties when Procter and Gamble, was vigorously becoming a global company, I recall that we found ourselves with operations in 58 countries, but our managers continued to be inward looking and behaved as though we existed in only one country—the country where they worked. In the larger subsidiaries they tended to be arrogant, suffered from the 'not invented here' disease, and were immune to learning from their peers elsewhere. Thus, we had the odd situation that 58 product managers in 58 countries were solving the same problems everyday.

To change this dreadful situation we embarked on a program called 'Search and Re-apply', which turned out to be so successful that in a few years it resulted in making Pantene, for example, the world's number one shampoo based on an advertising commercial that had been created in Taiwan. The behaviour change was so dramatic that managers stopped saying 'I did it', and instead began to say, 'I got this idea from Venezuela, and this is why I am successful'. Earlier, they might have said, 'Where is Venezuela?' This cultural change came about because top management began to reward unselfish behaviour or at least the appearance of it (not in terms of cash, but equally importantly through recognition, verbal strokes and brownie points). Narcissistic behaviour became unacceptable to the point that managers began to invent people to whom they could give credit for their own ideas. This is not an unusual thing in many large successful companies. Goldman Sachs, the famous investment bank, has been practising the most extraordinary levels of teamwork for generations, and it employs a relentless selection process wherein as many as thirty partners and associates will interview a new candidate in order to ensure his or her potential for unselfish teamwork.[32]

Does *nishkama karma* go against the capitalistic ethic?

There is rich irony in my ambition, I realize, to employ disinterest in the cause of the most self-interested institution in society, the private corporation. On the surface, *nishkama karma* would seem to go against the capitalist profit motive, and would appear to be hopelessly utopian, somewhat like socialism. In fact, it is not, if it is viewed as a motivational tool and not a replacement for material incentives, somewhat in the way of Abraham Maslow's framework of the hierarchy of needs, which has consistently resonated in the business world. Reading Maslow I was struck by the similarity between his 'peak experience' and this ancient Indian prescription. Enthusiasts of Ayn Rand, an unabashed apologist of capitalism, might recall that her protagonist in the *Fountainhead* did not want to put his name on the building; he was not driven by the desire for fame but rather by excellence in architecture. Similarly, I recall a number of senior managers in Procter and Gamble, who quietly and anonymously mentored dozens of younger managers through their long careers with no obvious rewards to themselves.

I have concluded over the years that there is a natural distribution of talent as well as of attitude. A group of persons (say, the top ten per cent) will perform in almost any society regardless; they are already motivated and they seem to be able to easily transfer their egos to the task and away from themselves. (It is somewhat ironic, I think, that American corporations think it necessary to shower excessive stock options on them—for they are precisely the ones who will perform without them).[33] Equally, another group at the bottom will fail to perform regardless. Where an attitude and behaviour change through *karma yoga* might be successful is amongst the vast majority in the middle, especially those on the margin of higher performance. If one could get, say the next ten to fifteen per cent from the top, to change there could be a huge pay-off to society.

Nasty Capitalist Myths

The focus of my paper is the individual and not society, but since I seek to apply it to capitalist society, I should like to briefly dwell on some recent changes within it. Capitalism is much misunderstood and much reviled, and it seems to put everyone on the defensive; hence, one of our defence mechanisms is to use euphemisms like "the market" to describe it. The governance scandals involving Enron[34], WorldCom, Arthur Anderson and others have confirmed to its detractors its evil nature. Even though I am not one of them, I have been deeply concerned with some nasty myths that have taken hold inside the corporation in the past 15 years, and about which Henry Mintzberg and others have recently written, and which might explain its recent failings.[35]

The first myth is that since we are all self-interested human beings, intent on maximizing personal gain, our only duty is to the bottom line, implying that everything goes and everyone has a price as long one stays within the narrow limits of the law. This myth ignores that a company exists in a social space and that man is a social animal, as Aristotle reminded us more than two thousand years ago, and integrity, self-respect and cooperation have been equally important values to the system's success. Leaders of the enduring companies have always known this and tempered dogmatic individualism with social engagement as a form of enlightened self-interest.

I have found that the lives of many successful entrepreneurs and senior managers are characterized by an ethic of ceaseless work combined with a ceaseless renunciation of the fruits of their toil. They work so hard that they have no time to enjoy their money. Aditya Birla, JRD and Ratan Tata, Azim Premji, Narayana Murthy — the more successful they became, the more they tend to live frugally. Max Weber had called this behaviour 'secular asceticism', and had used it to define the outlook of Protestant entrepreneurs, but it might easily characterise most outstanding business persons (and lawyers, doctors, artists, scientists.) Hence, the spirit that took hold in the nineties on Wall Street and in the dotcom world was pathological, and for the critics to characterise the system as synonymous with greed and selfishness is wrong.

Another myth is the notion that the corporation exists only to maximize shareholder value and the claims of other stakeholders in society — customers, employees, suppliers, and the community at large — are subordinate. Again, enduring companies have always believed that shareholders must receive a good return, but they are able to balance shareholder expectations with those of other constituencies. Successful companies know that they exist because of their customers; they don't serve customers by serving themselves, but serve themselves by serving their customers, and the more selflessly they do it the more successful their enterprise becomes.

Another fabrication is that the chief executive is the enterprise and must be rewarded disproportionately. This explains why CEO pay in the U.S. rose 570 per cent in the decade of 1990s, while profits rose 114 per cent and average worker salary went up 37 per cent.[36] Leadership is obviously important, but enduring companies understand that good leaders are often more quiet than heroic; they foster teamwork, work towards smooth succession and getting the best out of all employees. As the German playwright, Bertolt Brecht, aptly put it, "Unhappy is the land that needs heroes."[37]

These myths are seductive partly because they do contain a kernel of truth; but in the end they are half-truths. The governance failures of the past two years have highlighted the excesses that resulted from glorifying self-interest in the decade of the nineties, and that is why only 34 per cent of employees worldwide feel a sense of loyalty to their employers according to a recent study, and only 47 per cent view the leaders of their companies in the United States as persons of high integrity.[38] With the present churning in the system, I expect we will enact laws in many countries which better align the interests of producers and citizens and the balance in the system will right itself over time, as it usually does. But it will take an effort to do so and it will not happen on its own. In the end, I expect the old truth will re-emerge — that capitalism, like democracy, is by no means perfect, but it is better than any of the alternatives. There is a healthy search for model of behaviour within the capitalist system, and I wonder if *nishkama karma* might be able to contribute in this vacuum?

The governance failures in America have wounded the social myth that defines the moral terrain of corporate life everywhere. Given our deep suspicion of capitalism, we have had equally deleterious fallout in India. This social myth is, of course, Max Weber's 'secular asceticism' — an ethic of ceaseless work combined with a ceaseless renunciation of the fruits of one's toil — which I have already alluded to, but it is significant that this myth justifies the inequalities that follow the accumulation of wealth. Despite pervasive consumerism, this bourgeois ethic, I believe, continues to provide the foundations of capitalism. In this context my preliminary empirical work with business executives is significant. It suggests that *nishkama karma*, despite its limitations, might offer an answer to today's managers and is not intuitively inconsistent with the contemporary moral sensibility. Equally, Indian managers have found that this ancient ideal offers the possibility for improved cohesion, teamwork and for creating a high performance organisation. Much more empirical work, however, needs to be done on both counts. And even if one can succeeds in convincing executives that this is a robust and useful concept, the question remains in their practical minds, how to inculcate this attitude and behaviour, how become a *nishkarmi*.

Generals and Lovers

In concluding, I want to briefly point out that *nishkama karma* has obvious broader implications. It is the way to live one's life and in India for centuries it has been seen primarily as a way to spiritual enlightenment. If I do decide to pursue this, I should like to dwell upon and develop the varied applications of this notion for the contemporary secular world. In a light hearted moment I had thought of calling my paper, *Nishkama Karma: The Indian art of business, war, and love,* because I believed that it could also serve as guide for generals and lovers as well. Arjuna is, after all, a soldier, and as we sit here as spectators in the aftermath of this bizarre war with Iraq, I think Arjuna's moral dilemma might help inform the judgment of many thoughtful soldiers.

Similarly, *Nishkama Karma* might compete successfully with the *Kamasutra*, the famous ancient Indian self-help textbook of erotic love. I believe it can serve lovers because love essentially entails giving rather than taking and in that orgasmic moment the self does tend to disappear.

T.S. Eliot compared the *Gita* to the *Divine Comedy* in its greatness as a philosophical poem. In 'Little Gidding' in the *Four Quartets* he expressed the same notion of love beyond desire, and he saw in it the possibility of liberation from the future and the past:

> This is the use of memory:
> For liberation—not less of love but expanding
> Of love beyond desire, and so liberation
> From the future as well as the past.

In *nishkama karma* Eliot seemed to find the answer to the riddle of life and death and time. He agreed with Krishna that striving after an illusory and imaginary future was futile and could even be destructive. One must learn to live in the present like a *nishkarmi*, which was an attitude consistent with the existential ethic that became popular in

Eliot's time after the collapse of the Enlightenment project and the despair brought on by the absurd First World War. Hence, he advises one to act with the mind fixed not on the fruits (future) but on the pleasure one gets in performing the activity, in being alive and vital in the present. In the following, he imagines Krishna telling Arjuna:

> 'At the moment which is not of action or inaction
>
> You can receive this: "on whatever sphere of being
>
> The mind of a man may be intent
>
> At the time of death" – that is the one action
>
> (And the time of death is every moment)
>
> Which shall fructify the lives of others:
>
> And do not think of the fruit of action.[39]

Notes

1   This paper represents work in progress, rather than a finished product.

2   This project was born in October last year when I met a dozen senior corporate executives of a Fortune 500 company in a two-day meeting in Chicago, and I could not help but sense a palpable tension in the air, which was unusual for this affable group. In the evening one of them opened up and took me into confidence. He explained that the cause of the anxiety was that the auditors had found a problem, and when confronted, their CEO had lied to the auditors. The problem itself was minor, but the lie had compounded it. He was afraid that something terrible might happen to his company, and he emotionally asked me what he should do. I felt sympathy for his situation. I had not realized till then how much devastation had been wrought to the morale of the American manager by the governance scandals involving Enron, WorldCom, Arthur Anderssen and others. Later, over dinner, we began to discuss in a larger group, oddly enough, the *Bhagavad Gita*, the two thousand year old philosophical poem that I happened to be reading at the time. I am not sure how we got onto the subject but somewhat to my surprise these hard-nosed managers showed serious interest in *Gita*'s concept of *nishkama karma* or disinterested action, and they tried to imagine how one might behave when one is not driven by personal reward, and if this might happen in corporate life. By the end of the evening, they seemed convinced that if managers were to behave in this way, they would not only do the right thing (and 'we wouldn't have these scandals') but the quality of their work would improve. This Socratic dialogue gave me the confidence to pursue this line of thinking. This is how this project was born, believe it or not.

3   Traditionally, *nishkama karma* is regarded as a way to spiritual enlightenment and to freedom from bondage imposed by the law of *karma*, and in the way *karma* determines mundane happiness, suffering and repeated births and deaths. It is one of most celebrated ideas in Indian religion and philosophy and there is a long tradition of interpreting it over the centuries to suit different purposes. The brilliant Shankara offered an influential Advaita Vedanta reading; Ramanuja had an attractive 'modified non-dualist' interpretation, closer to the *bhakti* spirit of the *Gita*. The generation that struggled for freedom in the early 20th century had first Tilak's rendering, then Mahatma Gandhi's, both of who employed it to rally people for the purposes of Independence. In the same spirit I shall explore if this idea has relevance for our dispirited post-Nehru, post-Mandal, post-reform, post-modern times. Having said that, I believe, David Seyfort Ruegg's warning to the historian of ideas should be borne in mind: 'beware of anachronistically transposing the unsystematically imposing concepts of modern semantics and philosophy, which have originated in the course of particular historical developments, on modes of thought that evolved in quite different historical

circumstances and which have therefore to be interpreted in the first place in the context of their own concerns and ideas they themselves developed.' ('Does the Madhyamika have a thesis and philosophical position?' in B.K. Matilal and R.D. Evans eds, *Buddhist Logic and Epistemology*, Dordrecht Kluwer, 1986, p.236).

4   Some nations, it seems to me, have a national text that gives form to their national character and provides a clue to understanding them. Spain had *Don Quixote* by Cervantes; Italy had Dante's *Divine Comedy*; ancient Greece had the *Iliad*. America has Mark Twain's *Huckleberry Finn*. In the same why, I think, India has the *Bhagavad Gita*.

5   This is the *shloka* that begins *"karmyanevadhikara aste ma phaleshu..."* – editors.

6   Since I have only rudimentary knowledge of Sanskrit, I looked for a good English translation, but soon discovered that there were more than thirty translations to choose from, and like the Pandavan hero of the *Gita*, I became confused. So I spoke to scholars, talked to friends, visited libraries and dipped into different versions to help me make up my mind. An article by Gerald Larson, 'The song celestial: two centuries of the Bhagavadgita in English.' also guided me. Vedanta enthusiasts directed me to the slim Isherwood-Prabhavananda translation, which has an introduction by Aldous Huxley on perennial philosophy. While I thought it satisfying as literature—after all Christopher Isherwood is a great writer—I felt it was not the most accurate, and its interpretation was a de-ethnicised Shankara combined with western mysticism. Radhakrishnan's rendition I found to be dull and commentarial. Indologists recommended Zaehner, and although his translation turned out to be stilted, his wonderful discussions on Ramanuja, Shankara and the *Upanishads* that run parallel in the text make it quite exciting. Although an accomplished orientalist, Zaehner was clearly attracted to the notion of the love of a personal god. The most poetic is still the Victorian version of Sir Edwin Arnold, and it has the virtue of being the cheapest in the Dover thrift edition. Those seeking pure accuracy should read either Edgerton's translation or Van Buitenen's, who views the *Gita* as an integral part of the epic and challenges the traditional idea that it was inserted later. Don't trust Mascaro's version, which tries unsuccessfully to be poetic. Bhaktivedanta's rendition is a dull, sectarian, Sunday school textbook, reflecting the Vaishnavite values of Chaitanya. Since I am a beginner in Sanskrit, I found Winthrop Sargeant's very useful (but expensive); it is accompanied by an interlinear Sanskrit text, a word for word grammatical commentary and vocabulary. In the end, I chose Barbara Stoler Miller's translation because it is both accurate, poetical, and has the great virtue of simplicity. Before she died in 1993, she was professor of Sanskrit at Barnard/Columbia and she created the translation for our generation. Through this process of selecting I have come to realize that there is no right or wrong translation and each one serves its particular audience. Van Buitenen's version is no good to a follower of Sai Baba, as Arnold's account will not interest a Sanskritist. Mahatma Gandhi's or Tilak's use of the *Gita* in our freedom struggle is as valid as Edgerton's reading of the text as a Vaishnava Brahmin document of the 1st c. AD. Emerson and Thoreau used Wilkins translation. Hegel used Humboldt's (and Schlegal and Wilkins). Gandhi used Sir Edwin Arnold's, while post-Independence Indians turned to Radhakrishnan's. The translation for our generation is that of Barbara Stoler Miller, and I shall quote from it in this paper.

7   The Sanskrit doesn't say magic bow – it uses the name Gandiva – editors.

8   In addition, action undeserving of an *arya* – editors.

9   Teachers rather than elders – editors.

10 This is called *yoga*   "discipline" doesn't have the same nuance – editors.

11 Martha Nussbaum, "The Costs of Tragedy: Some Moral Limits of Cost-Benefit Analysis", *Journal of Legal Studies*, vol. XXIX (2) Pt.2, June 2000, pp (1005-1036).

12 "Consequentialism is the theory that the way to tell whether a particular choice is the right choice for an agent to have made is to look at the relevant consequences of the decision; to look at the relevant effects of the decision on the world," as Philip Pettit tells us in his fine collection of essays called, *Consequentialism* (Aldershot: Dartmouth, 1993, p.xiii).

13 T.S. Eliot, *Four Quartets*, London: Faber and Faber, 1944, p 31.

14   Amartya Sen, 'Consequential Evaluation and Practical Reason', *The Journal of Philosophy*, vol. XCVI, no. 9, September 2000, p 485.

15   Nussbaum 2000, p.1009.

16   Nussbaum 2000, p.1011.

17   G.W.F. Hegel, *On the Episode of the Mahabharata known by the name Bhagavad-Gita* by Wilhelm von Humboldt, Berlin 1826, Edited and translated by Herbert Herring, Indian Council of Philosophical Research, New Delhi, 1995. Hegel's first objection is what 'such indifference towards the result' might mean? He wonders 'if the result will be satisfactory without engaging the concrete individuality of the agent and the intensity of his will power for achieving the goal.' (p.13) The author of the *Manusmriti* had the same problem. 'Acting out of desire is not approved of, but here on earth there is no such thing as no desire; for even studying the Veda and engaging in the rituals enjoined in the Veda are based upon desire. Desire is the very root of the conception of a definite intention...for each and everything that he does is motivated by the desire for precisely that thing.' (*The Laws of Manu*, trans. Wendy Doniger with Brian K. Smith, London: Penguin Books, 1991, 2.2-4, p 17). Hegel's (and Manu's) objection might apply to the more extreme Buddhist interpretations of *nkk* (*nekkhamma* in Pali), where the agent is expected to eliminate the 'desire for desire', but how could Krishna mean to imply that the agent must totally eliminate desire or will power when he wants Arjuna to go out and fight? Rather, I think, he means to appeal to our common sense idea of disinterested or selfless behaviour. We have all known people to act in that way, including ourselves at times. Hegel's second objection is that 'to act means nothing else than to achieving some purpose; one acts to achieve something, some result. The realization of the purpose is a success; that the action is successful gives some satisfaction, a fruit inseparable from the performed action' (Hegel 1995, p 47). Hence, he is dubious about Krishna's principle about remaining indifferent to the fruits of action. In fact, he says 'the more senselessly and stupidly an action is performed, the greater the involved indifference towards success.'(p.47) Certainly it is normal to feel satisfaction for a job well done, but Krishna's advice to act without attachment for the results does not preclude this sense of satisfaction for the disinterested person. The agent might feel a sense of satisfaction and still act in a disinterested manner. Hence, this objection of Hegel's is also unsustainable. However, his third objection is sound—see above in the text.

18   Hegel, 1995, p.15.

19   I have since exposed this idea to half a dozen groups of executives with the same positive result.

20   Book 16, verses 1-3 provide a list of these virtuous traits; verse 4 lists some demonic traits.

21   Immanuel Kant, *Groundwork of the Metaphysic of Morals*, trans. H.D. Paton, New York: Harper and Row, 1964, I: para11, 399; para 14, 399-400.

22   Louis Dumont, 1960, 'World renunciation in Indian religions', *Contributions to Indian Sociology*, 9: 67.

23   T.N. Madan makes this point in his superb book, *Non-Renunciation: Themes and Interpretations of Hindu Culture*, 1996, Delhi: Oxford University Press, p2. He cites P.V Kane, to suggest that such was the challenge that the *dharmashastra* texts began 'to glorify the status of an householder and push into the background the two *ashramas* of *vanaprastha* and *sannyasa*, so much so that they are forbidden in the Kali age.' (*History of Dharmashastra*, vol II, Part 1, Poona: Bhandakar Oriental Research Institute, 1941, p.424.) Kane adds that some *dharamashatra* writers looked upon the householder's life as the only [authentic] stage of life. (*Ibid.*, p.640). To T.N. Madan I also owe the dramatic description of the renouncer at the beginning of the paragraph ('Religion in India' in *Daedalus* vol.118, number 4, p.120).

24   *Ibid*, p.9.

25   II:47-54.

26   M.K. Gandhi, (commentary on the *Gita*).

27 Aristotle also conceived of happiness (*eudaimonia*) as emanating from action and the excellence (*arête*) that attaches to it. *Nicomachean Ethics* II.7.1177b26.

28 Abraham Maslow, 'A Theory of Human Motivation', *Psychological Review*, 50, 1943, pp 370-396.

29 Mihaly Csikszentmihalyi, *Flow: The Psychology of Optimal Experience*, New York: Harper and Row, 1990, p.3.

30 Austrian psychologist, Victor Frankl, expressed the same thought when discussing success, 'Don't aim at success—the more you aim at it and make it a target, the more you are going to miss it. For success, like happiness cannot be pursued; it must ensue...as the intended side effect of one's personal dedication to a course greater than oneself.' Victor Frankl, preface, *Man's Search for Meaning*.

31 David Reisman and Nathan Glazer, *The Lonely Crowd*.

32 One of my former colleagues at P&G reminds me that TQA (Total Quality Approach) was also a marvellously liberating concept when we first encountered it in some of our plants in the 1980s. It broke work down into measurable parts, and guided one to achieve what was really important for a successful outcome. Hence, one's effort was productive. It fixed individual responsibility and created measures for monitoring one's progress (and in a Japanese factory even displayed it for all to see!). Rather than being a tool to push workers, it gave workers the means for self-assessment without the intrusion of a "boss" who decided how they were doing. In effect, workers began to self manage, with pressure from peers for higher performance. The bad apples got better or got out, and ordinary people went on to do extraordinary things. Teamwork also improved as a result, but unions resisted its broad scale application both in America and in India. Right behaviour will not result from moral exhortations, but an improved structure can help to shift behaviour.

33 Rewards for most middle and senior corporate executives (whether stock options, salary or benefits) are valued by the recipients more on a relative (or competitive) basis than for the intrinsic value of the reward. I think this largely explains why the compensation of senior executives in the United States has reached such ridiculous levels. These executives, and the Board of Directors who reward them, pay far more attention to pay comparisons versus other executives then they to 'absolute pay as a reward for results'. This also explains, I think, why senior managers don't take time to enjoy their money. It is partly because money is a much less valued reward—what is far more important is winning the race against one's peers.

34 I have a more than an idle interest in the infamous Enron corporation, which we know too well has a power plant in India, and which since inception has been dogged by criticism and rumors of ugly pay-offs. During its early troubles in India I had defended Enron in my Sunday column in the *Times of India*, arguing that it would be stupid for it to make pay-offs in its most visible investment in Asia. I had argued that the Foreign Corrupt Practices Act (FCPA) of the U.S. Congress was a huge deterrent, and I cited my own experience. When I became CEO of the Indian subsidiary of Richardson Vicks, my boss in Wilton, Connecticut used to remind me every six months that he would support me on any business issue, but when it came to this, I would be sacked within 24 hours, and most likely I would go to jail. 'So, it's not worth your while', he said, and I passed the message down the line to all my managers. When I attended the Advanced Management Program at Harvard Business School in the early eighties I recall thinking that the FCPA is working because American executives, especially in the aircraft and similar industries that depended on orders from foreign governments, used to complain constantly that they were disadvantaged by the FCPA against their European counterparts. After I naively wrote my column in the *Times of India*, Kenneth Lay, the worldwide head of Enron, who was on a visit to India, invited me to meet him. He thanked me for my article, and informed me that they were thinking of setting up an Advisory Board and wanted me to consider joining it. Months went by, but for some reason they never did set it up, and thank God for it, for when the truth came out about Enron's governance failures in the U.S. and the company collapsed, I felt deeply wounded. Although they have still not found the smoking gun in the case of the Indian investment, and although Rebecca Mark, the head of the Indian company, walked away

in good time with $82 million, Kenneth Lay will probably go to jail. I have since wondered if *nishkama karma* might have deterred him. Might he have behaved differently if his mother or someone had taught this to him when he was young?

35 Henry Mintzberg, Robert Simmons, Kunal Basu, 'Beyond Sefishness', *MIT Sloan Management Review*, 15329194, Fall 2002, Vol. 44, Issue 1.

36 J.S. Lublin, 'Executive Pay (A Special Report). Net Envy', *Wall Street Journal*, April 6, 2000, p. R1.

37 Bertolt Brecht, *Life of Galileo*, trans. J. Willett, ed. R. Manheim, New York: Arcade Publishing, 1995.

38 The media, always in search of celebrities, fosters this myth. For example, *Fortune* magazine typically wrote in its April 14, 1997 issue: 'In four years [Louis] Gerstner has added more than $40 billion to IBM's share value' (Cited in Mintzberg *et al*, 2002, who add aptly: 'Admittedly, Gertstner is a good CEO, but did he really do this all by himself.')

39 T.S. Eliot, *Four Quartets*, London, 1944, p.31.

11

A Vision for India

P.N. VIJAY

In this brief paper, I propose to give my vision of India of the future.

I would like to begin by talking about a free market economy and how it relates to our ethos. I am a great votary of the development of a free economy, which will give full support and encouragement for private enterprise and initiative to grow and flourish. The concept of a free economy with a strong private sector working in a globalized competitive environment is nothing new to us. It is based on our roots in Indian tradition, which has always held that a free system of commerce and industry is, but a facet of a free society. *The Rig Veda*, the oldest scripture of this country - and many would say the oldest scripture in the world - declares *"Aa No Bhadraah Kravato Yantu Vishvatah* (let noble thoughts come to us from every side)"*. Two thousand years ago sailors from the south took their ships into what we now call Indonesia and the Far East and set up sophisticated business enterprises, making them perhaps the first multinationals of this planet. Our silks adorned the wardrobe of Cleopatra and our gems the crowns of Roman emperors. We regard Chanakya as one of the most important political and economic thinkers that ever lived and draw inspiration from him. In his *Arthashastra*, he defines the role of the state as one, which essentially defends the country, maintains law and order and collects taxes, which it spends, on the poor. He did not envisage any role for the state in agriculture, manufacturing or services. In our vision of a great Indian nation based on the traditional values and principles of India, the role of private enterprise is central. For us freedom in business is but a part of the larger freedom of the Human Spirit. A free nation has to have a free economy.

My India will participate actively in a globalized economic environment and the blue print for that should include the following.

Good Governance

Good governance is good management. The cost of governance of India is Rs 1800 crores every day. About 800 MPs and 4210 MLAs run the Central and State Governments. And how do they run it? Let me give you some examples. There are 35 electricity boards in India and all of them lose money because of theft. In Delhi the capital's transmission loss was handed over to private hands. There are 10,000 municipal hospitals and not even one of them can be called well equipped or clean by international standards. More than Rs 1000 crores of food has been wasted in godowns of the FCI and the State Civil Supplies Corporations while people die of starvation deaths. One can go on and on.

About 18.7 million people work in Government, about 3 million in the organized private sector and another 353 million in the unorganized sector. A total of 380 million people work in India. Right now this huge resource of human capital is not productive. It should be made productive. We protect Government employees through Article 311 of the Constitution. This needs to be amended, as we cannot pamper 1.87 per cent of Indians at the cost of the balance 98.13 per cent. These employees are protected for life whether they work or not, whether they are honest or not, whether they are absent or not, whether they are efficient or not. They often sub contract their jobs and make money working somewhere else. They even disrupt other people's work, damage or sabotage the assets of Government enterprises to prevent any change that is brought in. So we should stop pampering these persons and make them do an honest day's work for the pay they get. They should be accountable to the people who pay taxes so that they can get salaries. If the government can be made efficient, the effect of this will be electric.

Improve Employee Productivity in the Private Sector

If there is sloth in the Government sector, there is greed in the private sector. If there is indolence in the Government sector, there is rapacity in the private sector. Fortunately market driven economics have largely taken care of the greed factor and today unless a business is efficient and keeps its employees happy, it has no future. In the private sector we should protect employment and not employees who do not come up to expectations or perform to standards of work culture and work ethics. We should drastically modernize our labor legislation, which now protects inefficiency, does not reward hard work and has prevented us from realizing the biggest competitive advantage we have, namely, our human capital. In an economy where capital is scarce and expensive, the only way to remain globally competitive is to make our labour force highly productive. Otherwise the 8 per cent growth rate that the 10th Five Year Plan talks of will remain only in paper.

Education

Fifty five per cent of Indians, some 550 million people are below the age of 30 and 730 million below the age of 35. How are we going to provide employment for them? While we need our IITs, IIMs and medical colleges, the real need is for primary, secondary education and vocational training. Primary and secondary education improve awareness of health, reduce animal instincts based on religion and caste, improve living standards and create better citizens as Kerala has proved. In China 99.1 per cent of the children attend school for nine years. Everyone cannot go to an IIT or IIM or become a lawyer or chartered accountant.

We need to impart vocational training so that there can be necessary correlation between our education and jobs. In Europe the Universities are empty and about 85 to 90 per cent of the students join vocational training institutes after school. They also work part time as apprentices with industry and trade, while they finish their vocational training. This way, business gets low cost manpower and the young men and women are getting trained and eventually gainfully employed in a trade they know well. Compare this with the situation in India where students after finishing school like a herd, join colleges without having a clue whether they will get a job after they get a degree and practically waste their 3 years in college only to come to terms with the stark reality of unemployment at the end of that period. Vocational training will create a formidable work force, which will make India feared all over the world. And will reduce the biggest scourge of modern India, *viz* unemployment.

Agriculture

Agriculture is India's backbone. 65 per cent of the population depends on it for its living, even though its share of the GDP is now only around 23 per cent. The tale of Indian agriculture is a saga of waste and mismanagement. We are the world's third largest producer of grains, second largest of fruits, flowers and vegetables and largest producer of milk. And yet the Indian farmer on the whole leads a marginal existence. Productivity is at an abysmal level. China with less cultivable land produced 415 millions tonnes of food grains while we produced just 184 million this year and slightly over 200 million last year. In the area of fruits and vegetables, we process less than 5 per cent of these and more than 25 per cent is wasted. Even in Malaysia, they process more than 80 per cent of the produce. If India is to be a great nation, we have to make agriculture efficient and viable.

Many things need to be done. I will just mention a few. Firstly we need to remove with one stroke of a pen all the plethora of laws that surround, subvert, subjugate and suppress Indian agriculture and create one free market for agriculture. These laws were made when we had an economy of shortages; today the scenario has changed and we are an economy of surpluses. All that these do is to fatten the purse of the middleman. The farmer in Mysore sells a kilo of tomato for Rs 1 but when the housewife buys it in Janakpuri, it is more than Rs 10. This sorry state of affairs has to be changed quickly and decisively.

Secondly we need to invest heavily in food processing. Agriculture today thrives on subsidies, which have played hell, wreaked havoc. Almost all the money we spend on agriculture is in the form of subsidies. These have no lasting value apart from having serious negative impact on cropping patterns. We need to invest heavily in storage, in processing, in value addition. This will strengthen the hands of the farmer by giving him holding power and make agriculture a highly profitable business. The side benefits are tremendous. Our agriculture exports, which were a pittance till a decade ago, are close to Rs 30,000 crores this year and constitute 14 per cent of our total exports. This will create rural prosperity and reduce the mindless influx of people into our towns and cities, making them living hells.

Infrastructure

We have to do a lot more on infrastructure. A lot has been done; telephones are available on tap and the costs have come down substantially. Gas connections are going abegging. But our roads and highways are still nowhere near international standards. True, the Pradhan Mantri Gram Sadak Yojana and the two national highway programs are making a dent, but not enough. The power sector has proved to be the Achilles heel of all governments, but after 55 years of Independence, our villages live in darkness for 18 hours of the day and our cities are only marginally better. Power costs for industry are prohibitive and crores of investment are made just for back up; something unheard of in any other part of the world. Almost every factory in India has a generator! The water situation is another sorry story. The picture of housewives standing in the scorching sun and fighting for water is something that tells more sordidly the Indian infrastructure story than any speech. We owe to our future generation at least decent drinking water and a light and a fan.

Vision

We can go on and on. But time is short and the story long. I am confident that in the next few decades we will cross many of these hurdles, as we have in the past. After that what? Is the India story over? No, far from it. India is not a part of this planet just to feed its people and provide software engineers to Silicon Valley and call centre girls to GE. We should represent the moral force of this planet. In the words of Swami Vivekananda, "There have been great conquering races in this world. We also have been great conquerors. Our conquests have been in the realm of the Spirit. When armies try to conquer armies they multiply and make brutes of humanity. Spirituality must conquer the West." Martin Luther King said, "When I go to other nations I go to preach. When I go to India I go to learn." We have and should continue to carry the message of the nobility of the spirit which made Carl Jung, Henry David Thoreau and Albert Einstein declare this land as the fountainhead of all wisdom. Each nation has its *Dharma*, that quality which is unique, which separates it from the rest of the nations; which is its very nature; just like heat is to the fire and light is to the Sun. The *Dharma* of U.S. is free enterprise and opportunity. The *Dharma* of Great Britain is its rich democratic traditions. The *Dharma* of India is its spiritual values, its ability to give solutions to the myriad problems that swell up in a man when his tummy is full and his feet are not bare. "Who Am I?"

asked the *Rishis* and they went into the Himalayas to meditate for years. They got the Self Realization - *Aham Brahman Asmi.* (I am Brahman). They took this message of hope, of the innate divinity of all creation to every corner of the world. From this arose the concept of universal brotherhood *"Vasudhaiva Kutumbakam"* It is our duty to carry on this torch. We should not lose sight of this noble endeavor, for if we do so, the whole world will suffer. We should spread the message of love, equality of man, faith in a Supreme Being to all lands. My India will not only be a prosperous economic power. It will be the Soul of Mankind.

12

The Idea of India and the Economic Tryst[1]

BIBEK DEBROY

SECTION 1

INTRODUCTION

Wiser and more informed people have tried to define what India means.

While historical explorations may help in understanding the historical context, they hardly seem relevant in defining modern India. After all, the *Sindhu* the *Aryas* confronted, excluded large tracts of modern India and included tracts that are no longer part of modern India. Depending on the century, the geographical coverage of *Aryavarta*, *Brahmavarta* or *Bharatavarsa* varied and in some cases was extremely limited. According to one *sloka*, Brahmavarta was the narrow region between the rivers Sarasvati and Drsadvati.[2] The geographical terrain covered in the *Mahabharata* was also limited, although the *Ramayana*'s coverage was wider. *Jambudvipa* might satisfy those who are more ambitious. But in all fairness, *Bharatvarsa* was only one of the nine *varsas* in *Jambudvipa* and barring *Kuruvarsa*, the others (*Ilavrta, Ramyaka, Hiranmaya, Ketumala, Bhadrasva, Harivarsa, Kimpurusa*) had nothing to do with what might be called India. Purely for purposes of record, the Gupta Empire (even if one includes tributary States) fell far short of modern India. Ashoka's Empire was a better approximation, but suffers from the problem of including areas that no longer belong. Hence, India is best defined as what it is post-Independence.

Nor do cultural definitions get us very far. Culture is not only an amorphous concept. It also implies homogeneity in language, ideas, beliefs and customs that India evidently lacks. The assimilative nature of India's evolution prevents a clear cultural definition and it is not surprising that parts of India have more cultural affinity with neighbouring countries than with other parts of India.

Culture also spills over into religion. A religious definition has the obvious disadvantage of imposing a majority religion's belief on the national identity.[3] Incidentally, in an etymological sense, the word religion has the nuance of monastic vows and obligations. The word *dharma*'s nuance of holding the world up is so much better. Every *dharma* has three core elements – a code of ethical conduct, a belief in after-life and a notion of God. Across religions, beliefs in the after-life differ. However, in their purest forms, there is little difference between codes of ethical conduct and notions of God.

What constitutes Hinduism? This is impossible to answer, because Hinduism is sometimes defined as a way of life rather than a religion. Interpreted as a religion, in the absence of a single sacred text, the choice of the text becomes important. For instance, the precepts of the *Upanisad*s (distilled if one likes in *Srmadbhagavadgita*) are not quite the same as the practice of Hinduism in the *Puranas* (or even the epics) and *Smrti* texts. In establishing the tolerance and pluralism of Hinduism, the usual recourse is to the *Upanisad*s or the *Gita*. Hence, Swami Vivekananda argued in September 1893, "We believe not only in universal toleration, but we accept all religions as true[4] ... The present convention, which is one of the most august assemblies ever held, is in itself a vindication, a declaration to the world, of the wonderful doctrine presented in the *Gita*: *"Whosoever comes to Me, through whatsoever form, I reach him; all men are struggling through paths which in the end lead to Me[5] "."*[6] And so on to the story of the frogs in the well on 15th September 1893.

The point is the following. If one accepts the Song Celestial as the core of Hinduism, there are three indicated paths to salvation – *bhakti yoga, karma yoga* and *jnana yoga*. Almost tautologically, *jnana yoga* is tolerant and not surprisingly, the 4/11 quote from the *Gita* is from the *jnana yoga* chapter. After all, the truth about the Godhead (and union with the Godhead) is generally unknown and my tentative probing of the elusive answer is as good (or as bad) as yours. *Jnana yoga* perforce implies this Catholicity. However, *bhakti yoga* is not necessarily tolerant. From the *Gita* itself one can cite, *sarvadharman parityajya mamekam saranam vraja.*[7] A convincing case can be made out that what distinguishes Hinduism's sacred texts from the sacred texts of other religions is the existence of *karma yoga* and the relative preponderance of *jnana yoga*. For instance, in the authorized version of the Bible, the teachings of the Essenes (there is a *jnana yoga* component there) are not included. These *jnana yoga* and *karma yoga* elements impart Hinduism its tolerance, quite apart from the fact that at the time of Hinduism's evolution, there were no other major religions to be intolerant towards. Hence, in the *jnana yoga* chapter again, the *Gita* says, *tadviddhi pranipatena pariprasnena sevaya.*[8] *Bhakti yoga* and a priestly class demand *pranipatena* and *sevaya*. Every priestly class hates *pariprasnena*, since it threatens their continued existence. In contradistinction to other major religions, Hinduism's sacred texts underline the existence of *jnana yoga* as a valid option. Belief in *jnana yoga* also ascribes importance to reason, unlike *bhakti yoga*, which imbibes all religions with the characteristic of blind faith.[9]

But the point is that *jnana yoga* is not for everyone. It is for the intellectual, for the thinking. For the vast majority, the path followed is *bhakti yoga* (and to a lesser extent *karma yoga*). In the practice of *bhakti yoga*, as opposed to the teaching of *jnana yoga*, it is not that easy to establish tolerance. After all, in the *jnana yoga* chapter, the Gita itself sanctions the caste system.[10] Had this intolerance not existed, Buddhism, Jainism and even Sikhism wouldn't have evolved. Nor would the Brahmo movement[11] have attempted to go back to the *Upanisads*. While on the Brahmo movement, the last section of Tagore's novel *Gora* bears mention. This is when *Gora* has discovered that he is the son of an Irishman and is hence, not a Hindu. Freed from this shackle, he realizes that he is an Indian. His god is the god of all Indians, the god of Hindus, Muslims, Christians and Brahmos and not the god of Hindus alone.[12] The Brahmo movement did a lot for the cause of women's education in Bengal. But isn't it significant that it didn't take root in the uneducated segments? This is in sharp contrast to the *bhakti* movement.

SECTION 2

THE CONSTITUTION

What does it mean to be an Indian?

In modern India, the core values that India represents should be the ones laid down in the Constitution. India is a sovereign, socialist, secular, democratic republic. India is committed to secure to all its citizens justice (social, economic and political), liberty (of thought, expression, belief, faith and worship), equality (of status and opportunity) and fraternity. More specifically, there are certain rights laid down in Part III (Fundamental Rights) and still others in Part IV (Directive Principles of State Policy). Is there enough in this to establish an Indian identity? Is there enough of a unifying thread?

The answer is probably in the negative.[13] Sovereignty is a desirable goal, but is rarely a unifying thread unless sovereignty is threatened. After all, this is a post-colonial world and 2003 is not the late 1940s or early 1950s. Except in rare instances of Pakistan being identified as the villain, there is no common external aggressor Indians can identify against. This is especially true of younger Indians, those born in post-Independent India. And with the end of the Cold War, the non-aligned movement also loses its identification.[14] Consequently, the young and urban Indian probably makes less of a fetish out of 26th January, 15th August or the Indian flag.[15]

Ditto for lack of identification in the democratic ideal. Fareed Zakaria argues that democracy should not necessarily be equated with core liberal rights.[16] Assuming this distinction, core liberal rights may or may not provide the unifying thread. But democracy cannot. Not unless democracy is itself threatened. At best, core liberal rights have provided identities to local communities, such as through various NGO movements.

Socialism is an elusive expression, although in more than one socialist country, socialism has sometimes been identified with specific goals and has therefore been a unifying thread as well as a goal that instills national pride. The Great Leap Forward or the Cultural Revolution periods in China or the literacy movement in Cuba in 1959 are examples. The Stakhanovite movement in the former Soviet Union is yet another instance. However, it is the goal rather than the expression socialism that leads to this identity. *Ipso facto*, the word socialism needs precise definition. The textbook definition of socialism as public ownership of means of production is *non sequitur*, especially now that liberal values have swept the globe. One might be able to argue that every socialist country has exhibited enormous strides in health and education. Hence, socialism in India should now be interpreted as attaining the Millennium Development Goals on health and education within a prescribed timeframe.[17] Alternatively, Lenin interpreted socialism as electrification of the former Soviet Union.[18] Electrification can be an acceptable national goal. In establishing such identities, the precise goal is critical. The adjective "socialism" is only incidental.

While an extremely desirable objective and no alien to the Hindu tradition of *jnana yoga*, secularism cannot provide the unifying thread either. In any case, other than the idea of all religions leading to the same universal goal, what does secularism mean? The word evolved in a country where there was a formal State and a formal Church and secular meant a separation between the two. What does secular mean in a context where there is no formal Church? One possible interpretation is something like the following. It is the State's job to provide for provisioning of public goods (those with positive externalities) and curb provisioning of public bads (those with negative externalities). Religion is a private good (or bad) and the State should therefore have no role to play in the religious domain. Even if there is no formal Church, except for those who take a purely intellectual *jnana yoga* type of view of religion, it is doubtful that the proposition of religion being a completely private good can be accepted. Delinked from State provisioning, there is the possibility of community provisioning of religious goods or bads and ignoring this completely is tantamount to ignoring an important element of Indian-ness. Nor does accepting this amount to necessarily accepting intolerance across religions. In Maharashtra in the 19th century, *Ganesh Chaturthi* celebrations played a major role in fostering a national identity.[19] Recognizing the public good characteristic of religion enables one to encourage positive externalities and curb negative ones, even though this intervention should not be State-driven in a secular country. But community-driven intervention is indeed possible. After all, there is an almost Keynesian angle in energy used for demolishing mosques. Shouldn't this be constructively channeled instead of ignoring it altogether?

The Preamble to the Constitution thus lacks any immediately identifiable national identity. What makes it worse is that other parts of the Constitution, in fostering unity in diversity, further fragment Indian-ness. While Articles 29 and 30 (cultural and educational rights of minorities) can perhaps be defended, an *a priori* defence for not implementing Article 44 (uniform civil code) cannot be advanced.[20] In similar vein, the case for positive affirmation is established. But shouldn't such positive affirmation be based on notion of class,[21] rather than on caste or tribal status? By splicing SCs and STs, with the undefined category of "weaker sections", Article 46 leads to further fragmentation. This argument also extrapolates to Articles 244 and 244A, or at the risk of even greater controversy, to Articles 330 through 342. And following the same logic, to Articles 369 through 371. To repeat, this is not an argument against positive discrimination. But it is indeed an argument against segmentation that prevents mainstreaming and prevents acquisition of a national identity. These Constitutional provisions are further compounded by other provisions that divide India (such as through State formation) along linguistic grounds. Is that the reason why sub-regional identities are sometimes stronger than national ones?

Here is a quote from a speech delivered by the Indian President on 30th March, 2003. "Got 10 minutes for your country? YOU say that our government is inefficient. YOU say that our laws are too old. YOU say that the municipality does not pick up the garbage. YOU say that the phones don't work, the railways are a joke, the airline is the worst in the world, mails never reach their destination. YOU say that our country has been fed to the dogs and is the absolute pits. YOU say, say and say. What do YOU do about it?" Slightly reminiscent of a speech delivered by an American President in the 1960s.[22]

The *quid pro quo* from the citizen is enshrined in Article 51-A of the Constitution, perhaps less weakly than it should be. However, Constitutional provisions alone don't lead to *quid pro quo* delivery. That requires national identity and national pride. Rather paradoxically, with freer inter-State migration and lower transaction costs to such migration among the young and the educated, especially in urban areas, sub-regional identities have probably been weakened and national identities strengthened.[23] Hindi films (and now television) have brought about a linguistic homogeneity that was earlier absent. There are more inter-regional marriages. The young and educated Indian is much more likely to describe himself (or herself) as an Indian, rather than as a Punjabi or a Gujarati.[24] If this identity does not find relatively desirable goals to identify itself with, identification and pride will be sought in relatively undesirable national goals like nuclear tests, lunar missions or India being the home to the tallest building on the planet.[25] Or perhaps that elusive permanent seat in the Security Council.

SECTION 3

THE ECONOMIC TRYST

"Long years ago, we made a tryst with destiny, and now the time comes when we shall redeem our pledge, not wholly or in full measure, but very substantially.... The service of India means the service of the millions who suffer. It means the ending of poverty and ignorance and disease and inquality of opportunity. The ambition of the greatest man of our generation has been to wipe every tear from every eye. That may be beyond us but so long as there are tears and suffeering, so long our work will not be done...We have to build the noble mansion of free India where all her children may dwell."

As every Indian knows, that was 14th/15th August, 1947. 2003 shows significant gaps between that promised economic tryst and the reality.

Human Development Report (HDR) for 2002 will suffice.[26] In a cross-country ranking of 173 countries ranked through the human development index (HDI)[27], India is ranked 124th, just behind Morocco and ahead of Swaziland. India's life expectancy of 63.3 years compares with 70.5 years in China. India's adult literacy rate of 57.2 per cent compares with 77.2 per cent in Botswana.[28] The combined (primary, secondary and tertiary) gross enrolment ratio of 55 per cent compares with 78 per cent in Namibia.[29] The PPP per capita income of 2358 US dollars compares with 9068 in Malaysia. Other indicators, not used in computing HDI, are no less stark. 16.7 per cent of the Indian population (at birth) will not survive till the age of 40, the figure is 7.8 per cent for Tunisia. 12 per cent of the Indian population doesn't have access to improved water resources, the figure is 3 per cent for Bangladesh. 47 per cent of children under the age of five are under-weight, the figure is 23 per cent for Kenya. 44.2 per cent of the Indian population is below the international poverty line of 1 US dollar per day, the figure is 3.1 per cent for Egypt.[30] 35.0 per cent of the Indian population is below the national poverty line, the figure is 10.1 per cent for Mexico.[31] 31 per cent of the Indian population uses adequate sanitation facilities, the figure is 73 per cent for Vietnam. 68 per cent of one-year olds are fully immunized against tuberculosis, the figure is 99 per cent for Egypt. 23 per cent of the Indian population is under-nourished, the figure is 6 per cent for Indonesia. The infant mortality rate (per 1000) is 69 in India, it is 17 in Sri Lanka. The maternal mortality rate (per 100,000 live births) is 540 in India, it is 60 in Venezuela. Understandably, these figures are worse if one considers inter-regional variations or gender biases or biases against SCs/STs.[32]

This noble mansion of free India does not lead to national pride. However, in a post-Cold War era, an explicit economic goal can perhaps be used to define the national identity. On 14th August, 1904, Sister Nivedita delivered a speech on "Nationality".[33] Here is a quote. "In talking to you this evening, on the subject of Nationality, I shall first of all tell you of some things that are not Nationality. You shall always bear in mind, as a lesson of the first importance, that there can be no nationality in a country where the people are always flying at each other's throats, for differences of opinion and sentiment. If the advocate of political agitation were always to revile the advocate of industrial re-generation; if the social reformer were to fly at the upholder of Hindu orthodoxy, if the orthodox Hindu, again, were to fight with the Hindu revivalist; if the literary man were to find fault with the educationist and vice-versa; if such were the state of affairs in a community, then it must be admitted that society has not yet learnt the first lesson of nation-building.... You, Indians, are very strong in the element of personal devotion; you can annihilate your own self even, for the sake of a parent, a brother, or a friend; and the European has still to learn this of you. But you have to learn a lesson from the European. He has the singular capacity of acting in concert with a person for whom, perhaps, he may have the greatest personal dislike – merely out of regard for the welfare of the party or organisation to which both of them belong. This power of self-suppression for the sake of an ideal is a virtue which the Indian has still to learn. For, it is evident that without this virtue, no considerable advance could be made in the direction of such popular organisations as the idea of nationality necessarily involves."

A coherent economic ideal is infinitely preferable to a national ideal that seeks to protect the bovine animal. Such an explicit goal missed articulation in the 1990s. If one divides the reform agenda into an external sector component and a domestic component, most reforms in the external sector have either been implemented or there is a clear timeframe for their further implementation.[34] It is therefore not surprising that external sector indicators have improved sharply.[35] These reforms were triggered by an external sector balance of payments (bop) crisis in 1990-91 and were therefore not driven by an explicit economic ideal. In hindsight, a goal that stated, "India vows to end foreign aid", would have introduced the same reforms, but would also have brought about a sense of identity.

"It is glorious to be rich" has found resonance in China. Before the East Asian currency crisis, the target of making Malaysia a developed country found similar resonance. The last goal, of making India a developed country by 2020, is mentioned quite often now, within the government system and without. There are three problems with this articulation.

First, the definition "developed" is not a precise one, even within the UN system. A goal that says, "Make India the third largest economy in the world" is more precise. Naturally, this is in PPP terms. Overtaking the United States or China is impossible in the foreseeable future. But given present GDP growth rates in India and Japan, overtaking Japan around the year 2010 (in PPP terms) should be no problem at all.[36] Alternatively, a goal can be in terms of per capita income. India's present per capita income is 500 US dollars.[37] While the definition of developed does not depend on per capita income alone, in all fairness, a country can't be called a developed economy until it has a per capita income of 2000 US dollars or even much more. The new Hindu rate of growth is between 5.5 per cent and 6.5 per cent, nowhere near the targeted 8 per cent.[38] If one assumes the 8 per cent rate as plausible (not just feasible as the Planning Commission argues) and also assumes the rate of population growth is going to be around 1.5 per cent, we have a per capita income growth of 6.5 per cent.[39] With a base level of 500 US dollars, 2000 US dollars is achievable around 2025, not around 2020. To the slogan of "overtake Japan by 2010" one can then add, "become developed by 2025". Both of these are more identifiable slogans than "8 per cent GDP growth". This ides not of course catapult India into the "high human development" category.

If religious imagery helps in this endeavour, why should one abjure religion, simply because religion is interpreted to be a private good? Rather than Lord *Rama*, Goddess *Laksmi* has much more utility in this context.[40] This is the counterpart of the "it is glorious to be rich" syndrome, although *Laksmi* does not stand for wealth or prosperity alone. Etymologically, goal (*laksma*) also has the same root as *Laksmi*. Unfortunately, the worship of *Laksmi* is equated today with the worship of *Grihalaksmi* (the *Laksmi* in the household). But *Laksmi* also has other manifestations, not just *Vijayalaksmi*, but *Rajyalaksmi* as well. Given the era of trade and globalization, *Laksmi's* origin from the ocean deserves mention.[41]

To get back to the goal of becoming a developed economy, a second problem is that the goal becomes meaningless unless a roadmap for progressing towards that goal is accepted. The agenda of reforms has been pending for a long time, now described as second generation reforms.[42] In this agenda, one should mention rural sector reforms[43], infrastructure[44], direct and indirect taxes[45], legal reform[46], the small-scale sector[47], targeting of subsidies[48], downsizing and making government more accountable[49] and public sector reform. *Per se*, the fiscal deficit should not be mentioned as a separate problem. While the fiscal deficit is indeed high, and the composition of the fiscal deficit is such that it is driven by revenue rather than capital expenditure, this problem cannot be addressed unless one solves the issue of interest payments, defence expenditure and subsidies.[50] In other words, the fiscal deficit problem will automatically be addressed once the other reforms take place. And in the absence of a consensus on those reforms, saying that there is a consensus on reducing the fiscal deficit (or the revenue deficit) is neither here nor there. The fact that there is no consensus on a minimum common set of reforms has been repeated *ad nauseam*. Perhaps the consensus becomes easier to generate if the liberalization package is specifically linked to an explicitly articulated economic goal. That is, the roadmap emerges from the goal. Despite more than a decade of economic reforms, this attempt hasn't yet taken place. In articulating this goal, the following quote is relevant. "India is a country of almost one billion people without a national agenda. Everyone, every party, every group has its own agenda – but there is no national agenda. If you ask 20 people what India should be, you get 40 different answers. India as a nation must decide what we want to do, where we want to go, and when we want to go down there…. This debate should start at the local *panchayat* or municipal level. From there, it could go to district, state, and finally the national level. It should of course also extend to people of Indian origin outside of India. This is the only way it will be the *people's* agenda. Otherwise, it will become Delhi's agenda!… It may take two or three years. That should not be a problem. But then we should come out with a national agenda that is more acceptable to the public… Once we get people talking, actions start to happen."[51]

Third, there is the matter of Gandhiji's talisman. One cannot forget that 26 per cent of the Indian population is poor. That amounts to 300 million households. Quite often, these poor households are located in certain specified districts in States like undivided Bihar, undivided Madhya Pradesh, Rajasthan, undivided Uttar Pradesh, Maharashtra, Karnataka, Andhra Pradesh, Orissa, West Bengal and the North-East. These are pockets of deprivation. Arguably, the decade of the 1990s has increased inter-regional disparities and these populations and these geographical areas have been bypassed and marginalized by the trickle down benefits of growth.[52] The national goal cannot be accepted as a national one without a buy-in by these deprived sections. Nor can the State abdicate from the responsibility of providing (or at least financing) a whole variety of social and physical infrastructure, including subsidizing households that are below the poverty line (BPL)[53]. In other words, the national goal should also have objectives like the following. Increase the literacy rate to 80 per cent and the gross enrolment ratio to 80 per cent by 2010. Reduce the infant mortality rate to 30 by 2010. These are precise goals and concrete deadlines people can identify with. Vague assertions like India becoming a developed economy will not do.

In the altered global environment, power flows out of the barrel of economics rather than politics. The national identity needs to be forged around an intended economic tryst. That's the noble mansion of free India we can strive towards. Where the pledge is concrete enough to be met in full measure.

Notes

1 This should be regarded as a paper with half-baked ideas rather than one that is polished and final. There is some similarity in argument with Bhikhu Parekh's "Re-imagining India", 6th Dr D.T. Lakdawala Memorial Lecture, 28th March, 2003, Institute of Social Sciences, Delhi. But Bhikhu Parekh takes a different line.

2 The land, built by the gods, and watered by the divine rivers Sarasvati and Drsadvati is *Brahmavarta*. Of course, the more common definition of *Aryavarta* (*cf. Manu Smrti* 2.22 or *Amarkosa* 2/1/8) is the region bounded by the Himalayas to the North, the Vindhyas to the South and the oceans to the East and the West.

3 Democracy ought to be about protecting the rights of minorities rather than those of majorities. Rights of majorities protect themselves.

4 Shri Ramakrishna's *jata mat, tato path* echoed the *Rg Veda's ekam sad, vipra bahuda vadanti*.

5 *Gita*, 4/11 – *ye yatha mam prapadyante tamtathaiva bhajamyaham*.

6 Response to the Welcome in Chicago, 11th September, 1893.

7 18/66. This is the *moksa yoga* or final chapter. Nevertheless, this is far more tolerant than Jehovah's wrath at the golden calf in *Exodus* 32.

8 4/34.

9 If belief in *nirvana*, code of conduct, belief in God (suitably interpreted) and blind faith characterize a religion, communism exhibits all the characteristics of a religion.

10 4/13 – *caturvarnyam maya srstam gunakarmavibhagasah*.

11 There are similarities with the Arya Samaj.

12 Tagore did not of course believe in the narrow definition of nationalism.

13 There are three things that unite India – cricket, hindi films and anti-Pakistan rhetoric.

14 See also, C. Raja Mohan, *Crossing the Rubicon: The Shaping of India's New Foreign Policy*, Viking, 2003.

15 It is certainly a mistake to presume that this urban Indian is an Indian who lives in the metros. The centre of the metro is increasingly spilling over into the periphery of non-metro urban India. Witness what has happened to the composition of the Indian cricket team or entry into the civil services.

16 Fareed Zakaria, *The Future of Freedom: Illiberal Democracy at Home and Abroad*, W.W. Norton & Company, 2003.

17 The Millennium Development Goals were adopted by the UN General Assembly in 2000, to be attained by the year 2015. There are eight Millennium Development Goals, of which, the first six are precise. In general, India is likely to miss the 2015 target, although progress is better on poverty reduction and education-related targets than on health or eliminating hunger. On eliminating gender disparity in education, the record is mixed. Instead of 2015, one can adopt more plausible deadlines, differentiated according to goal and region (meaning a region within India, such as a district).

18 Coupled of course with the system of *soviets*.

19 Less so, *Durga Puja* in Bengal. Although several Bengalis are likely to mention *Durga Puja* as an element of Bengali culture and Bengali identity.

20 There is no need to presume that such a uniform civil code should be the civil code of the majority community.

21 Implying an income criterion. Or even classification based on education or health indicators.

22 More precisely, John F. Kennedy's Inaugural Address delivered on 20th January, 1961. "And so, my fellow Americans, ask not what your country can do for you, ask what you can do for your country." There is a fairly strong religious under-current in this speech. Consider the following. "The world is very different now. For man holds in his mortal hands the power to abolish all forms of human poverty and all forms of human life. And yet the same revolutionary belief for which our forebears fought is still at issue around the globe, the belief that the rights of man come not from the generosity of the state but from the hand of God."

23 Paradoxically because the evolution of political parties leads in the opposite direction.

24 Quite understandably, this sentiment is stronger if the Indian is of the non-resident variety.

25 Which inevitably happens to be a temple.

26 *World Development Report (WDR)*, *Global Competitiveness Report* or Transparency International illustrate different dimensions of that same failed tryst.

27 Based on a combined indicator of PPP (purchasing power parity) per capita income, an indicator of education (literacy and gross enrolment ratio) and health (life expectancy). There are indeed problems of cross-country data comparability, especially if such data are from surveys rather than national accounts.

28 The Census of 2001 shows an adult literacy rate of 65 per cent, but *HDR 2002* usually has data for 2000.

29 In many physical quality of life indicators, India's track record is inferior to that in sub-Saharan Africa. The argument is not that there haven't been any improvements since 1947. While impressive, these improvements fall short of what several other countries have been able to achieve.

30 1 US dollar per day at 1985 prices.

31 This is before National Sample Survey (NSS) data for 1999-2000 came in. Once NSS (1999-2000) and Census (2001) data are incorporated in *HDR*, there will be a sharp jump in India's HDI.

32 Women don't hold up half the sky. Given a choice, the last thing a baby about to be born would want is to be born as a SC or ST girl, and this is not just a problem in the conventional BIMARU (Bihar, Madhya Pradesh, Rajasthan, Uttar Pradesh) States. Given foeticide (and infanticide) in Punjab and Haryana, there is a high probability of that baby not being born at all, were such a choice to be exhibited.

33 At the Dawn Society, Calcutta.

34 Phase-out of quantitative restrictions, reduction in tariffs, exchange rate changes, open policy on foreign investments (direct and portfolio) and rationalization of export incentives cum subsidies.

35 This is regardless of the indicator used – debt service ratio, foreign exchange reserves expressed as months of import cover, imports covered by exports, export growth rate or current account surplus. The Green Revolution eliminated the food constraint, the 1990s eliminated the foreign exchange constraint.

36 This is even if one assumes real GDP growth of 6 per cent in India, as against the Tenth Plan's (2002-07) 8 per cent.

37 Using official exchange rates rather than PPP.

38 The growth retardation since 1997 is of serious concern and cuts across the primary, secondary and tertiary sectors.

39 The rate of population growth is around 1.9 per cent now and should slow down further. Now does not mean the decadal (1991 to 2001) rate of population growth.

40   The issue of identifying Rg Veda's Sri with Laksmi or differentiating between the two is best left to Indological scholars. See, U.N. Dhal, *Goddess Laksmi: Origin and Development*, Oriental Publishers, 1978. However, consider the second half of sloka 7 from the *Sri Sukta* – *pradurbhuto asmi rastre asmin kirtimrddhim dadatu me*.

41   *Samudramanthana* or churning of the ocean. This is the common account of *Laksmi's* origin, mentioned both in the *Ramayana* and the *Mahabharata*, and embellished further in the *Puranas*. Some *Puranas* have a relatively uncommon account of *Laksmi* being born as Bhrgu and Khyati's daughter. There is also a famous nationalistic Bengali song, describing India (more accurately *Bharatavarsa*) as arising from the ocean – *jedin sunila jaladhi haite uthile janani bharatvarsa*. *Laksmi* is identified with agriculture and elephants. How many times have people sought the elephant imagery to describe the Indian economy? S.L. Rao (*Elephants Can Remember*) and Gurcharan Das (*The Elephant Paradigm*) even have books with elephants in the title. If national is interpreted in an economic sense, the national animal seems to the elephant rather than the tiger. But there is some danger of it also becoming the cow.

42   What "second generation" means is anyone's guess. The use of this expression suggests that "first generation" reforms are over. Yet, if one looks at reform measures listed by North Block in 1992 or 1993, most (barring ease of entry in manufacturing and financial sector reforms) continue to be on the agenda in the sense of not having been implemented. Hence, first generation can be identified with external sector reforms, while second generation can be identified with domestic reforms. Alternatively, first generation can be identified with Central changes, while (in a federal country) second generation concerns reforms that need to be implemented by States. The status quo is anti-poor and pro-rich. Logically, it follows that reforms should be pro-poor and anti-rich, if they are implemented. With non-implementation, the question of trickle down becomes somewhat meaningless. Having said that, the growth effects of trickle down are evident, with the percentage of population below the poverty line having dropped from 36 per cent in 1993-94 to 26 per cent in 1999-2000. There have been questions about comparability of NSS 1993-94 and 1999-2000 data. But such corrections only dampen drops in head count ratios and scale them down by a factor of around one-third. In addition to growth, the composition of growth is important.

43   Not just agriculture sector reforms. Such reforms are critical to broad-base income and consumption growth and thus drum up support for liberalization, as China has shown. That apart, GDP cannot grow at 8 per cent unless agriculture and allied sectors grow at 4 per cent. Other than macro growth retardation, the sorry state of India's agriculture should be of great concern.

44   Infrastructure is not just telecom and airlines. So far, despite the National Highway Development Programme (NHDP), there have been limited improvements in infrastructure sectors that matter most to the poor – roads, water (drinking and irrigation), power, sanitation, sewage treatment. Infrastructure reform does get into issues of subsidies and appropriate user charges. But had such reforms indeed happened, the pro-rich identification of the liberalization package would have been somewhat neutralized.

45   The two Kelkar Task Force recommendations are comprehensive accounts of what needs to be done in taxation.

46   This has several dimensions, extending beyond statutory law reform. There is the issue of speed of dispute resolution. While the *Civil Procedure Code* has been amended, the *Criminal Procedure Code* needs change. Of the 3,80,000 people in jail, 2,80,000 are under-trials and 95 per cent of these under-trials are poor, having been in jail awaiting trial for terms longer than the mandatory sentences for such crimes. That apart, administrative law (subordinate legislation) in the form of rules, orders and regulations is non-transparency and discretionary, leading to bribes and rent-seeking. Bribes are not distributionally neutral. In relative terms, they hurt the poor more than they hurt the rich. For rickshaw-pullers and vendors in Delhi, Madhu Kishwar has documented this corruption.

47   This is more than de-reservation. Satisfactory exit and the inspector *raj* are also problems.

48 Other than the power sector, several Planning Commission studies document leakage in anti-poverty programmes.

49 This includes decentralization.

50 In the Central component of the fiscal deficit, one should also mention pension payments. In the State component, one should also mention salaries and low cost recovery for services.

51 Sam Pitroda, *Vision, Values & Society*, Siliconindia, 2001. Sam Pitroda also uses the cricket metaphor. This was before the huddle became part of the Indian cricket team's strategy. The national strategy requires a similar huddle.

52 It is not surprising that much violent discontent is concentrated in these districts.

53 The form these subsidies take should of course be debated. There is also the matter of food security.

13

Law, Property Rights and Indigenous People

ARNAB KUMAR HAZRA

Introduction

Any conceivable Idea of India is perhaps incomplete without considering the indigenous people. It has been more than fifty-five years that we have gained Independence, but still these people are alienated from the mainstream. There are many aspects with regards to the indigenous people that are important and require urgent attention. Here we discuss the most fundamental aspect – the evolution of property rights and the corresponding legal framework within which they subsist. In today's Independent India, they lie outside the mainstream precisely because both the legal framework and the property rights are antagonistic to their very existence.

The coming of the Aryans is considered as the decisive historical factor to determine the original people of India. The most common habitat of these people have been the natural surroundings involving forest cover where they have, since ages, been traditionally protected from invaders, thus being able to keep their local ways intact to a large extent. The Anthropological Survey of India under the *'People of India Project'* identifies 461 tribal communities in India. They are enumerated at 67,583,800 persons constituting 8.08 per cent of the total population as per the 1991 census. The term *'adivasi'*, the Indian-language term for the indigenous people, has been used by social workers, missionaries and political activists, to refer to the tribal people.

There are three aspects, which are central to the conceptualization of the indigenous people. First, the indigenous are those people who lived in the country to which they belong before colonization or conquest by people from outside the country or the geographical region. Secondly, they have become marginalized as an aftermath of conquest and colonization by the people from outside the region. Thirdly, such people govern their life more in terms of their own social, economic and cultural institutions than the laws applicable to the society or the country at large.

In this paper there are two major aspects that are raised – law and property rights. First we look at the aspect of 'Law'. We begin with what is law and then describe the traditional system of governance that was prevalent in India and how it got transformed in the hands of the British who ruled India for nearly two centuries, giving rise to the modern legal system. As a result of this transformation, a certain type of justice delivery system, prevalent at the grassroots earlier, got completely obliterated. This created a vacuum in the justice system *vis-à-vis* the indigenous people who were unable to adapt to the requirements of the new modern legal system in Independent India. Expecting them to adhere to the perquisites was the major folly. Some experiments in the form of *Panchayats* were made, but these failed. This also brought about the alienation of these people, although it was not of their making.

At the same time, after Independence, a dual standard in property rights was adopted *vis-à-vis* forested and non-forested areas. While in the former all property rights were vested with the State, in case of the latter, private property rights were recognized and legalized, although the basis of such recognition, or the lack of it, was the same - occupancy of twelve years or more for entitlement to property rights. This completed the alienation. This aspect of property rights is elaborated next. The indigenous people remained 'tenants' with 'no rights' on their own land and thus at the mercy of the State.

This discrimination in property rights is exploited by various organs of the State, and typified by the forest department in India. A brief overview of the forest laws, operational in India today highlights the case in point. So the section on forest laws precedes the discussion on property rights, and in a way binds the two aspects of law and property rights. Finally, a brief conclusion sums up the discussion.

Law

Law is understood to be enacted by the legislative or executive organs of the State in the form of statutes, rules and regulations, or what emanates from the judiciary while resolving disputes. These legal instruments constitute the formal legal system that generally defines the political, economic and social contexts that encompass societal behaviour. However, it is not the only frame of allusion. A vast range of human activities lies outside the reach of the regulating arm of the State. Many human inter-relationships are regulated by 'non-State legal systems', a complex system of 'norms, institutions and culture', which parallel the substantive and procedural functions of State-made law. This body of law is variously defined as customary law, traditional law or local law-ways.

Distinguished from actual behaviour or practices, the term refers to 'norms and rules' underlying or determining behaviour, as well as 'procedures' that enable their application. Custom is generally understood to be that body of law, which is predominantly oral rather than written, and which derives its authority from sources other than the State.

Contemporary India is an example par excellence of the kind of society where a 'modern legal system' runs into close and extended encounters with traditional society and indigenous methods of (self and other) regulation. India is replete with all kinds of 'group' orderings, which are constantly subject to the strains of economic development and change; and, which provoke new patterns of group formation and social and occupational mobility. This 'modern legal system' seeks to define, constitute, reconstitute, sustain, re-align, transform and destroy these groups.[1]

The Traditional System of Governance

Hindu law is "older than any other existing legal system except perhaps the Jewish and ...[f]or three thousand years its outstanding characteristics have been the freedom of juristic discussion and the wealth and variety of custom"[2]. The traditional system of governance is largely to be found in the *dharmasastra* of the Hindus, which are credited with creating a general ideology and disciplinary framework, as well as a set of institutional arrangements that have held Hindu society together through the ages. The principles of equality were well enshrined in the ancient law of India. The legal theory of ancient India as evinced by the scriptures and *Dharmasastra* was a unique combination of religion, custom and morality.

In the traditional Indian jurisprudential framework, *Dharma*, Royal Order and Custom were the three sources of law. A delicate balance was maintained among the three sources, which reserved a distinct and specific authority for each. *Dharma* signifies the eternal laws that maintain the world.

Under Muslim rule, the judicial system remained a plural one. The Muslim population was governed by Muslim law in criminal, civil and family matters and disputes were settled before royal courts established in cities and administrative centres. Hindus were generally allowed their own tribunals in civil matters. When such matters came before royal courts, Hindu law was applied and was sustained by the sanctions of the State.

The King's function was to protect his subjects and guarantee their security. The royal sanction gave official recognition to local regulations; the king was to cause them to be observed; he could prohibit any regulations only if they were likely to breed disorder or if they were contrary to the interests of the State. This activity of the King was interpreted, not as 'legislative' in the domain of custom, but as 'administrative', the objective being the maintenance of peace. In theory, neither the king nor his council were legislative bodies in the modern sense of the term. The royal decrees that they issued were not new laws, but orders referring to special cases.

On the other hand, custom constituted a major source of law independent from all other known sources. The place that custom then occupied *vis-à-vis* other sources of law enabled and ensured a decentralized governance of natural resources. While *Dharma* pertained to the law that 'ought to be', custom was a purely social phenomenon. The rule of *dharma* did not become 'law' until it entered into behaviour and was accepted by the population as a customary rule.

No attempt was made to control the administration of law in the villages. Judges were called '*dharmastha*' – upholder of *dharma*. All these were to change fundamentally under colonial rule. Colonial administrators could not conceptually or administratively hold together the three interconnected planes of moral order, royal decree and local law-ways. English law rests on a fundamentally different foundation - on the primacy of written law, on statute or positive law. All other sources of law - case-law, legal doctrine, jurisprudence, custom - are only subsidiary to it, even if they play a role in the 'discovery' of law by contributing to the interpretation of statutory provisions.

The Evolution of the Legal System

Under the Anglo-Saxon legal system, which the British expounded in India by displacing the traditional ancient legal system, the three identified sources of law are statute, precedent and doctrine (in that order of precedence), with statute bearing over-riding authority over the other sources.

Three distinctive, if overlapping, stages can be discerned in the development of the modern Indian legal system[3]. The first, the period of initial expropriation, can be dated from Warren Hastings' organization in 1772 of a system of courts for the hinterland of Bengal. This period was marked by the general expansion of government's judicial functions and legislation was initiated. The second period, which began about 1860, was a period of extensive codification of the law and of rationalization of the system of courts, while the sources of law became more fixed and legislation became the dominant mode of modifying the law. This period lasted until Independence, after which there was a further consolidation and rationalization of the law and the development of a unified judicial system over the whole of India.

In undertaking to administer the law in the government's courts, the British initiated a process that might be called the 'expropriation' of law, which made the power to find, declare and apply law as a monopoly of the government. Two methods were employed to deal with indigenous law. Firstly, collections and translations of ancient texts and commentaries were undertaken. Secondly, Hindu *pundits* and Muslim *maulvis* were appointed as 'law officers' in courts to assist judges to 'root their decisions in traditional legal culture', and to fill up the gaps in their understanding of traditional law.

By the 1820's, courts began to be almost fully governed by the principle of *stare decisis* (decisions in earlier cases serving as precedents binding on later cases or lower courts), which worked as a counter-measure to the role of Indian law officers. They eventually became superfluous. Their posts were abolished in 1864. In their effort to make Hindu law more uniform, certain and accessible to British judges, the courts relied increasingly on translations, and on their own precedents. Regard for precedence was foreign to the Hindu system. Introduction of the rule of *stare decisis* diminished the flexibility of Hindu law by ruling out innovations to meet changes. British administration not only dissipated the techniques inherent in the *shastras*, but also narrowed the selection of authoritative texts. Consequently, with its innovative techniques stripped away, *shastric* law, like customary law, became more rigid and archaic as well as more uniform and certain.

The quarter of a century, following the takeover by the Crown in 1858, was the major period of codification of law and the consolidation of the court system. During this period a series of Codes, based more or less on English law and applicable, with minor exceptions, were enacted. It was estimated that during a period of seven years between 1862 and 1869, as many as 211 enactments were issued from the legislature.[4] By 1882, there was virtually complete codification of all fields of commercial, criminal and procedural law. Only the personal laws of Hindus, and Muslims were exempted.

In general three things happened – a) a centralized government assumed the monopoly power of 'finding', 'declaring' and 'applying' the law. Earlier, these functions were implemented at multiple levels. Textual law was given precedence over bodies of customary law and extended at the expense of the latter; b) the village lost its position as guardian of customary behaviour. Colonial courts could declare as unlawful decisions of traditional courts, whereas there was no appeal from these courts; and c) where indigenous law was applied, it was transformed.

Contrary to State law, customary laws emerge from the community, and command social acceptance and observance or compliance. One of the remarkable and unanticipated results of the British administration of Hindu law was the elevation of the textual law over lesser bodies of customary law. While some really widespread and long-standing customs gained recognition, "the most distinct effect of continued judicial construction has been greatly to extend the operation of semi-sacred collections of written rules at the expense of local customs which had been practiced over small territorial areas".[5]

The British courts, with their heritage of common-law hostility to local customs, applied requirements for proving the existence of a custom that were onerous to Indian litigants. To prevail over the written law a custom must be "proved to be immemorial or ancient, uniform, invariable, continuous, certain, notorious, reasonable (or not unreasonable), peaceful, obligatory and it must not be immoral nor opposed to an express enactment or to public policy". As more learned to use the official courts, the authority of the village tribunals was displaced. Over time the modern system encroached on the traditional system. Court law replaced village law, on more topics of law, for more groups, and over more territory.

Modern law is thus a political creation. The signal achievement of the Raj was to bring the entire social and political economy within the shadow of its law and legal institutions and processes. Most of the changes that emerged did not result from errors of understanding but constituted deliberate and adaptive re-creations. To that extent, they are a part of a general effort to codify Indian Law as well as to displace the traditional legal system, which was otherwise statutorily achieved through the efforts of Macaulay, Maine, Fitzjames Stephen, and others. This process of discovery was as inexact as it was purposive. Its inexactness led to what Gandhi later described as the 'egregious blunders' committed by the British in their interpretation of native law.[6]

The legal System in Independent India

The Anglo-Saxon legal system is the foundation of the Indian legal system. The formation of an independent Indian nation provided a basis for further integration and consolidation of the hitherto operating legal system. With the coming of independence, enclaves previously outside the legal system were integrated into it. A layer of constitutionalism was superimposed on the existing legal system and structure of government. The Constitution (1950) established India as a secular federal republic with a parliamentary system in the British style and a strong central government. The framers of the Constitution rejected the various proposals to construct a government along 'indigenous' lines. The Constitution established powerful legislatures at the centre and in the states. It also established a unified judiciary covering the whole of India under a Supreme Court as a court of final appeal in all cases. The Parliament soon passed a series of legislations known collectively as the Hindu Code, which affected a wholesale and drastic reform of Hindu law. The Code marked the acceptance of Parliament as a kind of legislative body for Hindus in matters of family and social life and brought in a degree of uniformity unprecedented in Hindu legal history.

The Constituent Assembly (1947-49) contained no spokesman for a restoration of *dharmasastra,* or for a revival of local customary law as such. An attempt by Gandhians and 'traditionalists' to form a polity based on village autonomy and self-sufficiency was rejected by the Assembly, which opted for a federal and parliamentary republic with centralized bureaucratic administration. The only concession to the Gandhians was a Directive Principle in favour of village Panchayats as units of local self-government.

The local customary component of Hindu law is also a source of rules at a few isolated points, but it, too, was abandoned as a living source of law. There was but one significant attempt to promote such indigenous law, by devolving certain judicial responsibilities to the local elective village Panchayats. But these elective Panchayats were quite different bodies from the traditional Panchayats.

Panchayats

In the late 1950s the Government adopted the policy of community development, whereby elective village *Panchayats* were established as instruments of village self-government in the hope that they would increase initiative and participation in economic development. The eager promotion of these administrative *Panchayats* secured the acceptance of judicial *Panchayats* or *Nyaya Panchayats* in almost all the states. Either the administrative *Panchayats* themselves, or allied bodies elected directly or indirectly, were given judicial responsibilities in specific categories of petty cases. Almost uniformly lawyers were barred from appearing before these tribunals.

As might be expected, judicial *Panchayats* enjoyed little favour with bar or bench. They were largely ignored and disdained by lawyers and were strongly criticized by judges. In reviewing their work on appeal, courts tolerated some departure from ordinary judicial procedures, but they also restricted the powers and discretion of *Panchayats*. In particular, the Supreme Court has held the exclusion of lawyers in cases where a party has been arrested for a crime as unconstitutional. It is not clear however, whether there has been any strong movement away from the courts in favour of the *Panchayats*.

Rather than inspiring a resurgence of indigenous local law, the judicial *Panchayats* or *Nyaya Panchayats* served more as agencies for disseminating official norms and procedures, further displacing traditional local law by official law within the village. The *Nyaya Panchayats* established in the 1950s and early 1960s are for the most part moribund. They had low caseloads and enjoyed little public or official regard. Although lack of government support undoubtedly made an important contribution to their demise, it is clear that they never attracted significant support from the villagers in whose name they were established. They withered away because they represented an unappetizing combination of the formality of official law with the political malleability of village tribunals. Subsequently, there has been a disintegration of the post-Independence efforts to revive the *Nyaya Panchayats* or the village tribunals.

Thus, while the process of displacement of the traditional legal system has taken place completely and the efforts to revive the *Nyaya Panchayats* also failed, there has not been the demise of traditional norms or concerns among a vast section of the Indian population – the *adivasis* or indigenous people. However before proceeding further, one also has to look at legislation pertaining to forests. This is important, as the most common habitat of the indigenous people has been the natural surroundings involving forest cover and so 'Forest Laws' directly affect them. Moreover it is directly linked to the issue of property rights, which is central to this paper.

Forest Laws

The modern legal framework on natural resources is entirely statute-centered. However, natural resource use in India and its associated institutions and law have their origin in an entirely different jurisprudential base. The governance of natural resources, which was essentially decentralized in character, had its legal basis almost entirely in 'local custom'.

The colonial rulers had established state property rights over the forests in the 1860s, prior to which there existed unrestricted use rights in them. The forests continue to be under state property rights and therefore under the Forest Department instituted by the British in 1864. Ramachandra Guha (1983) has argued that before 1947, our forests served the strategic interests of British imperialism, and after

Independence, they served the needs of the mercantile and industrial bourgeoisie.

One of the important objectives of the entire exercise of implementing the Anglo-Saxon system of jurisprudence was to further the interests of the crown or the ones who represented the crown, by bringing in momentous changes in the institutional structure and changing or twisting the legal mechanism to achieve it. This is typified by the *1865 Forest Act* and then more pronouncedly in the *1878 Forest Act*, wherein the tribal customs, practices, relations and dependency on the forest and thereby their traditional customary rights on the forests, was totally and blatantly neglected. In enacting these legislations, the British Government did not wait for public opinion of the indigenous people. These codified British laws were akin to Austinian concept of positive law, having the element of certainty, definiteness, effective enforcement and sanction. In this strict Austinian sense, the *Forest Acts* exemplified sanctions that were imposed in the name of 'justice according to law'.

British forest consciousness in India had begun to take concrete shape around the middle of the nineteenth century, when in keeping with the bourgeois outlook towards forests, the British turned towards maximizing the revenue. Consequently a full-fledged forest department was created. The assertion of state monopoly right and the exclusion of forest communities have marked the organizing principles of forest administration, since its inception in 1864. Towards this end, the first *Forest Act* was passed in 1865.

Section 2 of the 1865 Act contains the purpose for which the Act was promulgated. It gives powers to the Governor General of India, as well as to the Local Governments, to declare any land covered by trees, brushwood or jungle, to be declared a 'Government Forest'. What Section 2 provided, was a simple methodology by which any wasteland covered by trees or brushwood could be declared as 'Government Forest'. It must be recognized that the term 'jungle' is itself obscure. The Act merely sought to establish state-property rights, which translated into the right to cut down the forests for its imperialistic pursuits.

By specifically declaring certain activities as illegal or regulated, the legislation aimed at restricting access of the local people in the forests. So, in effect, this section aims to put forth the exclusive claims of the

Colonial Government over the forests. The villagers traditionally carried on activities like collection and removal of leaves, fruits, grass, honey, *etc.*, for centuries, and sometimes for mere subsistence. The Colonial Government failed to recognize this aspect. The Government had no interest in such forest produce either, at the time of the promulgation of the Act. Restricting access by banning activities inside the forests was the *modus operandi* of establishing State-property rights.

Revenue generation and commercial exploitation became all pervasive and continued to be the edifice on which the legal system for forests was built and on which the machinery of the forest department operated. The process totally annihilated the community. The policing orientation of the forest department excluded villagers who had the most long-standing claim to the forests.

The 1865 Act was replaced by a much more repressive Act in 1878, as the 1865 Act was thought to be 'inadequate', with commercial considerations and revenue generation becoming overriding. The 1878 Act was a comprehensive document. The Act was entirely different, both in form and in content, as compared to the previous legislation.[7]

For the 1878 Act, establishment of absolute state property rights and so a firm settlement between the State and its subjects over their respective rights in the forests represented the chief hurdle to be overcome. Towards this end, the classification of forests – into reserved forests, protected forests and village forests – and the procedure for forest settlement in these, were the twin features. At the end of the settlement, no "rights" remained in the reserved forest. After Independence, Indians not only accepted these classifications, but also attempted to enforce them with greater zeal.

In reserved forests, the lands were the absolute property of the Government. In protected forests, although the lands were the property of the Government, the use-rights of the villagers remained. What distinguished the reserved forests from the protected forests was that "in a reserved forest everything is an offence that is not permitted; while in a protected forest everything is an offence that is not prohibited".[8] In village forests, the Government held only the rights of management and these consisted of residue forest wastelands. With time, the area under reserved forests increased. Protected forests were designated with the ultimate goal of converting them to reserved forests.[9] And as the demand for forests resources increased, the conversion took place. There were 14,000 square miles of state forests in 1878. This increased to 56,000 square miles of reserved forests and 20,000 square miles of protected forests in 1890 and to 81,400 and 8,300 square miles respectively in 1900.[10] There was a bar on the further accrual of rights. The chapter on village forests remained a 'dead letter'.

The laws enacted by the British, which realized total control over common property resources never mentioned 'reserved' for whom, 'protected' against whom, and in favour of whom; nor do the 'revenue' land laws mention as to who the beneficiaries of revenue are going to be. This is because the British had a straightforward purpose in declaring land, which generated wealth for the local people, as 'revenue' land and in so doing, the wealth available to the local people as 'revenue' became available solely to the Crown.

The procedure of forest settlement of the customary rights of the villagers further strengthens this argument. The Act outlined a detailed settlement procedure, at the end of which, no 'rights' were to remain in the reserved forest. A distinction was made between 'rights' and 'privileges'. 'Rights' referred only to those that unquestionably existed earlier and were perhaps recorded in earlier land settlements, giving it a strictly legalistic interpretation. On the other hand, 'privileges' were more of concessions, for example, the use of grazing, collecting firewood, *etc.*, and which were "always granted by policy of the state for the convenience of the people". The distinction, "by one stroke of the executive pen, attempted to obliterate centuries of customary use by rural populations all over India".[11]

The several amendments to the 1878 Act and the ambiguous language used necessitated a single piece of legislation that would do away with all kinds of ambiguity. So the 1927 Act was promulgated. In fact there are only minor differences between the 1927 *Forest Act* and the 1878 *Forest Act* (read along with the various amendments).[12] The 1927 Act continues to be the basis of Indian forest legislation.

Sufficient anthropological and sociological data was available to explain the institution of communal possession or ownership amongst tribals, as well as about occupancy rights granted to them by earlier rulers. But in enacting the forest laws, the British chose to ignore all such data for economic purposes that are now generally classified as colonial.

The shortsightedness of the Indian government after Independence also highlighted, as no further amendments were made to the basic Act of 1878. The 1894 policy spoke about the rights of the rural communities over forest produce. Slowly it became 'rights and privileges', which was given a legal status in the *Indian Forest Act* of 1927. One would have expected the post-Independence Government to undo this damage. But the 1952 policy turned it into 'rights and concessions'. Forests are not perceived as a whole, and the focus is on timber, which is but a component of the complex whole. The colonial government turned land without individual titles into state property. Consequently, the forest laws turned the forest dwellers into 'encroachers'. After Independence, the process intensified.

At the same time, the Government came up with a new *Forest Policy* in 1988, which was a historical turn-around in forest policy. The rights and needs of the forest dependent communities were prioritized over other aspects. However, the 1988 amendment to the *Forest Conservation Act, 1980* places all the forestland under the jurisdiction of the forest department. Thus while on one hand, the Indian Government has adopted a policy sympathetic to the needs of the forest dwellers, but on the other hand, enacted laws which restrict access of these people to the forests. "In the case of the Government of India, the left hand does not know what the right hand is doing. As regards forest development, the right hand is undoing what the left hand is trying to do".[13]

Forest laws are thus colonial and capitalistic in nature, with scant regard for the original inhabitants, their rights, livelihood aspects and even to their existence.

The Question of Property Rights

Historically, forest dwellers have never truly owned the forest in the modern legal sense. What they have had is 'occupancy rights', *i.e.* rights to possess the forest and use its products. The *Atharva Veda, Brihat Parasara* and other related texts clearly reveal that in the Vedic period the Aryan kings, after they conquered an area, realized taxes for land granted, but did not usurp occupancy rights. This tendency became more pronounced in the Mauryan and Buddhist periods. Forest dwellers were granted life tenures. Later, Hindu and Muslim monarchs continued this tradition, even though they proclaimed sovereignty over all land under their jurisdiction. The British used monarchical claim over land to introduce the institution of state property over which the sovereign has absolute rights. For non-forested areas, the *Land Acquisition Act* was enacted. For the regulation and acquisition of common property, the parallel set of regulations came to be known as the Forest Laws.

In the strict legal sense, even the *Zamindars* had only an occupancy right and were mere tax collectors. Although the British vested property rights in the *Zamindars*, they did not do this for forest dwellers. This was despite the fact that, legally, the land granted to forest dwellers by earlier monarchs generated similar occupancy rights for them, as it did for those who cultivated non-forest lands.

We see thus that the same fact - of having occupancy rights - is interpreted in two different ways, both to assert and deny property rights, to achieve similar ends. In the first case, it represents the desire to simplify the procedure for revenue collection. In the second, since forests were virgin lands with massive resource potentials and since the tribals living in them were not educated enough to set up administrative machinery for revenue collection, it represents the desire to directly usurp the land. Consequently, the *Forest Act* declared common lands as 'revenue' lands and complete control was gained over the resources.

After Independence, various land reform Acts were promulgated in different states. The *Land Acquisition Act* of 1894, enacted by the British earlier, was also amended in various ways to allow land reform. Together with this came the *Abolition of Zamindari Act*. An essential aim of all such Acts and amendments was to give property rights to those who had toiled or lived on the land for long, but who remained mere occupants at the mercy of the landlords; in other words, to convert occupancy rights into property rights. The Acts required occupancy of twelve years or more for entitlement to property rights. Without going into the success or failure of such land reform measures, if those who have occupancy rights on cultivable land for more than twelve years are entitled to property rights, why does this principle not apply to forest dwellers who have had occupancy rights on non-agrarian lands for centuries? Indians, like the British, have continued to use double standards with occupancy rights, and for similar ends – the exploitation of resources from the common land.

The *Indian Forest Act*, which adopts the procedure of the *Land Acquisition Act*, 1894, for the settlement of rights, does not take the dominion status of the land dependent on the settlement of such rights. The government can simply proclaim the land to be 'forests' by notification and declare it to be government land without defining what a forest is and acquire dominion status over it without compensation to the original title holders, something which is not possible under the *Land Acquisition Act*.

According to Singh (1986), "The Indian Forest Act represents a point in the dialectics which is neither discoverable nor applicable in this manner. Hence, strictly it lacks all the characteristics of law. It is merely a decree by political fiat being passed off as law within a political system that permits this."[14] The realization of the rights is the *sine qua non* for the realization of distributive justice. If property rights are restored in the favour of forest dwellers (or the indigenous people), then, even if the destruction of forests continues, a much greater part of the resulting income will go back to the native dwellers than has hitherto been the case. Unless solutions to the problem of distributive justice are sought in the wider context of property relations, the problem of forest degradation will remain unresolved. Prior to the colonial period, benefits from common property resources were widely and fairly equitably distributed. But in the neocolonial situation, the distribution became fairly skewed.

Tenurial security is an important precondition for sustainable resource management, principally because it encourages long-term planning and greater investments of labour and resources. In the words of economist Theodore Panayotou (1989), "Property rights need to be secure. If there is a challenge to ownership, risk of appropriation (without adequate compensation), or extreme political or economic uncertainty, well-defined and exclusive property rights provide little security for long-term investment such as land improvements, tree planting, and resource conservation." And security can only be brought about by proper legislation. Forests have great economic value and are a sustained source of income to many people. So, they can be seen as contested resources over which many different sectors of society seek to assert control. Accordingly, the allocation of property rights assumes importance. In legal terms, to have a right is to have the capacity to call upon the collective power of some authority system to protect the right if the need arises. To have a property right, therefore, is to have secure control over a future benefit stream.

Environmental problems like degradation of forests are property rights problems. Most conflicts in forests arise because of difficulties in clarifying the property regimes (Bromley, 1991). It has been argued that "(d)ifferent bundles of property rights, whether they are *de facto* or *de jure*, affect the incentives individuals face, the types of actions they take, and the outcomes they can achieve." [15]

Then the question arises as to what form of property rights should be adopted – private property rights, state property rights or common property rights. The situation of no property right is ruled out, as this leads to, in Hardin's parlance, "tragedy of commons".[16]

Many economists have argued the efficacy of private property over common property. Common property regimes have been presumed to be inefficient on three counts. One is rent dissipation. No one owns the products of the resource until they are captured, and everyone engages in an unproductive race to capture these products before others do (Cheung, 1970; Dasgupta and Heal, 1979). The second is the high transaction and enforcement costs expected if communal owners were to try to devise rules to reduce the externalities of their mutual overuse (Demsetz, 1967; Coase, 1960). The third is low productivity, because no one has an incentive to work hard in order to increase his or her private returns (North, 1990).

The debate on the relative advantages of private property over common property has been marked by confusion that pertain to the difference between common property and open-access regimes, but which has been made explicit by Ciriacy-Wantrup and Bishop (1975) in a now classic article.[17]

In a common property, the members of a clearly demarcated group have a legal right to exclude non-members of that group from using a resource (Bromley, 1991). In the absence of such a right, if the resource generates highly valued products, there will be no incentive system to conserve their use for anyone and so misuse and over-consumption will follow leading to the situation called open-access regimes (*res nullius*).

Ostrom (1990) argued that common property regimes controlling access and harvesting from forests had evolved over long periods of time in all parts of the world, but were rarely given formal status in the legal codes of developing countries. On the other hand, the institutional arrangements that local users had devised to limit entry and use lost their legal standing, although the national governments lacked monetary resources and personnel to monitor the use of these resources effectively. Thus, resources that had been under a *de facto* common property regime enforced by local users were converted to a *de jure* government-property regime, but reverted to a *de facto* open-access regime leading to disastrous consequences. The result has been summarized by Bruce (1996) as follows: "In many parts of the world the national state has rejected or simply refused to recognize indigenous common property regimes, and by undermining them, has returned large areas to the relative chaos of open access. It has then often responded to this chaos by insisting that the state must assume control of the resource." The impact of state intervention has often been intensified by failure to understand the functioning of the existing systems.

On the other hand, private property and common property need not be mutually exclusive, but can be seen as two types of property with a good deal in common (Bruce, 1996). As access to use of common property is confined to members of a defined user group, which excludes other potential beneficiaries, the common property therefore has some of the attributes of shared private property. Put another way, common property is a way of privatizing the rights to use a resource without having to divide the resource into individual holdings (McKean, 1995). Moreover, the factors which encourage collective action, and the self-regulating capabilities of groups of users makes this form of property rights and management control over the forests all the more relevant. (Runge, 1986).

While no single type of property-rights system will be successful in managing every type of common property rights (CPRs), that it is possible to identify certain 'design principles' employed in efficient governance of CPRs. "There is a huge body of literature that documents where people have overcome these CPR problems," (Ostrom 1990). Some of these are the size of a group and its homogeneity, clear monitoring rules and authority to impose sanctions. Behavior in social dilemmas is affected by many structural variables, including the dependence of the participants on the benefits received, their discount rates, the type and predictability of transformation processes involved, the nesting of organizational levels, monitoring methods, and the information available to participants, besides face to face communication. On the other hand, at a behavioral level, levels of trust, reciprocity, and reputations for being trustworthy, are positively reinforcing and affect levels of cooperation and net benefits. If the CPRs are able to achieve most of these, and there exists ample examples in support of it, then there is no reason to believe that common property rights are inferior to others. Moreover, in Indian forests it is very difficult to envisage private property rights.

Breakdowns in common property systems may reflect deficiencies in policy or its implementation, rather than their appropriateness for managing a resource. Common property seldom has the same degree of support in law, or elicits the same response from authorities when threatened, as private property (Bromley and Cernea, 1989). On the other hand, these groups are typically very small, often based in single ethnically homogeneous hamlets and function within broader hamlet-level management activities.

There has been a failure in recognizing 'common property' as a regulated form of resource tenure and use, managed by a group of users with exclusive rights to do so. Consequently, the presumption that such use is destined inevitably to lead to degradation of the resource, has had a profound impact on thinking, policy and practice related to control and management of forests and other natural resources. In particular, it has contributed powerfully to the pursuit of land distribution policies that favour individual private landholdings, and has helped to justify state control of forest resources, ostensibly to ensure protection and productive use.

Conclusion

Traditional law - Hindu, Muslim and customary - has been almost entirely displaced from the modem Indian legal system. As a procedural-technical system of laws, a corpus of doctrines, techniques and institutions, *dharmasastra* is no longer functioning. This is equally true of Muslim law. The local customary component of traditional law is also a source of official rules at a few isolated points, but it too has been abandoned as a living source of law.

Strict criteria were imposed to prove the legal validity of custom. It is in this general context of the changed inter-relationship between law and custom, in terms of their respective validity and exclusivity, and the impact of the one on the other, that the issue of natural resource use and management in India is located.

According to the Hindu law, where there was a conflict between custom and *shastra,* the custom overrode the written text. Custom was a body of orally transmitted precepts and precedents. English law perceived custom through the eyes of law, through the notion of legality. Thus, custom, even if it had been a source of law, had to be sanctified by statute declared by the State. In other words, custom has no existence outside statute law. It had to be discovered and asserted, case by individual case before courts.

From a body of orally transmitted percepts and precedents subject to variable interpretation and quasi-legislative innovation at the discretion of village notables and elders, it became a fixed law to be construed by a professional court. Judicial enforcement of custom rigidified it and stripped it of its quasi-legislative character. Official courts were and are reluctant to permit the creation of new binding custom. Derrett observes that "the *dharmasastra,* as a living and responsible science died when the courts assumed full judicial knowledge of the Hindu law in 1865".[18] But the demise of traditional law does not mean the demise of traditional society.

The most significant difference between these two systems of law, which has a bearing on the subject under review, is the relative importance given to the sources of law. The significance of the imposition of Anglo-Saxon jurisprudence on the Indian legal environment lies not only in the characterization of the sources of law, but also in the inter-relationship between them.

Laws and their interpretation change over time. Law is a dynamic concept and should change with the evolution of society, under different socio-economic and political conditions. A pragmatic approach has to be incorporated. The forest laws in India are outdated and repressive for the village communities who survive on them. Property laws like forest laws should not just be geared towards achieving greater efficiency of economic transactions, but also on the principles of distribution. Wealth redistribution as a goal is better than efficiency as an objective. The survival of the village communities depends on the forests, in and around of which they live. But the British drastically changed this. One must not underestimate the changes in forest ecology that resulted from the shift in management systems. Significantly, the species promoted by the British - teak, pine and deodar in different ecological zones - were invariably of little use to the rural population. The species they replaced, like oak or terminilia, were invariably used for fuel, fodder, leaf manure and small timber.

Jurists usually seek its roots in the Latin maxim of Roman law: '*Salus populi est suprema lex*', *i.e.*, the welfare of the people is paramount law. This has been farthest from the truth *vis-à-vis* the indigenous people. We need to abandon the out-dated forest law. The forest question can be addressed only if the restoration of the rights of the people is placed on the agenda. The various schemes which are aimed at encouraging the people to participate in forest management, even if they succeed in enlisting the support of the local inhabitants, cannot be a substitute for the rights of the people who have the customary rights in forests and are traditionally dependent on forest produce. This is not to suggest that tribals, forest dwellers and pastoralists can be made to go back to a primitive economy. What one would like to emphasize is that the state or the forest department cannot have a decisive say in the matter of determining how forests are to be managed. The absolute right claimed by the State is based on the historical extinction of customary rights in forests by the colonial state. This was detrimental not only for the indigenous people for the forests as a whole. Today they have reached such a state that they cannot be neglected any longer. The forests have been managed traditionally as common property resources. This is very different from the commons and the two should not be mixed up. Property right is not just a single right, but also a bundle of rights. It should include (1) right to manage the forests, (2) right to use and sell its products, and (3) right to residual income and its disposal.

Notes

1 Rajeev Dhawan (1989), "Introduction" in *Law and Society in Modern India* by Marc Galanter, Oxford University Press, Delhi, pp. xlviii – xlix.

2 Vesey-Fitzgerald, 1998, p.257.

3 See Marc Gallanter (1989), *Law and Society in Modern India*, Oxford University Press, Delhi.

4 Vani M.S. (2002).

5 Marc Gallanter (1989), *Law and Society in Modern India*, Oxford University Press, Delhi, pp.23.

6 Dhawan, R., *op cit*, pp. xiv – xv.

7 The colonial bureaucracy was unanimous that the 1865 Act exercised only a tenuous control over forest estates, and the search for a more stringent and inclusive piece of legislation started quite early. In fact Brandis, the first Director General of the Indian Forest Department, prepared a new preliminary draft as early as 1869.

8 Gadgil and Guha, 1992, p. 125.

9 Initially only three kinds of trees, deodar, teak and sal were used for railway sleepers. However, around 1912, research proved that the blue and chir pines were also suited for this purpose. In the next few years, the extensive pine forests of Gharwal and Kumaun regions were reserved.

10 Gadgil and Guha, 1992, p. 134.

11 Gadgil and Guha, 1992, p. 134.

12 For example, the word 'State Government' has replaced the word 'Local Government' throughout the Act. Again 'Land Acquisition Act, 1870' has been replaced by 'Land Acquisition Act, 1894' in the 1927 Act. Wherever a substantial deviation has taken place, it is highlighted in the analysis.

13 Singh 1995, p. 185.

14 p. x.

15 Schlager and Ostrom, 1992, p. 256.

16 The term was coined by G. Hardin (1968), "The tragedy of commons", *Science*, 162, pp. 1243-48. Hardin argued that it was in the interest of individuals to over-extract benefits from a commonly held resource. Even if a particular individual exercised restraint – others would not, leading to the resource being degraded in any case. In this formulation of the problem, the resource can be sustainably managed only through state regulation or privatisation. As noted by many, this formulation of the problem closely parallels the prisoners' dilemma game or Olson's collective action problem (Ostrom, 1990).

17 For a detailed exposition on this subject see Bromley, Daniel W. 1991, *Environment and Economy: Property Rights and Public Policy*, Oxford: Blackwell Publishers.

18 Quoted in Marc Gallanter, *ibid*, pp.24.

References

Baden-Powell, B.H. (1882), *A Manual of Jurisprudence for Forest officers*, Government Press, Calcutta.

Bromley, Daniel W. (1991), *Environment and Economy: Property Rights and Public Policy*, Oxford: Blackwell Publishers.

Bromley D. W. and Cernea M. M. (1989), *The Management of Common Property Natural Resources, Some Conceptual and Operational Fallacies'* World Bank Discussion Papers No 57, The World Bank, Washington DC.

Bruce, J. W. (1986), *Land Tenure Issues in Project Design and Strategies for Agricultural Development in Sub Saharan Africa*, Land Tenure Center, LTC Paper 128, University of Wisconsin-Madison.

Cheung, S. N. S. (1970), "The Structure of a Contract and the Theory of a Non-Exclusive Resource", *Journal of Law and Economics*, 13/1: 49-70.

Ciriacy-Wantrup, S.V., and Richard C. Bishop (1975),"Common Property As a Concept in Natural Resource Policy", *Natural Resource Journal*, 15(4), pp.713.

Coase, Ronald (1960), "The Problem of Social Cost", *Journal of Law and Economics*, 3, pp.1.

Dasgupta, P. and G. Heal (1974), "The Optimal Depletion of Exhaustible Resources", *Review of Economic Studies*, Symposium on the Economics of Exhaustible Resources, 41: 3-28.

Demsetz, Harold (1967), "Towards a Theory of Property Rights", *American Economic Review*, 57, pp. 347.

Dhawan Rajeev (1989), "Introduction" in *Law and Society in Modern India* by Marc Galanter, Oxford University Press, Delhi.

Gadgil, M. and Ramachandra Guha (1992), *This Fissured Land: An Ecological History of India*, Oxford University Press, New Delhi.

Galanter Marc (1994), *Law and Society in Modern India*, Oxford University Press, New Delhi.

Guha, Ramachandra (1983), "Forestry in British and Post-British India: An Historical Analysis", *Economic and Political Weekly*, 29 October and 5 November.

Guha, Ramachandra (1990), "An Early Environmental Debate : The Making of the 1878 Act", *Indian Economic and Social History Review*, 27, 1

Hardin, G., (1968), "The tragedy of commons", *Science*, 162, pp. 1243-48.

McKean M.A. (1986) "Management of Traditional Lands ('Iriachi') in Japan" in National Research Council, *Proceedings of the Conference on Common Property Resource Management*, Washington DC, pp533-589.

North, D. (1990), *Institutions Institutional Change and Economic Performance*, Cambridge University Press, Cambridge.

Ostrom, E. (1990), *Governing the Commons: The Evolution of Institutions for Collective Action*, Cambridge University Press, Cambridge.

Panayotou, T. (1988), "Comments on Kenneth Ruddle's *The Organization of Traditional Inshore fishery Management Systems in the Pacific*", in P. Neher, R. Arnason, and N. Mollett (eds.), *Rights Based Fishing*, Kluwer Academic Publishers, Dordrecht, pp. 86-93.

Ribbentrop, B. (1900), *Forestry in British India*, Government Press, Calcutta.

Runge, C. F. (1986), "Common Property and Collective Action in Economic Development", *World Development*, 14/5, pp. 623-35.

Shlager, Edella and Ostrom, Elinor (1992), "Property-rights regimes and natural resources: a conceptual analysis", 68(3) *Land Economics*, pp. 249-262.

Singh, Chattrapati (1986), *Common Property and Common Poverty: India's Forest Dwellers and the Law*, Oxford University Press, New Delhi.

Singh, Gurdip (1995), *Environmental Law*, Lawman (India) Private Limited, New Delhi, pp. 185.

Vani, M. S. (2002), "Customary Law and Modern Governance of Natural Resources in India – Conflicts, Prospects for Accord and Strategies", Mimeo, Paper Submitted for the Commission on Folk Law and Legal Pluralism XIIIth International Congress, held in Chiang Mai University, Thailand, April 2002

Vesey-Fitzgerald, Seymour, "Hindu Law", *Encyclopedia of Social Sciences*, p.257-62.

Voelcker (1897), "Report on the Improvement of Indian Agriculture", Government Press, Calcutta.

14

My Vision of India: 2047 AD

BHALCHANDRA MUNGEKAR

The topic I have chosen, relates to an enterprise of speculation. For an individual or a society it is desirable to speculate and sometimes it becomes even a need. But in that case speculations become objectives or dreams to be achieved over a period of time either by the individual or the society. Now, being a professional economist I am aware of John Meynard Keynes' warning that *'in the long run we all are dead'*. But economics is just one aspect of complex human life. I, therefore, tend to temporarily overlook Keynes' warning and venture to set out the scenario in our country in the decade to follow. But before I do so, it would be pertinent to make mention of few aspects of our immediate past and deal with some of the major issues presently surrounding us as a society, for it is only in that background it would be possible to do some justice to the theme on which I have chosen to deliberate.

Freedom came to India in the midst of turmoil. It was accompanied by the partition of the country, probably the greatest tragedy human society has so far witnessed, to be followed by its disastrous and horrendous consequences. Lakhs of people were killed, millions were injured, property worth crores of rupees was destroyed, millions of people lost their homes and, for the first time in the human history, millions were compelled to cross the artificially created borders. Though this stupendous loss can be apportioned between Hindu and Muslim communities, in terms of 'human values' such distinction is irrelevant and also immoral.

India became a **Sovereign Democratic Republic** on 26th January, 1950 and later also **secular** and **socialist**. The Indian Constitution is the reflection of the dreams and aspirations of the millions of countrymen and women who courageously threw themselves in the long-drawn freedom movement, which reached to its highest stage under the historic leadership of Gandhiji and withstood to all sufferings to which the mighty colonial power had subjected them. True, modern democracy based on individual as the **unit** is the gift of Europe to human civilization and I am proud of Europe on that account as it paid heavy price for that. However, taking into account the nature, structure, spirit and content of the Constitution of India, particularly in the background of social and institutional structures and rigidities prevailing in the country for centuries arresting her overall progress, I venture to describe the Constitution as a silent liberal democratic revolution and hold the people of this country in highest possible esteem who brought such Constitution in existence.

Let me justify this proposition.

Earlier, in no country practicing formal democracy as the way of governance, **adult suffrage** came at one go. It came only with the advent of the Indian Constitution without any discrimination on the basis of class, caste, sex, race, language and so on. The infamous untouchability, unknown to human species anywhere in the world, was abolished by the Constitution. The Constitution bestowed on every citizen, again without any discrimination, certain basic fundamental rights. It contained Directive Principles of the State Policy spelling out the future course of national governance in every sphere of life.

The country adopted economic planning as a strategy to secure economic advancement at as high a rate as possible, by ascribing a pivotal role to the state as the initiator of growth. It was thought that neither unrestricted market economy nor would a totalitarian economy be relevant for securing economic growth and social justice, on the one hand; and realization of political freedoms guaranteed by the Constitution, on the other. This was consistent with the broad 'development consensus' emerged after the end of the Second World War. India, thus, adopted the course of mixed economy, representing the co-existence of private and public property, manifested in the form of private and public sector. The genesis of the evolution of the mixed economy adopted in our country is too well known to repeat here. Suffice is to say that to a substantial extent, India's post-Independence economic policy with all its characteristics, was influenced by and, an outcome of the political and economic thinking of the pre-Independence Indian National Congress, the main instrument of India's freedom struggle, on the one hand; and the various post-war compulsions, on the other.

It is unnecessary here to deliberate on how our economy was brutally subjected to the colonial exploitation for about a century and a half. Briefly said, during the colonial period our agriculture was pauperized, starving for investment and our indigenous industry was debased, making agriculture the source of infamous **disguised** unemployment, and industry incapable to help solve the problem of unemployment. Our savings and interest rates were miniscule, and the overall state of technology was far from satisfactory. The means of communications and transport were grossly inadequate except some railway coverage and shipping. Life expectation of both men and women was miserably low, the death rate being alarmingly high. Health facilities were not only totally inadequate, but of absolutely poor quality. In the post-war world, divided into conflicting ideologies subscribed by the competing super powers, foreign aid was not immediately available.

Viewed in the background of socio-economic and political conditions prevailing in the country at the time of advent of freedom, our achievements in all spheres of national life may not be stupendous, but at the same time, by no means can they be considered unsatisfactory.

India has succeeded in transforming its colonial economy with all attended ills and scenario mentioned above in more ways than one. In the course for more than five decades of economic planning, with its all inherent limitations, the economy has performed somewhat better. For instance, our savings and investments rates have reached to nearly 24 to 25 per cent of gross domestic product. The rate of economic growth could break the vicious circle created by 'Hindu Rate of Growth' (about 3.00 per cent per annum) and for a period of overall five decades during the planning era, it works out to be around 4.3 per cent per annum. Agriculture, due to technological breakthrough and other structural reforms such as land reforms, mainly the abolition of the *zamindari* system in the north, could quadruple foodgrain production. Whether we achieved 'self-sufficiency' on the front of foodgrain production, would be, according to me, a debatable proposition. But taking into account the 'effective' demand for food, the country is relieved from moving with a begging bowl for food-aid from the surplus food-producing countries. Agriculture has also diversified its cropping pattern in-as-much as newer regions are brought into the mainstream of technological break-through and thus, the latter is somewhat widely spreading.

Today, the Indian economy reflects a broad-based, complex, versatile, and dynamic industrial structure. Our industrial economy consists of very large, medium, semi-medium, small and tiny industrial units and enterprises encompassing the whole range of industrial activities, making India one of the few industrialized nations in the world, including the highly industrialized nations of the west. Means of communication and transport are so well spread that probably, today, there may not be a single village in the country that has no access to State transport facilities.

India's achievements in the field of technology are self-evident and indeed gratifying. The establishment of several scientific research organizations after Independence have proved very fruitful, credit for which needs to be given to the immediate post-Independence visionary political leadership, our innovative scientists and scientific personnel, and young scientist men and women undertaking research with a sense of commitment and dedication. India's success in the field of software technology has acclaimed her an enviable position in the world.

We also could achieve some success in the field of education and health. We could evolve somewhat elaborate and comprehensive arrangements for providing health and education facilities to our people, compared to the scenario prevailing at the time of Independence. Special constitutional provisions made for the disadvantaged social sections, such as the Scheduled Castes and Scheduled Tribes, helped them to relax the shackles of social and economic bondage and join the mainstream socio-economic order though, at a slow pace. I venture to describe the progress made by our women-folk as stupendous and this is indeed gratifying for every right thinking Indian.

One of the notable successes of the nation is the stability of our democratic order, notwithstanding all shortcomings to which our democracy is presently subjected by all sorts of vested interests, about which, I shall say something later. But there is no denying the fact that democracy as a system of governance has come to stay in India. The people, at least till now, have succeeded in preventing the rulers of the country from changing the basic structure of the Constitution which consists of: (a) supremacy of the constitution, (b) republic and democratic form of governance, (c) secular character of the Constitution, (d) separation of powers between the legislature, the executive, and the judiciary, and (e) federal character of the Constitution.

About Secularism

Whatever may be the debates and controversies either in the realm of philosophy or with respect to actual functioning of the society, India has inherited a pluralistic society. Acknowledging this and also taking into the imperatives of modern democracy, and also the multi-cultural nature of society, the founding fathers of the Constitution, without explicitly incorporating the word secular (it was done in 1976 by the 46th constitutional amendment) gave us a secular Constitution. And notwithstanding, all attempts by some, at least till now, we, as a nation, have succeeded in preserving the secular character of our society.

Now, while setting out the vision of future India it is also necessary, rather compulsory, to refer to some of our glaring failures.

Whether India could have adopted a model of economic growth based on complete social ownership of means of production is not only hypothetical, but also a debatable proposition, particularly in view of the nature and composition of ruling classes at the time of Independence, in whose hands power descended from the colonial rulers. However, the result of accepting the model of economic growth in the midst of the mixed economy primarily based on the private ownership of means of production and the 'trickle-down theory', in terms of distribution of benefits of economic growth was inescapable, notwithstanding economic planning, some land reforms and nationalization of key and strategic industries in the course of time. Thus, the benefits of post-Independence economic growth mainly accrued to the sections of the society in whose hands came to be concentrated means of production, including knowledge and, decision-making or bargaining power in different economic areas and activities; be it agriculture, industry, trade, finance, or any form of economic and business activity. In terms of 'interest' categories, they comprised industrialists, traders, big and surplus farmers, politicians, bureaucrats, technocrats, organized workers in better-paid professions, doctors, professors and so on. Again, in terms of their caste composition, they invariably belong to the upper and intermediate castes, as they are recognized in Indian society. On the other hand, an overwhelmingly large section comprising agricultural labourers, marginal, and dryland small and even medium farmers, rural artisans, low-paid industrial workers in the unorganized sector, mostly belonging to the so-called lower castes, remained neglected.

I mentioned that in the 1950s several state governments enacted legislation giving way to various kinds of land reforms. However, not only were these reforms inadequate in their content, but whatever legislation was enacted, was also not implemented with a strong political will. As a result, today, about one-fifth of the large, medium and semi-medium farmers own and cultivate nearly 70 per cent of the cultivated land in the country, while 80 per cent of the farmers, being small and marginal, cultivate remaining 30 per cent of the land. Similarly, most of all other productive assets and inputs in agriculture too are mainly possessed by the affluent sections of the rural community, manifesting the interlocking of factor markets. Given such glaring unequal distribution of land and other productive assets in rural areas, there is no wonder that today nearly one-third of the rural people remain below the poverty line in the presence of about 60 million tons of foodgrains remaining idle in the government godowns for want of adequate purchasing power in the hands of the rural poor.

Though several industrial policies helped achieve broad-based industrial growth, due to state-sponsored industrialization giving several concessions, one of the most important being the sheltered market from foreign competition, Indian industry exploited the concessions against the interests of the consumers. For instance, private sector industries got virtually unrestricted pricing power which, among other things, reflected in their high profit margins that came to be recognized as the index of efficiency of the private sector *vis-à-vis* the public sector, overlooking altogether the fact that the latter were made to operate under diametrically opposite conditions and, yet, were dubbed as inefficient entities. The onslaught of criticism of the public sector became a professional commitment of the many economists and policy-makers particularly after initiating economic reforms. I urge that serious economists in this country sometimes should explore objective criteria to dispassionately evaluate the relative performance of the public and private sectors since Independence and come to some meaningful conclusions that would enlighten the people of India.

I have mentioned about the stability of parliamentary democracy in our country and yet, not only are many disturbing trends visible, but some are well-entrenched. The way, of late, we came to operationalize our parliamentary democracy where not only individuals keep their interests above the interest of the parties to which they belong and the parties keep their interests above the interests of the nation, but the whole democratic structure and particularly the process of election is suffering from serious distortions and ignominies. In the absence of genuine electoral reforms, expenses of contesting elections have increased to such alarming levels that right to contest an assembly or parliamentary election has become meaningless; while the use of muscle power and growing criminalization of politics in several parts of the country has come to underestimate even right to vote as also force people to vote against their conscience. Thanks to the sustained efforts of our Election Commission, the sanctity of electoral process is sought to be maintained.

Though we have achieved some success on the front of social and gender equality, there is no room for complacence. For instance, untouchability was abolished by law, and yet there are thousands of registered cases of violation of basic civil rights that the Constitution has given to the socially disadvantaged sections, such as the Schedule Caste and Schedule Tribes. Annihilation of caste was never on the agenda of this country either in pre-or post-Independence era, but as I said above, our political and administrative machinery is failing even in protecting the basic human rights of the *Dalit* communities in the country. I am proud of the achievements of our women-folk in every walk of life, perhaps the single achievement of our country since Independence, thanks to the Constitution makers, who gave women equal rights with men and to various women's organizations in the country who helped in a sustained way raise the consciousness of women and also agitate for establishing their rightful place in the society, women are still victims of male-dominated patriarchal family and social organizational structures.

Though we have made strides in the field of education at every level, our efforts in the field of elementary and primary education are grossly inadequate, as a result of which, nearly 16 per cent of the world's total illiterates are living in India. Differences in the various levels of education between men and women, between the so-called upper castes and lower castes, and between the majority and minority communities, are rather glaring and hence disturbing. Thus, on the one hand, we are, and rightly so describing 'knowledge as power', and on the other hand, are witnessing a scenario where nearly one-third of our population is illiterate for want of access to elementary and primary education. Till recently, we preserved the higher education system, introduced by Lord Maculay as early as in 1835, without questioning its contemporary relevance. Our inability to evolve an appropriate education policy relevant to the requirements of building up of a strong and egalitarian nation has been one of the major failures of our country since Independence.

While discussing numerous challenges facing the country today, I must add to the list two more. The first relates to growing communalization of politics; and second, the country's post-1991 wide-ranging economic reforms based on liberalization, privatization and globalization.

An attempt is being made by some sections of the society to redefine nationalism in terms of its cultural manifestations. Briefly, it is described as **cultural nationalism**. In this context, a question is raised as to what would be the cultural foundation of India's nationalism. It is feared that if any specific religious culture happens to be the basis of Indian nationalism, this would pose a serious problem to the unity and integrity of the country characterized by a multi-religious and multi-cultural spirit. So far as economic reforms are concerned, much has been written and said about their pros and cons for the Indian economy and society. Now, if there is a distinction between economic theory and policy, and there **is** such distinction, the only given economic policy cannot be considered as sacrosanct. However, the sole criteria, for judging the usefulness of economic policy lies in its efficacy to solve, to the greatest extent possible, economic problems of the society, mainly the poor, at a given point of time. Viewed in this context and judged by the criteria which I have mentioned above, I am of the considered opinion, notwithstanding the necessity of some economic reforms even with some element of inevitability, and further notwithstanding the fact that some of the benefits that the reforms have been instrumental to bring to the economy, their nature and focus at the aggregate level, sequencing, and implementation during the last ten years or so has made one thing apparent: the **welfare state** implicitly embodied in the Constitution of India, and also operationalised in the pre-reforms period, is being considerably eroded.

In view of what I have said so far, as a conscientious citizen of this country, I am constrained to observe that our entire socio-political and economic arrangement is not only at stake, but is also rendered largely ineffective and perhaps irrelevant for solving the basic material problems facing large sections of our society.

Where do we go now from here?

I would like to postulate two alternative scenarios. First, some of the challenges and distortions in the system mentioned above may aggravate beyond repairs, undermining our post-Independence achievements and create chaotic conditions in the country, threatening thereby the very foundation of our social fabric. The second scenario may witness overcoming the challenges, removing the distortions and strengthening our post-Independence achievements, making India a strong united nation. But there is a caveat. If the things are left to themselves, the first scenario will be inevitable. And if that is to be prevented, there will have to be a positive and thoughtful intervention from all those who are concerned.

It is in this background that I spell out the nature of positive intervention and its various ingredients.

Elimination of Poverty

In an economy experiencing wide-scale and abject poverty, the purpose of economic growth should obviously be to improve the material conditions of living of the poor and not to increase the privileges of the affluent sections of the society. For this to happen, the poverty removal policy must be an integral part of the development policy and not its by-product, which unfortunately has been the case over the years. Professional economists too did not lag behind in-as-much as, in India, they concentrated their entire academic energy in quantifying poverty. Being a student of economics it would be naive on my part to underestimate the importance of serious academic efforts of quantification of poverty, which is a necessary exercise to identify the target groups or the beneficiaries of welfare policies on the priority basis. And yet, according to me more important and fundamental question is **'why poverty'?** than **'how much poverty'?** or **'how to measure poverty'?** This is because due to the neglect of the question **'why poverty'?** and failure to identify factors causing its perpetuation, various poverty alleviation programmes, though helping to some extent in reducing poverty, could not succeed to the desired level. The political economy of poverty would make it amply clear that the most unequal distribution of means of production is the basic cause of wide scale poverty in our country. Here, a detailed discussion on the measures to be adopted to secure more egalitarian distribution of such means of production is not possible. One immediate and often argued solution, is to carry out the unfinished agenda of various land reforms, particularly implementation of ceiling legislation. Even today, land being the primary asset of production in agriculture and also a major determinant of access to various other productive and income generating assets, any talk of meaningfully reducing poverty in the rural areas without land reforms would be self-defeating. Many countries in South East Asia implemented with full commitment and zeal various land reforms, which helped them in a big way in their efforts of removing poverty. However, the emergence of India's rural power structure dominated by the rural ruling classes and coalition of ruling classes at the national level, it is very much doubtful whether such land reforms would be, at all, now feasible.

Creation of Employment Opportunities

Due to several interconnected factors, the problem of unemployment in the country has become virtually insoluble. What is distressing however is the fact that unemployment does not any more appear to be a serious concern of the rulers, and policy makers both at the center and at the state levels, and also to the 'reforms friendly' economists in the country who consider employment as a by-product of growth. Particularly, attempt is made in the annual budgets of the Central and State Governments to incorporate some policy measures intending to create employment opportunities as the Prime Minister's or Chief Minister's Programmes. But as I mentioned above, the scale and intensity of the problem of unemployment is probably the single most worrisome economic issue facing the country today and which, regretfully, has virtually become invisible in the post-economic reforms discussion in the country. Serious attempts and policies of more fundamental nature are required to solve the problem of unemployment.

Restoring Welfare State

Those who still subscribe to political revolution may not find themselves comfortable with the concept of the Welfare State, which in the radical circles is considered bourgeois in nature. I do not want to go into a debate here on the feasibility of political revolution, though a meaningful and serious debate on that issue is needed in the present context of the prevailing socio-political processes in the country and also in the background of what has happened and what has been happening at the international level *vis-à-vis* neo-colonialism on the one hand, and the collapse of the former communist/socialist regimes, on the other. At this juncture and given the economic suffering of the masses, I would expect that state must undertake the responsibility of providing to the poor basic amenities such as health, education, drinking water, sanitary facilities, shelter *etc.* which are the pre-conditions of their material existence. I say restoration of the welfare state, for there is sufficient evidence to suggest that in the post-reforms period, as I mentioned above, the welfare role of state is suffering from erosion.

Social Equality

The caste system in India has, for centuries, played havoc with millions of downtrodden sections, officially known as the Scheduled Caste and Scheduled Tribes and popularly *Dalit*s. The whole political management in the country is becoming insensitive to the social and cultural sufferings of these people, nor are there attempts made to adopt meaningful policies and programmes that would loosen the tentacles of caste system. What is further distressing, only the *Dalit* communities speak about the caste atrocities and offences with respect to the practices of untouchability, which make socio-cultural life of the *Dalits* miserable. A long-drawn thoughtful national agenda, therefore, needs to be adopted to secure the annihilation of caste, as also to prevent the atrocities perpetrated on the *Dalit* communities with a strong and genuine socio-political will.

Removal of Gender Bias

I am aware that it would not be possible to attack and remove the centuries-old male-bias which discriminates against women in each and every walk of life, and yet more rigorous and systematic efforts need to be made with a view to reforming our family structure and property rights and relations and functioning of the labour market. The debate in the country on uniform civil code is mostly used as a potent political instrument to score over the opponents and to communalise the political process, rather than the genuine concern towards removing hardships and sufferings of women arising due to social, religious and cultural customs and traditions.

Indian Nationalism and Composite Culture

My primary acquaintance with the spirit of the Indian Constitution has made to me clear that it subscribes to a cosmopolitan Indian nationalism whose foundation is each and every man and woman in the country irrespective of his/her religion, caste, class, gender, language and so on. In other words, the Constitution is based on 'Indian Nationalism' and, according to me, India's composite culture, transcending any specific religious denomination is its cultural foundation. Though the Indian Constitution nowhere uses the words 'Indian Nationalism' or 'Indian culture' or 'composite culture', but according to me that is the cultural basis of our Constitution. I am aware that political parties in a parliamentary democracy are not groups of *Sannyasis*, and therefore, there is nothing wrong in their making efforts to capture and retain political power. But some of them must introspect and ensure that while doing so, they are not destroying the very spirit of Indian Nationalism or India's long drawn heritage of composite culture. Lastly, examples of Germany and Italy have shown that fascism is the most pervert, devastating and inhuman form of nationalism, the fact, if forgotten, would pose a serious challenge to the unity and integrity of the country.

Electoral Reforms

Right from the passage of *the People's Representation Act* in 1951, discussion is going on in the country about electoral reforms, but our actual achievements are disproportionately low *vis-à-vis* the scale of discussion. It is not possible to touch upon the nature of such electoral reforms, nor am I competent to deal with them. I leave it to the experts and various agencies in that field. But as a common citizen, I would suggest that something needs to be urgently done to regulate the electoral expenses which are so alarming that they make the right to contest election a mere farce. I am also painfully aware of the nature of our semi-backward polity, which is in transition and therefore use of such primordial identities such as religion, caste, language *etc.* cannot be totally ruled out, at least in the immediate future. But unfortunately, during every successive election since the first held in 1952, misuse of these identities is increasing at a geometric speed. The use of muscle power and criminal elements is also increasing very fast. All these developments are unquestionably and seriously undermining, if not destroying, the sanctity of our electoral process, which is the only constitutional mechanism to reflect the political choice of the people with respect to political parties governing the country and people managing that party. As a conscious citizen, therefore, I urge that all those concerned should seriously do something immediately to ensure the sanctity of electoral process in the country.

Reduction in Imbalance in Regional Development

Due to uneven factor endowments and wide variations in other requisites of economic development, it would be impossible for any country to secure balanced regional development. Whatever may be theoretical framework prescribing balanced regional development, suggesting practical policies to achieve it, it is possible to argue that development is somewhat inherently uneven, and yet there is no justification whatsoever to perpetuate that unevenness. In other words, in a country like India where regional variations are many, systematic efforts need to be made at every policy level to reduce the natural imbalance in regional development, keeping in view the environmental considerations. This is necessary not only for enabling people to share benefits of economic development at large, but also a necessary consideration for maintaining India's territorial integration. States such as U.P., Bihar, Madhya Pradesh, Rajasthan, Orissa and all North Eastern states, to mention a few, as also backward regions of the advanced states must get some priority from the planners with respect to investment policies and those fiscal corrective measures. In some of the above states, exploitation of vast potential of economic development such as mineral and water resources, tourism, *etc.* can help achieve faster economic growth, generate income and provide employment opportunities to the people of the region.

National Population Policy

Not that India had any serious population policy after Independence, but whatever policy we had, was abandoned since the mid 1970s. Philosophically, it is a well accepted proposition that an individual is an **end** in himself or herself, or in terms of economic theory and policy, that human capital is an indispensable factor of production, yet in a labour-surplus country like India, control of population growth appears to me inevitable. I don't deny that somebody may develop a model for India's economic development where present size of labour force may prove to be inadequate; but certainly that is not the case at present. Progressive economists in the country have always held that population was no more a problem for India, and in this regard, they always gave an example of China, overlooking the fact of total dissimilar model of development adopted by China and particularly the stringent measures China has adopted to control its population growth. Briefly, what I would like to suggest and, somewhat emphatically, is that we should have a comprehensive, genuine and serious population policy, of which, basic objective should be to ensure some balance between the demand for labour in various economic activities and its supply.

Role of Intellectuals

In every society, intellectuals are accorded a place of esteem and I think they deserve it. Intellectuals try to first raise the questions facing the society, understand and analyze them and try to suggest solutions keeping in view the interest of the society of which they are integral part. But Gramsci has wisely written about the concept of 'organic intellectuals'. By this Gramsci meant that generally intellectuals find it very hard to rise above the interests of the class (or caste) to which they belong. Taking this into account, the commitment of Indian intellectuals at large towards making efforts for establishing an egalitarian social order may be disputed. I think this causes a serious concern. I am painfully aware that intellectuals do not bring social change, but certainly they act as facilitator, of social change. This is epitomized in the words of Napolean, who said that had there been no Rousseau, there would not have been the French Revolution. I, therefore, urge that Indian intellectuals must introspect their role in the contemporary Indian society and decide which way they want to facilitate the change of the Indian society.

15

An Ideal India

A View from Below

D. SHYAM BABU

Soon after the First World War, Britain floated a new idea; the idea of self-determination of people. The motive was to break up the Ottoman and Austro-Hungarian empires. But the idea was pregnant with other possibilities, such as giving birth to a new era that would include the disintegration of the British Empire and the imperialists in the foreign office were quick to foresee the dangers in it. One such imperialist questioned: what did it mean by self-determination? He went on offering the answer, "It would logically lead to the self-determination of Gibraltar to Spain, Malta to the Maltese, Cyprus to the Greeks, Egypt to the Egyptians, Aden to the Arabs or Somalis, **India to chaos**, Hong Kong to the Chinese, South Africa to the Kaffirs, West Indies to the blacks, *etc*. And where would the British Empire be?"[1]

India to chaos? Apart from being offensive to Indians, that prognostication, in hindsight, may be more appropriate in other cases of 'self-determination'. India has not only managed to avoid chaos, but emerged as a major power to be reckoned with. However, that doesn't appear to be a source of satisfaction. Irrespective of the current euphoria on the turnaround in the economy, as well as its status as a nuclear weapon state, the country is ranked 127th in the United Nations Development Program's Human Development Index, sandwiched between Morocco and Vanuatu. The point is not that India finds itself in bad company, but its human development accomplishments are similar to that of these two countries, that have no comparable fertile soil or natural resource-base. That the country produces more than sufficient quantity of food grains to feed its billion-plus population becomes a moot point when considered in the light of starvation deaths and widespread malnutrition.

There are similar contradictions galore. Chaos might have been avoided, but it does not mean that India has become a cohesive, functioning nation-state, in peace with itself as well as its neighbours and confident of the future. In some places, whether geographic or policy areas, the State is collapsing or has no will to assert its authority. The Indian State, which succeeded British India, is a construct of national consensus embodied in the Constitution, enshrining modern ideals of equality, freedom and justice. The prescription of the founding fathers was that remaining dedicated to these ideals would be the pre-requisite for the nation never to lose its Independence.

What is our track record? Caste and communal violence, left-wing extremism, ineffective polity and unconcerned bureaucracy are some of the fruits of the failure to abide by the Constitutional mandate. Therefore, not much has changed to challenge the description of India, by John Kenneth Galbraith, as a "functioning anarchy."

Moreover, Rajni Kothari's "India-Bharat" dichotomy has worsened over the decades. For him, India represents the miniscule minority of English-speaking upper and middle classes, and Bharat symbolizes the vast rural masses caught in the spiral of illiteracy, poverty and deprivation. Development policies mostly benefit 'India', thus creating a tiny island of prosperity amidst the vast ocean of poverty and ignorance that is Bharat. And the 'tiny island' together with urban sections that depend on it and get some succor, cannot account for more than 20 per cent of the total population. That means no more than 200 million people and this section has come to be insulated from the rest of the country. Hence the talk, sometimes, of a 250-million strong Indian market!

The image of the nation, projected exclusively by 'India', is increasingly at variance with facts. Claims of economic progress or increasing military might are not false, though they portray an incomplete picture. Economic prosperity coexists with widespread poverty and a nuclear India is saddled with internal violence and external aggression. Therefore, when one considers the nation as a whole, every claim of accomplishment is challenged by a counter-fact. In other words, while cities and towns are in self-congratulatory mode about progress, villages are untouched by that progress. The life of contradictions also neatly fits into India's caste structure. Euphoria found at the top of the caste hierarchy turns into despondency at the bottom.

Where shall the twain meet? The purpose of this paper is not exactly to highlight the all-too-familiar contradictions between urban and rural India, but submit how the failure to address the problem will have deleterious consequences. How does India fare from the perspective of the one-fourth of the population at the bottom?

Past Imperfect

It is submitted here with equanimity that much of the problem arises out of the uncritical estimation of our past. Leaving aside the colonial period as if it is not part of our heritage or mostly as a national trauma we should come out of, has helped in unleashing forces that were at least partly responsible for the nation losing its Independence in the past. And, for most Indians, the 'colonial contribution' is a contradiction in terms. It is not the purpose of this paper, however, to chronicle the 'achievements' of colonialism, but to point out how the exclusion of this period pushes the nation back a few centuries in real terms. It doesn't hurt to be truthful and it may lead to some much-needed re-evaluation of the direction the nation is taking. Moreover, such an endeavor is relevant to the advancement of minorities, *Dalits*, Tribals and other marginalized sections.

Though the Indian State and its Constitution, the top soil in Ambedkarite terminology, are formally successors to British India, the way we have attempted to construct nationalism, solely based on our traditions[2] has come to legitimize obscurantist forces and accentuated intolerance of all kinds. Consider the case of villages and the related issue, decentralization. There is a widespread culture of idealizing villages as self-sustaining entities where social and economic life is guided by customs of equality and brotherhood. This is not the case now and it was never the case in the past. Ambedkar drew the wrath of 'nationalist' sections when he said in the Constituent Assembly, "What is the village but a sink of localism, a den of ignorance, narrow-mindedness and communalism? I am glad that the Draft Constitution has discarded the village and adopted the individual as its unit."[3]

Ambedkar's satisfaction of taking the individual as the unit was short-lived as the village, with all its primordial identities incompatible with rationalism and modernity, struck back with vengeance. The intelligentsia could not have simultaneously glorified the village and condemned it as a fen of stagnant waters. The question 'what is happening to the village' gets a clear answer if one asks, 'what is happening **in** the village'. Scholars, politicians and common folk untiringly speak of ancient Indian village republics to establish that democracy is not alien to the land and, in fact, democracy existed here much before Athens came into existence. As with other contradictions, the contention is partly true. The village republics were caste assemblies, strictly confirming to caste hierarchy. This fact again was highlighted in the Constituent Assembly, this time by Sarangdhar Das:

I disagree with most of my friends, particularly the Hindu friends who expatiate on the existence of the republican system of government, *i.e.*, republics in our old Hindu polity. I disagree with them. My contention is that our lower classes, the lower castes of our society, whom we call Harijans, have all along been kept in a depressed condition. Consequently, there was no democracy. If there was democracy, if there was a republic, it was amongst the higher classes, what we call the higher castes...[4]

This is by no means an academic point. Even after more than four decades of experimenting with *Panchayati Raj* and even after the system was given Constitutional status more than a decade ago, our villages remain village republics of the distant past. When *Dalits* and other lower strata try to claim their rights of equality and freedom, granted by the Constitution, they are taught a 'lesson': intimidation, socio-economic boycott and violence. This has become routine in States such as Bihar, Tamil Nadu, *etc.*, that the political process and its vehicle, elections, are pitting lower castes against upper castes and tradition against modernity.

Ironically, the very process of political empowerment of the *Dalits* – reservations in the legislature — is responsible for tensions between the community and the caste Hindus. In fact, several welfare measures designed for the community's upliftment are more often leading to bitter resentment among the rest of the society. The process is clearly evident in the rural areas.[5]

Intimidation of *Dalit* voters and mass violence on them as a warning before elections (so as to influence their preferences) or as punishment after the elections (for not heeding the 'advice' of the dominant caste) are fairly well known. In its pioneering report, the National Campaign on Dalit Human Rights has meticulously documented several recent instances of large-scale violence on *Dalits* during elections. Its case studies from Kerala, Tamil Nadu, Gujarat, Punjab reveal a familiar story:

- In Pathanathita District of Kerala, CPI and CPI(M) cadre unleashed mob violence against the *Dalits* as the latter allegedly switched loyalties in favour of a new *Dalit* party.

- During the 1999 Lok Sabha polls in the Chidambaram (reserved) constituency in Tamil Nadu, the dominant Vanniyar caste violently prevented the *Dalits* from exercising their vote, as the former feared that they would vote for a major alliance in which the Dalit Panthers India party was the main partner.

- In 1998, Devalia village of Amreli district in Gujarat witnessed a social boycott of *Dalits* by Patels who were incensed by the *Dalits'* political assertion, coupled with tensions over land reforms.

- During the 1999 parliamentary polls in Faridkot, the Shiromani Akali Dal supporters, including the son of the then chief minister of Punjab, unleashed violence on *Dalits*, demolished their dwellings as they felt that the *Dalits* voted for the Congress candidate.[6]

Paul R. Brass, in his electoral study of Uttar Pradesh, mentions that "Jats and Gujars do not permit the low castes to vote as they wish, but caste (*sic*) their votes for them."[7]

The case of elections to local bodies is in no way different. In fact, the vehemence of the caste Hindus to *Dalit* representation in the local bodies is more intense as the effect of the reservations is felt locally. For example, in 1996 the post of the president of a *Panchayat* (local body) in Madurai district in Tamil Nadu was reserved for the Scheduled Caste. The dominant Kallar (Thevar) caste opposed the move and prevented *Dalits* from contesting as the president. When, after a few months, a *Dalit* contested and elected as president, he along with five *Dalits* was brutally hacked to death. The Human Rights

Watch visited the village and recorded that the new *Dalit* president of the *Panchayat* was not being allowed to function as president and the Thevars had imposed an economic boycott on the *Dalits*.[8]

Similarly, many *Dalit* massacres, such as the one in Laxmanpur-Bathe, are at some level related to their political assertion. However, it may be noted that poll-related violence is not confined to the reserved constituencies alone. As a majority of the *Dalit* voters live outside of the reserved constituencies, they are also the targets of violence.

Where does the intelligentsia stand? Is political violence against *Dalits* a law and order problem? Can there be a solution without attacking the fundamental feature of our social existence, namely the caste system? When was the last time one witnessed a Hindu scholar attempting to de-legitimize *Manusmriti?* Or, is it the problem of the lower castes alone to fight caste discrimination and its scriptural sanctity, because they are the victims? Can India emerge as a cohesive modern State with the millstone of obscurantism firmly around its neck?

It is not only India. Many other countries periodically attempt to recall and artificially reconstruct the past to suit present requirements, albeit with unfortunate consequences. National identity built around religious identity is increasingly becoming anachronous. Take the case of secularism, which was sought to be constructed as a synthesis of Hindu-Muslim heritage and cultures. It has almost fallen apart as it ignored the fundamental intolerance written into caste system. The result is that lower castes, particularly *Dalits*, are the victims of casteism as well as communalism, since a majority of Muslims and Christians, against whom attacks are taking place of late, are lower-caste converts. Can one, then, solve communalism without eradicating casteism?

Can there be a forward movement towards national unity without that humbling experience, namely, the recognition of colonial contribution? Rajni Kothari's 'India' is thriving thanks to the British legacy of modern English education, made possible by the 'western' institutions of governance, though many find fault with them for precisely being what they are — alien to Indian culture. And the only hope for Kothari's 'Bharat' is to emulate 'India'.

The systematic attempt to deny historical facts such as the adoption of modern civil and criminal procedure codes, in fact the rule of law itself, as a radical forward movement in our history, has proved to be disastrous. Not many Indian scholars have studied the impact of customs and traditions, seeped in religion, that determine the place and role of individuals and on their economic development. What Satu Kähkönen calls 'institutions' ("formal and informal rules and practices"[9]), social norms based on the caste system, present the most insurmountable obstacle to economic development. What appeared as given to outsiders like Max Weber, Gunner Myrdal and others, have miraculously escaped the attention of Indian academia.

However, a troubling aspect of that tiny part of India that has become triumphant at home and abroad is the irrational yearning for things past, a constant attempt to hail obscurantism as patriotism. No doubt, inheritors of an ancient civilization cannot possibly shun their heritage. In their search for identity, they cling to their own and rationalize it as almost infallible. How else can one explain the fact that communalism gets its moral and material support from these well-off sections? With what result?

Economic development, which was hoped to blur all other identities, has failed in the task[10]. There has been reluctance to deny rural masses the same benefits of modernity that the elite have monopolized for themselves. More to the point, while benefiting from modernity, the elite seek to debunk it. Devoid of development and modernity, rural India is mired in caste-communal divisions, poverty and destitution and spewing the same onto urban areas. Priority sector lending, lending bank policies, *etc.*, defunct now, could not have lifted rural India out of poverty and ignorance, without ridding it of obscurantism first.

Future Direction

Economic development can wait, but not the fight against obscurantism. Because emancipation of *Dalits* and Tribals, the bottom fourth of the population, is not only about providing employment or other economic opportunities, it is about creating a modern Indian nation where rationalism, rule of the law and the recognition of individual's worth are treated as self-evident truths.

Such a transformation is only possible if we ensure certain preconditions without which development strategies and liberalization are bound to fail.

One, we should be more discriminating when we attempt to define our identity. Not everything is glorious about anybody's past. Intellectual honesty demands that we discard elements from our heritage that are incompatible with modernity. Whether the caste system has religious sanction or not, it should be attacked as an evil practice. The pervading intolerance — against minorities, women, *Dalits*, Tribals, *etc* — has to be tackled in its totality, not as the case now. Fight against communalism and fight against untouchability cannot be treated as mutually exclusive. What is needed is an intellectual culture where intolerance and xenophobia do not enjoy any credence.

Two, the fight against intolerance can only be possible when we rededicate ourselves to Constitutional morality by insulating public institutions from caste and communal prejudices. The State machinery suddenly, though rightly, becomes very efficient when nabbing terrorists who happen to be Muslims. The same efficiency is conspicuous by its absence when dealing with communal and caste violence against minorities and *Dalits*. Our record is dismal in punishing perpetrators of atrocities as well as officials who fail to dispense their duties.

Three, we should create an enabling environment in which egalitarianism, social justice, non-discriminatory policies and equal opportunities can be made use of by people solely on merit and without regard to their caste/communal identities.

Conclusion

This paper is intended to make only one submission, namely, we should extirpate whatever is wrong with our heritage, whatever is responsible for our losing our Independence, and construct a cosmopolitan identity for India as a vibrant Nation state, not oblivious of its past and not unconcerned either about its future. Dr. Ambedkar's farewell address to the Constituent Assembly in 1949 sums up the task ahead:

"It is not that India was never an independent country. The point is that she once lost the independence she had. Will she lose it a second time? It is this thought which makes me most anxious for the future...

This anxiety is deepened by the realization of the fact that in addition to our old enemies in the form of castes and creeds we are going to have many political parties with diverse and opposing political creeds. Will Indians place the country above their creed or will they place creed above country? I do not know. But this much is certain that if the parties place creed above country, our independence will be put in jeopardy a second time and probably be lost forever.[11]

Notes

1 Note of Colonel Maurice Hankey, the Cabinet Secretary, to Under-Secretary of State for Foreign Affairs Lord Robert Cecil, cited in Paul Johnson, *Modern Times: The World from the Twenties to the Nineties*, New York, Harper Perennial, 1992, p. 41. Emphasis added.

2 "...More or less xenophobic political campaigns calling for Indian nationhood to be based on the dominant religion," see, Barbara Harris-White, "India's Religious Pluralism and its Implications for the Economy", *Queen Elizabeth House Working Paper Series* Number 82, Oxford: Oxford University, February 2002, p. 7.

3 *Dr. Babasaheb Ambedkar Writings and Speeches, Vol. 13*, "Dr. Ambedkar: The Principal Architect of the Constitution of India", Bombay: Education Department, Government of Maharashtra, 1994, p. 62.

4 *Ibid*, p. 1191.

5 P. R. Rajagopal, *Social Change and Violence: The Indian Experience*, New Delhi: Uppal Publishing House, pp. 114-5.

6 *Atrocities against Dalits in India* Case Papers: Volume I (Summary), National Public Hearing held on April 18-19, 2000, Chennai, Madurai: National Campaign on Dalit Human Rights, 2000.

7 Paul R. Brass, *Caste, Faction & Party in India*: Volume Two: Election Studies, Delhi: Chanakya Publications, 1985, pp. 187.

8 *Broken People: Caste Violence against India's "Untouchables"*, New York: Human Rights Watch, 1999, pp. 89-99. See also *Atrocities against Dalits in India* Case Papers, Volume I, op cit. pp. S 98-S 102.

9 Satu Kähkönen, *Understanding Rural Institutions*, Working Paper No. 215, (College Park, MD: Center for Institutional Reform and the Informal Sector, University of Maryland, June 1998), p. 1.

10 Jawaharlal Nehru said: '[T]he real thing ... is the economic factor. If we lay stress on this and divert public attention to it, we shall find automatically that religious differences recede into the background and a common bond unites different groups.' Cited by Barbara Harris-White, *op cit.*, p. 5.

11 *Dr. Babasaheb Ambedkar Writings and Speeches, Vol. 13, op cit.*, p. 1214.

16

The Idea of India – Bollywood Style

MADHU KISHWAR

India evokes strong feelings and responses among Indians as well as non-Indians. India may be loved or hated, maybe an object of devotion or derision, but there is hardly anyone who remains indifferent to or lukewarm about India.

"You can take Indians out of India, but you can't take India out of Indians" – so goes a popular saying. Most people of Indian origin stay obsessed with India, no matter how far they move away from India in geographical terms. This engagement takes many forms – some express it through anger and outrage at the raging corruption, inefficiency and lack of will to set things right. Some others make a profession of critiquing the many real and imagined ills and evils of Indian society while many others turn rabid apologists. And some actually sustain their faith in India by remaining emotionally and intellectually nostalgic about its "glorious" pre-colonial past, its unique heritage and "The Wonder that was India".

However, India defies definition because of the incredible diversity of its people, religions, belief systems, languages, social structures, topography, weather conditions and knowledge systems. It is not just a nation, it represents a distinct civilization and universe of values. India does not lend itself to easy generalisations. India is not very easy to know and understand and yet Indians are very simple people who wear their hearts on their sleeves and recognise 'Indian-ness' by their tuning into people's hearts rather than any external trappings. Raj Kapoor expressed it very aptly in the famous song from the film *Shree 420* in the heydays of "Be Indian, Buy Indian" variety of nationalism being forced by the government in the 1950's:

> *Mera Joota hai Japani,*
>
> *Yeh patloon Englishtani,*
>
> *Sur pe lal topi Russi*
>
> *Phir bhi dil hai Hindustani*

Four decades later Alisha Chenoy echoed the same sentiment in her equally tantalising popular song *"Made in India"*. In this song video Alisha wears a skin-tight western outfit with a plunging neckline and bare shoulders. She herself looks like a night club dancer from a Hollywood film but she croons her heart away for a "Made in India heart":

> *Dekhi hai saari duniya, Japan se lekar Russia, Australia se lekar America. Dekha hai pyar ka sapna, Dil chahe jo ho apna, Mil Jayega ek sathiya, ek Deshiya, Made in India, Made in India, Dil chahiye bus Made in India.*

The message is clear - you may dress and dance like Madonna or Michael Jackson, you may wear jeans or mini skirts, you may look like a vamp or a night club dancer - all those are external trappings. What really matters is that your heart stays Indian. Any time our NRIs get deeply nostalgic or sentimental, they proclaim their deep attachment to their Indian roots not by showing their investment portfolio or the number of times they visit India every year, but by proclaiming that if they could tear open their chests like Hanuman did for Ram and Sita, people would find the map of India inscribed on their hearts.

India indeed defies comprehension especially for those who try to understand it through books, research studies and as an intellectual exercise. The "Real India" can perhaps only be understood intuitively, by tuning in to the emotions of its people, (as did Mahatma Gandhi more successfully than anyone else in recent times) by understanding what touches their hearts, what makes them perform miraculous feats, or what makes the people of this land indulge in the most brutal violations of human rights; what makes Indians accept corruption as a way of life or what makes them rise in rage and indignation. The 'Real India' can only be understood by coming to understand what triggers off large-heartedness, tolerance for others, no matter how different their values and appearances and what evokes vicious and mean responses; in what role are Indian men willing to worship and revere women as *Saraswatis*, *Lakshmis*, and *Durgas* incarnate or what makes them turn so women hating that they will kill their own daughters as unwanted burdens and torture their daughters-in-law to death.

In my view, despite large doses of vulgarity and mushy melodramas, Bollywood films are perhaps the best guide to understanding what values the Indians of today endorse as quintessentially Indian and what moves the Indian heart.

When one travels to Europe, North America or Australia, for the average white citizens of these countries, India is synonymous with wife murders, dowry torture, burning of widows, killing of baby girls, communal riots, caste atrocities and all pervasive human rights abuses. This is because their basic sources of information about India are their newspapers, T.V. channels and select intellectuals from India who act as native informants interpreting and informing the white world about the many "social evils" and problems faced by India.

Western media has made India's "dowry murders" and *sati* far more wonderous, exotic and famous than the, Taj Mahal, Konarak Temple and other such renowned symbols of India's heritage. Not surprisingly before India produced the great IT success stories, it evoked derision and contempt among the average European, American or Australian white citizens.

However, whenever one travels to any of the non-European countries from the Middle East to the Far East, from the backwaters of Africa or to the troubled waters of Russia — people know India mainly through Bollywood *masala* films which are not a native informant's version of India churned out for the benefit of the outside world. Bollywood films depict Indians sharing with other Indians their hopes, fears, romantic aspirations, their critique of their own society, their anger against what they perceive as unjust and unacceptable as well as the kind of transformations and social reform they aspire for and their notion of good life and fair-play. From Kashmir to Kanyakumari, from California to Kuala Lumpur from South Africa to Singapore, from Trinidad to Tokyo, from America to Australia, from Dubai to Dublin, Bollywood films have become the heartbeat of the Hindustani *dil*, both of the resident or non-resident variety. They have welded the emotional life of NRIs living in distant and diverse cultures and made them feel "Indian" by making them feel connected to their cultural values. Indians of all age groups have overcome linguistic barriers and made Hindi film songs act as the vehicles for expressing their myriad emotions and sentiments.

I began taking Bollywood films seriously only after I experienced their popularity abroad and saw how this industry had positioned itself as the most powerful cultural ambassador of India without any official endorsement to this effect; how they have built emotional bridges with people of diverse races, nationalities and languages and made them feel deeply connected with the Indian world view and way of life, though often in crude caricature form, if they are to be judged by the yardstick of "high" culture.

Bollywood film industry is the largest churner of popular entertainment films every year. And yet unlike Hollywood, Bollywood did not start off with global aspirations. Hollywood spends a good deal of money and energy on capturing world markets; Bollywood could never afford that kind of international publicity. Bollywood films are made primarily for Indians and are characteristically Indian in their values. And yet Bollywood films have travelled far and wide without extensive, high cost publicity campaigns – all through word of mouth. In the entire non-European world Bollywood *masalas* have come to acquire much greater emotional appeal and fascination than American films. Ours is the only film industry in the world, which has offered real tough competition to Hollywood and seems poised to emerge as the winner. For example, Hollywood has captured 80 per cent of the film market in Germany. But in India, Hollywood has captured only 10 per cent of the entertainment market.

Amazing Outreach of Bollywood

One could even say Bollywood films are loaded with the Hindu worldview and yet they have acquired amazing popularity in the entire non-European world. They are exported to more than a 100 countries. This when Bollywood has had to deal with various disadvantages. It has had hardly any legitimate sources of funding. Bollywood film directors have had to rely on black money and finance from the underworld because it was denied industry status and could not raise finances legally. It has had to deal with unimaginative and bureaucratic Censor Boards. Till recently, India's closed door economy necessitated the export of these films through illegal channels. Dubai became the centre of distribution for Indian films. That is how the grip of the underworld strengthened further. And yet this underworld dominated industry has chosen to churn out moral fables as entertainers and taken on the mantle of inculcating what are commonly believed to be Indian *sanskars*.

Bollwood has conquered hearts and minds of people of even those countries whose governments have long been hostile to India. When the Pakistan government recently banned the telecast of Bollywood films to Pakistan homes, Pakistan's cable operators went on strike and forced their government to withdraw the ban. This was at a time when the Indian and Pakistani governments were locked in serious conflict over the issue of cross-border terrorism and had severed even normal diplomatic ties. Even at the height of Indo-Pak hostilities, one saw Bollywood films playing in the homes of Army generals as well as ministers. This when they reach Pakistan through illegal channels, courtesy smugglers. One heard Bollywood film songs being played in the jeeps of police officers as well as ordinary buses, taxis and auto-rickshaws. At the time of the Lahore Bus Yatra, Prime Minister Atal Bihari Vajpayee was reported to have been received by a group of young Pakistanis with the following chant: "*Madhuri de do, Kashmir le lo*".

In Afghanistan, after the fall of Taliban one of the first acts of celebration was people queuing outside cinema halls to see Bollywood films. In all of the Islamic countries, including those where the ruling regimes have imposed very oppressive forms of religious fundamentalism that mandate keeping women veiled and in seclusion, people are addicted to Bollywood films showing skimpily dressed heroines dancing in parks, in the streets and in night clubs.

Bollywood films are influencing bridal dresses, and marriage and other festival rituals in all our neighbouring countries. Be it in Africa, the Middle East, or small towns and even villages of Indonesia and Malaysia, I have found young kids break into Hindi film songs on seeing a visitor from India in order to communicate their welcome and a sense of bonding despite the language and other barriers. Amitabh Bachchan, Madhuri Dixit, Shahrukh Khan, Kajol and Aamir Khan are far more popular icons than any of the Hollywood heroes or heroines have ever been or could ever hope to be in the non-western countries. They are not just cult figures, they are also perceived as role models, as moral exemplars on the strength of the values they propagate as characters in various hit films. Films like *Dilwale Dulhaniya Le Jayenga, Hum Aapke Hain Kaun, Mission Kashmir, Amar Akbar Anthony* and *Zanjeer* don't just tell entertaining stories. They are treated as moral fables that propagate a consistent set of what are seen as "quintessential" Indian values — despite all the *dishum dishum* scenes and the sexy *latka jhatka* dance numbers.

The Indic Worldview

An important reason why Hindi films resonate so deeply despite the use of very predictable stories and low brow melodrama is that the two great epics of India—the *Ramayana* and *Mahabharata*, which are also the two foundational texts of the Indic civilisation, have provided a very widely acceptable base for the artistic development of Indian commercial cinema. They are critiqued, their values often challenged, even parodied—but the stories within stories of these great epics remain the foundational discourse of Bollywood cinema. They function as meta texts of Indian tradition and *dharmic* values. The worldview they propagate and values they uphold have proved remarkably resilient despite pressures for change.

As my colleague, Dhirubhai Sheth puts it: "Bollywood films have come to play the same role than *Pauranic kathas* (tales) and the *Bhakti* movement did in the medieval period when Vedic knowledge went into decline and the original sources of the civilisational moral code began drying up. At such a time the *Pauranic kathas* took on the task of preaching morality and giving people a spiritual anchor through narrative accounts of mythical heroes and heroines whose lives demonstrated through personal example the desired social and moral code."

This is the epoch in which Tulsidas wrote the *Valmiki Ramayana* as *Ramcharit Manas* in the *Bhakti* idiom, and presented the mythic hero Rama as the *Maryada Purushottam* as opposed to the very humanly flawed Rama of *Valmiki Ramayana*. This is the period when India faced repeated invasions and the polytheistic Indic civilisation faced ideological, theological and social onslaughts from monotheistic Islam. This historic clash was very creatively resolved through powerful socio-religious movements—the *Bhakti* movement within the Hindu fold and Sufism within Islam which built bridges of communication between the two contrary worldviews. The shrines of Sufi-Sants became common centres of worship for Hindus, Sikhs and Muslims.

In the 20th century when India faced another major ideological onslaught from the imperialist triumphant West, Bollywood came to perform the role that *pauranic kathas* once did—to reaffirm a distinct moral code. Bollywood films reiterate—often in crude caricature but nevertheless popular form—a distinct worldview and set of values which in the mind of common people have come to be identified as the core, essential values and moral code of the Indian civilisation.

Unity in Diversity

For the newspaper reading intellectuals across the world India is often associated with recurring communal riots and ethnic strife between Hindu-Muslims, Christians and Sikhs. However, in the minds of ordinary people in all the non-European societies whose idea and perceptions of India are shaped by Bollywood hits, India is seen as a place where an incredibly large spectrum of diverse, religious, linguistic and ethnic castes, communities coexist on the basis of deep bonds of affection based on making respectful space for each other's unique cultural and religious identities. Film after film has obsessively reiterated the quintessential oneness of people of diverse faiths—be they Hindus, Muslims, Christians or Sikhs—and shown them cherish their close bonding as neighbours, friends, colleagues and fellow citizens.

The positive and often romantic portrayal of non- Hindu religious minorities in Indian films is a major reason for their international popularity. Bollywood has shown the world how Hindus, Sikhs, Christians and Muslims joyfully join in each other's festivals, lay their lives for protecting each other, and share each other's joys, griefs and even family secrets. The theme song of the film *Dhool ka Phool* made in the late 1950s: *Tu Hindu bangega na Muslman banega, insaan ki aulad hai insaan banega* (you should grow up to be neither Hindu nor Muslim, you are the child of a human being and should remain a human being) echoes the sentiment of *Bhakt* Kabir. This sentiment has been repeated in film after film strengthening the message that Hindus, Muslims, Sikhs, Christians are all sons and daughters of Mother India and, therefore, inseparable no matter how hard the politicians try to break their unity and sense of oneness.

The Sikhs are invariably depicted as generous, large-hearted, jovial, sincere friends, neighbours colleagues—always ready to help. They are portrayed as men of raw courage and willingness to take great risks for their friends and neighbours. Dialogues like, "He is a Guru *ka* Sikh – he can't be a cheat"—are fairly typical dialogue in Bollywood films.

Indian Christians are presented as God fearing simple people. If they are Goan they are also shown as fun loving. Christian priests are invariably depicted as kindhearted, providers of charity, help and shelter to those in need. Churches are always shown as places that provide spiritual, emotional succour to any one in distress. Hindi films are replete with scenes of Hindus walking in a Church at a time of crisis and seek Mother Mary's blessings.

Similarly, true believers in Islam, the *mazhabi* Muslims are invariably depicted as pious human beings whose faith teaches them to treat all human beings as equals and who are steadfast in their loyalties and commitments, including their loyalty to the land of their birth.

A repeated popular device for portraying Muslims as not less if not more patriotic than Hindus is to depict them in roles of great responsibility taking on anti-national elements and battling terrorists from across the border – as defenders of village, ethnic or national solidarity.

For example – a film made to honour the martyrs of the Kargil war – *Ma Tujhe Salam* – opens with a young Muslim army officer being put in charge of the most sensitive border post along the Indo-Pak border. In the very first scene his village-based mother sends him a letter saying, "Always remember you have two mothers – me and *Bharat Ma* (Mother India). Your duty towards *Bharat Ma* comes before your duty to me." In the same film, a reformed terrorist defends Kashmir from invaders from across the border hand in hand with a Hindu army officer when he realizes that the foreign *jehadis* wanted to destroy mosques and promote internal strife among the people of Kashmir. To convey that religion does not divide them he proclaims: "Our *mazhab* may be different, but our *mulk* is the same."

In *Mission Kashmir,* the man in-charge of anti-insurgency operation in Kashmir is a Muslim Inspector General of Police, who is married to a Hindu woman and their relationship is portrayed as an idyllic romance. Even while the Hindu wife keeps her Hindu identity intact; she goes to the Hindu temple, and retains her Hindu name, but adopts a Muslim orphan whose parents were killed inadvertently by her own husband. When her adopted son becomes a terrorist to avenge the death of his parents, she does not stop loving him. She gets killed by a bomb planted by her adopted son to kill her husband to underscore that terrorism is not the right path for redressing political wrongs, the politics of hate destroys not just the targets of hate but also those who act out of hate. He finally joins hands with his father to save his homeland, Kashmir, when he realises that his terrorist colleagues were planning to blow up an important mosque in order to foment communal trouble.

Compare it to the demonised stereotypical portrayal of Muslims in Hollywood *masalas* which deal with such themes and one cannot help but be impressed by the instinctive wisdom shown by Bollywood directors, script-writers and producers in not using a powerful medium like cinema to generate feelings of hatred and phobic mistrust. It is also a proof that the average citizen of India endorses this view. Or else Bollywood could not afford to sink crores of rupees in such films.

Bollywood has shown enormous wisdom in driving home the message that Pakistani may be playing evil games and have to be dealt with as enemies but Muslims are not to be blamed or scapegoated for the political mischief of a few Pakistanis. *Bombay, Mission Kashmir, Sarhad* and a host of such films dealing with cross-border terrorism take pains to distinguish between ordinary Muslims and ideological *jehadis* who are shown as misguided youth rather than as demons. When Indian Muslims (or Sikhs) take to political violence, they are almost always shown as reluctant terrorists who are pushed into the arms of external *jehadis* (who remain anonymous as forces of evil) after witnessing human rights violations and abuse of power by security forces resulting in the torture or death of close family members or friends. (*eg. Maachis, Mission Kashmir, Roja and Sarhad*). And since they too have an "Indian heart", it does not take long for them to b e reformed and return to the fold of Indian nationalism. Thus even Muslim terrorists are not denied their humanity, if they are Indian.

This gives the average Muslim outside India an image of a country where Hindus-Muslims, Sikhs and Christians not only cherish their friendship and social/civilisational bonds but also a proven ability to work out very sophisticated norms of co-living. Where else in the world do you see people of different religious faiths worship at common shrines? Which other cinema of the world would show very matter-of-factly an 8-10 year old Hindu girl child kneel before the *Quran* with due respect and appropriate rituals and pray for a boon to Allah and Allah gracefully answers the call of this *kafir* child as in *Kuchh Kuchh Hota Hai*? Which other non-Islamic country would project an underworld Muslim don as in *Ghulam-E-Mustafa* as essentially good hearted and god fearing person who is trapped in the world of crime due to force of circumstance? The cinematic device used for establishing the genuine piety of this underworld don is to show him in the introductory shot itself in solitary prayer in an ancient mosque.

Not surprisingly, Muslims of even those societies where religious fundamentalism of a very intolerant variety is pushed down people's throats by very authoritarian regimes, rejoice in the India that Bollywood takes to them. They rejoice in the liberal Islam that took roots in the Indic civilisation. The portrayal of Muslims does not offend their sensibilities and self-view and India appears as a land of freedom, of love and romance, of mutual respect and tolerance, of celebration of diversity, a land of song and dance.

If an average Indonesian, Malaysian, Saudi or Kuwaiti is asked to list two-three prominent things associated with India- he or she is unlikely to name Babri Masjid demolition Hindu-Muslim riots or the Gujarat carnage. His/her idea of India is informed by Bollywood films depicting the quintessential oneness of *Amar, Akbar, Anthony* and their unbreakable friendship and love. They are shown a world where Rehman *Chacha* (uncle) is invariably a loved and respected elder of whichever *mohalla* (neighbourhood) he is living in even when it is mainly inhabited by Hindus and Sikhs. They see India as a land where people of different religions join in celebrating each other's festivals. They see Hindu actresses Aishwarya Rai and Preity Zinta play hot love scenes opposite the Muslim super stars of Bollywood - Shah Rukh, Aamir Khan without evoking any hysterical responses.

Of Humans and Divines

Bollywood as the most effective cultural ambassador of India has also kept people reminded that in the Indic world view, there is no sharp dividing line between the hum and the divine. God is not a distant, entity who sits somewhere above in the Heaven giving orders and commandments expecting unconditional obedience, dolling out reward for obedience and punishment for those who dare work out their own code of ethics. In the Indic civilisation, gods and goddesses take avatar and descend on earth. They come and live in the world of ordinary men and women in their human *avatar*—sharing their joys, sorrows, trials and tribulations. And in their human incarnations the very same yardstick judges them that human beings apply for each other. If Krishna as the avatar of Vishnu plays naughty pranks as a child, his mother has a right to give him a good thrashing. If as an adolescent he harasses young *gopis* and village women, they too take him to task in their own ways. *Bhagwan* Rama is worshipped as *Maryada Purushottam*—the best among men for observing his *dharmic* duties as a son, as a brother, as a king and as a friend. But even when this avatar of Vishnu treats his devoted wife Sita unjustly, ordinary people have the right to criticise his unfair actions and the freedom to create script their own versions of *Ramayana* which depict him acting more honourably than he did in the original *Ramayana* created by Sage Valmiki.

In other words, it is Bollywood more than any other agency or group which has resisted the attempts by vested interests to make our gods and goddesses above criticism and reinterpretation. They keep reminding people that even gods are not to be credited with perfection. They too have flaws and they too make mistakes. It is for the devotees to demand and ensure improved behaviour every time gods make errors of judgement or act whimsically. In film after film, we are shown a devotee come and chastise his/her favoured deity for allowing evil people an upper hand in life or permitting injustice to thrive. And the *ishta deva* or *devi* is expected to respond and come to the aid of the devotee in times of need. This might come through the agency of a human or animal or even a reptile. Dogs, horses, birds and even snakes are depicted in our films as active players coming to the aid of human beings who like Draupadi appeal for divine intervention. Such an interplay should not be dismissed as mere gimmicks. They carry an important message that Indic gods are not distant creatures. They are willing to be at the beck and call of devotees who reach out for their deities as they would for close relatives in times of stress. This happens not only in popular mythologicals like *Jai Bhawani* or *Shiva Purana* which shows the personal deity as constantly coming to the aid of the harassed devotee and defeating the evil designs of all those who seek to harass him/her.

This constant interplay of the human and divine takes many forms. On the one hand it shows gods and goddesses display very human failings as for example in *Jai Santoshi Ma*, Lakshmi and Parvati are shown as being jealous of a new upstart goddess like Santoshi Ma and do all kinds of mean things to harass her devotee till they realise their mistake and make peace with Santoshi Ma giving space for her in the pantheon of goddesses. On the other hand, films also depict ordinary mortals play and have fun with divinities. Scenes of *raaslila*, of Krishna playing *holi* with *gopis*, or those depicting Radha-Krishna love or the Shiva Parvati romance with Parvati enjoying the right to veto and change any number of decisions of the all-powerful Shiva are a source of immense fascination for people trained to see God as a distant figure to be feared and obeyed unconditionally. Bollywood has no hesitation in showing people make fun of gods, crack jokes about them or even treat them as a nuisance as in the film *Yehi Hai Zindagi*. The hero played by Sanjeev Kumar is very proud of the fact the he is a "self-made" man – a typical rags to riches story. The film portrays a very charming relationship between him and Lord Krishna—who keeps appearing to mock at him for his arrogance in thinking that he alone shapes his destiny and that of his family. Sanjeev Kumar as the hero treats Krishna as an unwelcome pest and keeps shooing him off through most of the film till the life choices his kids make (example, his pampered daughter chooses to marry her horse riding instructor while Sanjeev Kumar nursed the ambition to marry her to a wealthy high status man) brings in the hard realisation that Krishna's message about the need for humility should have been heeded. Even in this film, the purpose is not to show the victory of the divine will over the human but the need for humility and graceful acceptance of how each person's destiny unfolds for him/her rather than attempt to play God.

Many people in several Islamic countries told me they were fascinated by the freedom with which Hindus poke fun at their gods, quarrel with their favourite deities, and provoke the gods to prove their worth to their devotees by actually coming to the aid of good over evil. In societies where power wielders project Allah as someone to be feared and held in total awe, where Islam or the *Quran* cannot be criticised openly from public platforms, let alone through films, the ease with which Hindu gods and goddesses are openly depicted allowing liberties to their devotees appears very attractive.

Happy Marriage of Tradition and Modernity

Bollywood films have become the staple emotional diet of people in most of these societies that are getting "westernised" and "modernised" without being comfortable about it. They are popular because they don't just play on those anxieties. They always attempt to resolve these conflicts and present a world where a happy balance is possible and even desirable—provided certain "eternal" core values are kept intact—which allows for maintaining a healthy, creative relationship with tradition while adopting modernity in appropriate doses. The success of Bollywood lies in its offering what appears like a viable alternative to a narcissistic variety of individualism that often comes with westernisation which people in non-western cultures feel threatened by because it undermines traditional institutions, especially the institution of the family.

"Modernity is disavowed even as it is endorsed. Tradition is avowed even as it is rejected". This echoes Mahatma Gandhi's advice: "To swim in the waters of tradition is healthy but to sink in them is suicide". Bollywood tries to show how to swim in the waters of both tradition and modernity.

Let me describe how Bollywood performs this role by recounting a small but revealing incident. About two years ago I was sitting at a neighbour's house — The entire joint family — including the 80 year old grandmother and a couple of grand aunts were watching some film award function. For one of the awards Karishma Kapoor was invited to act as the ceremonial host. Her job was to announce the winner of a particular award and call upon ageing Sunil Dutt to do the honours. She appeared on the stage in a sexy skin-tight mini dress with a revealing neckline. When ageing Sunil Dutt in visibly poor health came up the stage, she rushed not only to assist him but bent down to touch his feet. The entire family, including the grandmother and grandchildren spontaneously exclaimed: "See how Indian she remains despite all the westernisation and stardom."Thereafter, the mother gave her own little speech to her children on the importance of respecting elders and remaining forever humble in life, no matter how successful one becomes. It was revealing to me that even the old grandmother showed no disapproval of Karishma's seductive and revealing outfit. That one gesture of spontaneous respect giving to an elder far beyond the call of duty (given that Karishma was not acting the role of a Hindi film *bahu* on stage but acting herself) endeared her so much to everyone in that room that it did not matter whether she wore a bikini or a Hawaiian dance outfit.

Family Values and Respect for Elders

While Bollywood has been obsessively propagandising the value of stable and harmonious families, as the hallmark of Indian culture, it has been as steadfast in dealing with inter-generational conflicts in values and aspirations. Our filmmakers are obsessed with resolving the inter-generational conflict in a way that leads to greater understanding and harmony in the larger family rather than a breakdown or nuclearisation of it. Young people are encouraged to revolt against parental tyranny but not disown responsibility for the care and respect of their parents and other elders.

A large majority of Bollywood films since the 1940's depict the hero and heroine asserting their right to choose their marital partner while parents resist their choice on grounds of economic and social status, caste or religion. However, this clash is by and large never allowed to lead to a permanent rift or estrangement. Even while rebelling against the authoritarian mindset of parents, children are expected to win over parents to their point of view with patience and love. *Dilwale Dulhaniya Le Jayenge* provides the most well-worked out role model of a healthy inter-generational equation. The NRI patriarch of the family is outraged at discovering that his daughter has fallen in love with a young and boisterous NRI played by Shah Rukh Khan. He forcibly takes her to his native village in Punjab so that she could be married off to a real *desi* Indian who, in his view can only be found back home in India. The rest of the film is a heart-warming story of how Shah Rukh Khan works hard to win over the love and respect of his authoritarian father-in-law. He does domestic chores, wins over the hearts of each member of the family with love, cheerful service and good humour. So much so Kajol's mother offers to help them elope because she fears her husband's wrath and believes he can never be made to change his mind. But Shah Rukh Khan refuses to elope for that would mean humiliating his beloved's father and causing a permanent hurt to a father-figure which would rule out a mutually respectful and trusting relationship between them for the rest of their lives. Sure enough, his Gandhian method of winning over the ostensibly hard-hearted and tyrannical man whose daughter he wishes to marry through love and uncomplaining suffering results in a happy and voluntary change of heart. However, he could do that only by undergoing a whole series of self imposed trials/tests to demonstrate that he may have been raised in England and from the outside may look and behave like a boisterous London teenager but in his heart he is far more Indian and far more committed to family values than the Punjab born and raised groom selected by Amrish Puri for his daughter. The Punjabi groom is finally rejected because he proves that he is actually a non-Indian Resident, has adopted a very decadent life style and was merely interested in using his NRI bride as a means to get a British visa and a passport to a licentious life-style.

By contrast, our Indian-hearted hero, though living in Europe is so steeped in "Indian values" that he does not stoop to pre-marital sex with his beloved, even when they share the same bed and she is in an inebriated condition. Why? Because he knows that a sexual encounter against her wishes would make her lose trust in him and get her into deep trouble with her parents. He also has a very special and close bond with his father who gives him full support and encouragement in going and winning over the heart of his beloved's family. The film clearly holds up this relationship as an ideal between parents and children.

Bollywood has conveyed this message with untiring zeal and consistency that a happy and stable family is the bedrock of our civilisation – and that a family cannot be happy if it is a site of oppression and injustice. While our films have been obsessive in teaching young people the value of sacrifice, commitment to family well-being and respect for elders, it has been no less steadfast in telling parents and other elders that they have to earn the respect of young people by understanding their aspirations and the demands of changing times. Film after film reminds audiences that to command slavish obedience from children is to destroy family well-being.

Portrayal of Women

Bollywood depicts Indian families in all permutations and combinations. There are those in which some women are the domineering matriarchs (*eg.* Deena Pathak in *Khoobsoorat*) and those where women have little or no say (*eg.* Raveena Tandon in *Daman*) and are brutally oppressed.

They present you with a whole range of *Mother Indias* – women who are strong, and resilient in the face of greatest adversity while retaining the nurturing qualities and compassion associated with Parvati-Sita like mother goddesses who can at a minute's notice also turn into real Durgas. We see devoted Sita like wives assume *Chandi roop* and stand up against wrong doers – even if that involves challenging their own husbands as does Madhuri Dixit in *Mrityudand* in a memorable confrontation with her husband when she challenges him with a stunning verbal blow: *"Aap pati hain, Parmeshwar banne ki koshish mat Kijiye!"*

They show us wronged daughters-in law as well as those who become tyrants for the whole family. We see domineering mothers-in-law who protect their *bahus* even against their own son's tyranny or caprice as in *Biwi No 1* as well as those who ruin the lives of their daughters-in-law. Thus, there is a larger range of female incarnations than available in the writings of social historians and journalists.

It is through Bollywood films that people have understood that Indian women are able to assert their rights without leading to a breakdown of families. That every woman desirous of recognition of her self hood does not have to walk out of her home in order to win freedom. That a woman can win over everyone to her point of view rather than be despised for her assertiveness. It is through our films that the message gets communicated that an Indian woman's role in life is not to suffer indignities and tolerate injustice, that it is in her to rise like Durga and destroy evil and conquer evil doers, that such a Durga-like woman is not despised for her strength but revered even by men.

It is through Bollywood that the world gets to see that the Indian culture allows for a whole diversity of roles and personas for a woman. She can choose to be a steadfast spouse like Sita or besotted lover like Radha who throws all social restraints to the winds or be a fearless, awe-inspiring Durga—that in each of these varied incarnations a woman is reverence worthy. That even if she chooses to be a devoted and long-suffering wife – it is not because suffering is a woman's fate but because she wishes to be the instrument of reform of her unreasonable and other tyrannical members of her family.

Bollywood keeps transmitting this message with perseverance that a woman need not be frozen into a stereotype. The same woman who could defy the world in her *Radha roop*, can easily transform herself into a domineering wife like Draupadi or assume *Chandi roop* to avenge wrong doers — as in *Insaf ka Tarazu*.

The ease with which Indian film heroines switch from jeans to miniskirts to traditional *sarees, ghagra cholis,* tennis shorts and on to biknis as a normal daily routine is an indication of the diverse role allowed to them. The same woman who is on crooning away with *jatka thumka* number in a night club one hour, will be shown singing a melodious *bhajan* with her family in a *mandir* the next hour and then perhaps move on to being an efficient manager of her family business. She could be a Rani Roopmati or a Rani Jhansi. She could be a Mirabai or an Indira Gandhi as in *Aandhi*. These multifaceted *roops* or incarnations of femininity derived from mythology, history and legend and given contemporary coinage in film after film churned out by Bollywood have enthralled audiences in many parts of the world, including those that have come to impose very oppressive and restrictive norms of behaviour on women. The depiction of free lifestyles of women in Hollywood evokes sharp fearful responses in many conservative Muslim countries - but Bollywood films are embraced warmly.

In most academic tracts and studies, Indian men are projected as cruel patriarchs who are insensitive to the needs of women and subject them to all kind of oppression and misery. In recent decades Indian men have gained international notoriety for committing atrocities on women, for denying women their basic human rights. Bollywood goes beyond this simplistic stereotype and shows the soft and sentimental side of the Indian male.

It is through Bollywood films that message is being conveyed to the world that in India even men are expected to value family ties and happiness more than wealth and careers. It is our films which have reiterated the message time and again, that you cannot be a good human being without being a devoted son, a doting brother, a caring husband and a good father who puts the happiness and interests of his children above his own. You may defy God but you do not act against the wishes of your mother. Even if a mother slaps her grown up son in righteous rage, a good son never holds a grudge, leave alone retaliate or abuse his mother. Bollywood films have reiterated this message a million times that the status of a mother is higher than that of God. So her commandments need to be taken more seriously than that of any divinity.

The Bollywood hero may be a great doctor or a feared dacoit, a gangster or an upright police-officer, a Gandhian social reformer or a feudal aristocrat –he has to have some essential family values to qualify as a hero. He has to be a devoted son and specially reverential towards his mother including his step mother, who may like *Kaikeyi* suddenly turn vicious. For example, in *Hum Saath Saath Hain* the step-mother is goaded into breaking the close bonding of the three brothers in favour of her own biological son, so that her eldest step son is not made the head of family's business empire. But the three sons remain steadfast in their mutual devotion, just like Rama, Lakshmana and Bharata of *Ramayana*. More importantly, the eldest son, in the footsteps of the hero of *Ramayana*, willingly undergoes all kinds of privations and adversities in the interest of family well-being and unity. Never for a minute grudge, his step-mothers injustice towards him. Finally, like Valmiki's Rama, he too through love, generosity and patient suffering is able to make his stepmother realise her mistake and accept the superiority of a well-bonded joint family over an individualistic nuclear family. Our filmy hero may be a don on the streets, but at home he becomes a goody-goody sentimental son who will defy heaven and earth to fulfil his mother's wishes. He also has to be a devoted and fond brother who will shed blood and sweat to put together the required money for the decent marriage of his sister, pamper her like a little princess if she is younger and be a Hanuman like devotee if she is older. The unique emphasis given to the brother-sister bond as symbolised by *raksha bandhan* is celebrated in numerous Bollywood films. In the worldview of Bollywood, a man, who respects and cherishes this bond, can never be evil even if he is in criminal activities.

To Sum Up

It is indeed ironic that Bollywood has received only disdain and ridicule from those who claim to represent the high culture of India. The new Brahmins of India are both embarrassed by worldview and of Bollywood and are aggressive in the disapproval of its value system.

Review of Hindi films cinema in *avant-garde* intellectual journals like *EPW* accuse our film makers of spreading religious obscurantism, Hindu fundamentalism, anti-women attitudes, animosity towards minorities and as conservative defenders of an anachronistic *status-quo*. Is it not a case of a re-play of the hostility of the Brahminical orthodoxy towards the popular upsurge of *Bhakti* in the medieval period with just this difference that the new Brahmins of today are not rooted in Sanskrit learning. They are the products of elite English medium schools and colleges and whose manners and tastes resemble those of their intellectual masters in the West.